Management of Competency Based Learning

By the Same Author

Governance and Management of Technical Institutions.

About the Author

B.L. Gupta, is Professor in Education Management at National Institute of Technical Teachers' Training and Research, Bhopal. He completed B.E. in Civil Engineering in the year 1982 from Shri Govindram Seksaria Institute of Technology and Science, Indore. He completed LL.B. from the College of Law and Legal Aid Shahdol in the year 1988. Then he completed Master of Technical Education in the year 1992 and Ph.D. in 2002 from Technical Teachers Training Institute Bhopal. Professor Gupta has 24 years of experience in the field of teaching and training. He is trained in Great Britain. He has received training from well-known personalities of the country. He has conducted more than 250 management development programmes for various clients such as teachers of technical institutions, trainers and managers of industries. He has guided more than 15 theses in the field of technical education and management of industries. He has published more than 30 papers in national and international journals. He has developed print and non-print instructional material for teachers of technical institutions. He has worked on various World Bank assisted projects. Earlier to this book he has written four books.

Management of Competency Based Learning

Dr. B.L. Gupta

Professor, Education Management
National Institute of Technical
Teachers' Training and Research, Bhopal

CONCEPT PUBLISHING COMPANY, NEW DELHI-110059

Cataloging in Publication Data—DK
Courtesy: D.K. Agencies (P) Ltd. <docinfo@dkagencies.com>

Gupta, B. L.
Management of competency based learning/ B.L. Gupta. — 1st ed.
p. ; cm.
Includes bibliographical references (p.)
Includes index.
ISBN-13: 9788180694523
ISBN-10: 8180694526

1. Competency-based education. 2. Instructional systems. I. Title.

DDC 378.01 22

ISBN: 13-978-81-8069-452-3 (HB)

First Edition 2007

Published and Printed by
Ashok Kumar Mittal
Concept Publishing Company
A/15-16, Commercial Block, Mohan Garden
New Delhi-110059 (INDIA)

Phones : 25351460, 25351794
Fax : 091-11-25357103
Email : publishing@conceptpub.com

Preface

In the comtetitive world the whole concept of education has changed significantly. The engineering education is required to produce technically competent professionals. Here the word professional is very important in the sense that professional is required to satisfy and delight the customer in the competitive, changing and challenging world of work. They are required to work in uncertainty, recession, fluctuating market, diverse culture, and different environment. They are required to work to long hours and without tension, stress and anxiety. They are required to satisfy customers as well as stakeholders. The definition of professionalism has changed over the years and still it is in fluid because the whole world is changing very fast. In the changing world of work it is very difficult to predict the status of the profession. The concern for safety and conserving environment has also increased significantly. The laws governing all the professions are being modified to control and regulate the unwanted and undesirable act of the companies.

In order to develop technically competent passouts from institutions efforts have been made from micro level to meta level and the results are encouraging. There is a need to bring professional approach in the institutions then only institutions can think of producing professionals. The professional skills can only be developed in the actual world of work. Professionals develop the professional skills. Not to say that institutions are not having professionals but there is a need of working professionally. Along with technical competencies the students are required to develop variety of professional competencies such as accepting the challenge, risk taking, working in a team, quick learning, problem solving, effective decision-making, negotiating, collaborating, networking, working in uncertainty, predicting the future, visualizing the whole on the basis of available data, accepting accountability, managing change, coping with situation, influencing the customer, undertaking research and projects for quick response, adjusting in new environment and new culture, learning new and different competencies, forgetting fast, and so on. Not to say that all the competencies listed here will require to be developed in students of all the disciplines but this is the need of the day.

There is a fast change in technology and way of working in the professional world. Companies are diversifying, changing, merging, expanding, collaborating, networking and withdrawing from the market place. This requires continuous refinement, updating and learning new technical competencies. This demands for quick revision of curriculum may be every semester for every batch. Accordingly there is a need of adjusting the subsequent processes of learning and supporting process to learning. The technical institutions have to fulfill the technical as well as professional demands of the industries then only it would be said that professional institutions are performing professionally.

This book on 'management of competency based learning' is written keeping in mind the professional performance of technical institutions to manage learning and satisfy the needs of the industries and young students who have visions, ambitions and aspirations in their career and profession. This prime focus of this book is managing learning within and outside the institution. This book is based on researches, experiences, theories and philosophies of various disciplines but they are not described in this book. The application part of the learning is the main focus of this book. The institutions and teachers irrespective of their qualification, training, exposure, experience can use this book. It is very difficult to give any prescription without any specific case so no prescription is given but guidelines are noted everywhere for easy application. All the chapters are kept open to use individual creativity and innovations in managing learning.

Teachers can assess their competence on various aspects of management of learning using self-assessment exercises and can reflect on the same individually and in a group. Apart from self-assessments guidelines would definitely help and improve the performance of the teachers for managing learning. Teachers will find this book very stimulating and encouraging so for management of learning is concerned. The message of whole book is to remove redundant process that is teaching and work on directly producing learning. I hope reading of this book would contribute to enhance professional competence of the teachers for managing learning. Wish you a very good luck.

Dr. B.L. Gupta

Acknowledgements

This book on 'management of competency based learning' is outcome of many precedent learning experiences and research studies conducted in past. I wish to record my sincere thanks to following persons:

Dr. Mahendra Singh Chauhan, Chairman, Governing Body, National Institute of Technical Teachers' Training and Research, Bhopal for approving sabbatical leave and encouragement Governing Body members for continuous encouragement.

Prof. K. K. Shrivasta for extending guidance and support generously Ex-Principals and Directors of National Institute of Technical Teachers' Training and Research, Bhopal for providing opportunities to get international exposure.

Prof. R.K. Mani, Ex Director, National Institute of Technical Teachers Training and Research, Bhopal who formally taught, trained, encouraged and guided me to pursue the career in education management.

Dr. D.V. Chandrashekhara, Retired Professor, National Institute of Technical Teachers Training and Research, Bhopal for mentoring me on the job during conduction of training programmes.

Prof. (Mrs.) M. Saxena Head of Education Management Center, National Institute of Technical Teachers Training and Research, Bhopal for nurturing, guiding and providing constructive feedback for thirteen years.

My colleagues at National Institute of Technical Teachers Training and Research, Bhopal for openly sharing the experiences.

Director Technical Education, Governing body members, Directors and Principals of Engineering Colleges and Polytechnics, faculty members of technical institutions, research scholars and administrators, who shared experiences openly. Supervisors, guide and research scholars for systematically studying various issues and documenting the outcomes of the research work.

Prof. S.R. Ganorkar for going through the first draft of the book and offering suggestions for improving the presentation.

Library staff of National Institute of Technical Teachers Training and Research, Bhopal.

Shri Vipin Bhatnagar, for providing photographs for cover page.

Shri Ashok Kumar Mittal for accepting the proposal to publish the book.

My wife Mrs. Suman Gupta, sons Kumar Gandharva and Kumar Gaurva for supporting me during the writing work.

Contents

List of Exhibits

Summary

The 'management of competency based learning' is a practice-oriented book written for technical teachers. The book emphasizes to develop professionals through professional learning processes. The focus of the book is to offer competency and proficiency development education along with professional and entrepreneurial competencies. The book emphasizes on shifting from teaching to learning and use learning methods matching to learning styles of the students. It stresses on shifting the responsibility of learning from teachers to students and empowering them for their own learning.

The book on management of competency based learning is divided in seven chapters. Chapter one emphasizes on management of curriculum that describes the concept of competency based curriculum, shift required from content oriented curriculum to competency and flexibility-based curriculum. It spells out the model of competency based curriculum supported by research studies on technical education. Chapter two focuses on concept of learning, characteristics of learning, learning process, learning styles, shift required from teaching to learning and role of a teacher in management of learning. Chapter three describes the learning in the classroom. It describes various learning methods such as lecture, team teaching, question answer, demonstration, learning in groups, buzz group, in basket, panel discussion, case method, seminars, symposium, role-play, simulation, game, force field analysis, tutorials, assignments, action learning, self learning, drill and practice. Chapter four emphasizes on management of learning in laboratory. It explains about learning in laboratory, principles of learning used in laboratory, mode of learning in laboratory, guidelines for effective learning, development of attitudes and assessment of learning in the laboratory. Chapter fifth describes learning through projects. It explains learning projects, classification of learning projects, purpose of project, learning from projects and guidelines for effective learning from projects. Chapter sixth describes management of learning at work place. It describes the objectives of learning at work place, types of learning and role of teacher and resource person. Chapter seventh describes the role of the teachers to manage the learning process. It describes the competencies of a teacher, shift from training of teachers to learning organisation, dimensions of learning organisation, motivation and commitment of teacher, role conflict and time utilisation, performance appraisal and competencies of a teacher.

The author has quoted numbers of research studies conducted in technical education to support the content presented. The book should be considered as guidelines and reference book for the management of learning.

1

Management of Curriculum

Objectives: The readers will be able to:

1. Define the curriculum in context of technical education
2. State the need and importance of designing a curriculum
3. Explain the concept of competency in context to technical education
4. Define the competency in context to technical education
5. Explain the shift required in the process of curriculum management of technical education
6. Explain the model of curriculum management
7. Describe the characteristics of curriculum document
8. Describe the meaning of flexibility in curriculum
9. List the competencies possessed by passouts irrespective of their discipline
10. Explain the method of evaluating the impact of curriculum

1. Introduction

The rapid modernisation of industry in the wake of the economic and technological liberalisation has made it essential to produce competent and professional passouts. The information and computer technology has changed the way of working in production and service organisations. Every organisation is continuously changing and updating itself to stay in the market place. The globalisation of economic, technological, social, cultural and educational dimensions has significantly affected the functioning of corporate sector and even government sector. Thereby it is affecting the curriculum and core business of technical institutions. The change in environment is in fluid state. In some technical sectors the change has initiated and in other technical sectors it is taking shape. The continuous change in environment is profoundly affecting the core business of the institutions. The concept and philosophy of curriculum is continuously evolving with the changes in environment. The old concept of curriculum development that is design a curriculum for 5 years and make modifications as per needs has to go. Now there is a need to reengineer the curriculum every year as per evolution in technology and need of the corporate sector.

The concept of value addition in the corporate world needs to be considered in education sector to make its products and services effective, efficient and satisfying. The concept of value addition in technical education should be seen from many dimensions such as additional technical competencies, entrepreneurial competency, managerial competencies, research competencies, social competencies, linguistic competencies, coping competencies, change management competencies, learning competencies, thinking competencies and so on. The value addition needs to be considered from enhancing proficiency level in core competencies. It can be seen from reducing the time of learning, cost of learning, stress of learning and so on. It can be seen from increasing joy in learning, interest in learning, achieving self actualisation level, pursuing hobby, career and so on. It can be ensuring minimum competence level in all the students, placement of students, providing more opportunities for interactions and hands on experiences.

The corporate sector is investing cores of rupees in tuning its business to suit the demand of the market. It is pouring money in terms of technology, techniques, manpower, research, marketing and so on. It is obvious that the corporate sector would prefer and employ competent, proficient and entrepreneurs in their business.

2. Concept of Curriculum

The curriculum document is a link between the institution, students and industry. It reflects the needs of the employers, needs and ambitions of students, and programme offered by institution. It is a menu that tells about the products and services of the institute. It clearly spells out the quality parameters imbibed in the products and services of the institution. It is an educational plan for managing the learning in the institution. It sets the ultimate learning outcomes in terms of competencies, proficiency level in each competency that is acceptable to employers. It indicates broad strategies to achieve the stated learning outcomes and resources required for the same. It spells out the significant learning activities that are to be carried out in order to implement the strategy and achieve the learning outcomes. This is the base plan for which rest of the supporting plans, processes and activities are performed to supplement and compliment the curriculum implementation strategy. The institute organizes all six types of resources that are man, material, machine, minutes, methods, maintenance and information to implement the curriculum. The men are influenced to perform the learning events using resources. They are influenced to assure the competency and proficiency development through learning events. They are influenced to take preventive measures to prevent learning problems. They are trained to early diagnose the learning problems and solve them through remedial actions. The outcome of the curriculum in the form of learning outcomes is evaluated and necessary modifications, refinements, fine-tuning, and value additions are carried out. If necessary the complete curriculum is reengineered.

3. Concept of Competency

The competency is derived from the role of the potential position the passouts are expected to occupy in the industry or in her/his enterprise. The competency is a link between the role and the role holder. It enables the role holder to perform competently, proficiently, productively, creatively, innovatively to assure quality of products and services at minimum price, without waste, on right time, with minimum efforts and without stress. Experts have defined competency in different contexts. Some of the significant definitions of the competency are stated in Exhibit 1.1

Exhibit No. 1.1: Significant definitions of competency

- Competency is ability to do or perform or take responsibility —*Phil Race*
- Competency is ability to perform the activities within an occupation or function to the standard accepted within employment and a competency statement is a full and complete description of something, which a person who works in a given occupational area should be able to do and achieve —*Paul Ellis*
- A competent individual can perform a particular function or satisfy a particular role in diversity of setting, over extended period of time, and

(*Contd.*)

(*Contd.*)

respond effectively to irregular occurrence in environment having different characteristics
—*Graham Debling*

- Competence is something that we can observe directly. If we are going to assess the people in terms of competencies, we will have to develop observable measures and use them to collect evidence, that can support an inferential leap from the observed consistency to a construct that account for the consistency
—*Alison Wolf*
- Competency is described in general terms as being able to perform "whole" work role to standard expected in employment in real working environment
—*Bob Mansfield*
- Competencies are composite skills behaviour or knowledge that can be demonstrated by the learner and are derived outcomes of learning. The emphasis in competency based education is on competencies, on the ability, develop and demonstrate a total performance not just the mere learning on specific kills
—*Hall Johnes*
- The concept of competency based instruction is based on idea that student must be able to demonstrate that they can successfully perform job competencies to the standards accepted by industry. The job "competencies" are the skills. Task. knowledge and attitudes that students must learn to perform a job successfully
—*G. W. Maxwell and Lind Nunes*

A critical analysis of the above definitions reveals the following basic features of competency in Exhibit 1.2.

Exhibit No. 1.2: Features of Competency

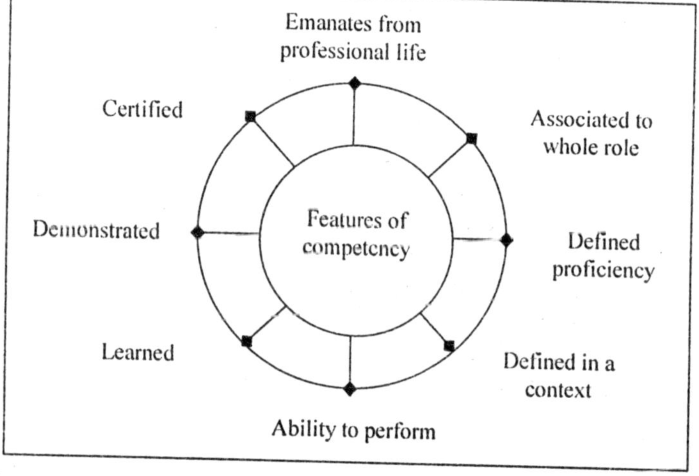

Competencies are derived from the real life professional role and it is based on whole work of the role holder. Proficiency level for each competency is defined and it is related to expected standards of performance and behaviour. Competencies are defined in a specific business or context. It means for different business the same competency will have different meaning. Competencies are ability to perform a role in a real life situation. Students or employees learn competencies through formal and non-formal educational programmes. Students demonstrate competencies repeatedly and consistently in real life work situation for getting it certified from competent authority. The competent authority certifies the competency and proficiency in core competency based on evidences of acquiring the competency and demonstration of it.

4. Paradigm Shift in Curriculum

In the light of above discussion there is a need of shift in curriculum approaches. The shift is stated in Exhibit 1.3.

Exhibit No. 1.3: Paradigm shift in life cycle of curriculum

Criteria Curriculum Design	*Existing Curriculum*		*Curriculum of 21st Century*
Philosophy of design	Designed by experienced teachers		Designed by professionals and stakeholders including teachers
Approach	Blue print approach Job and task analysis Present and near future considerations Principles of educational psychology Principles of teaching Supply driven No benchmarking	⇨	Process approach Role analysis, organisational analysis, innovation plans and major changes Long-term consideration Principles of androgogy Principles of learning Demand driven Benchmarking with the best
Focus	Teacher Content Content and skills testing Broad based		Employers and Students Competency development Demonstration of competency Specific

(*Contd.*)

(*Contd.*)

Criteria	*Existing Curriculum*	*Curriculum of 21st Century*
Duration	Rigid Fixed	Flexible
Responsibility of learning	Teacher	Students
Curriculum Implementation		
Implementation plan	Generally not prepared Teachers rely on their experiences	Cluster of competency/competency plan is prepared
Learning resources	Generally not developed	Developed according to requirement of competency
Course/competency offerings	Rigid	Multiple and flexible options
Learning	Passive learning	Active learning
Role of teacher	Directive	Participative
Motivation	Teacher influences the behaviour of the students	Promote self motivation for learning
Power	Enjoy administrative and expert power	Empower students for learning Learning to learn concept is promoted
Emphasis	Curriculum completion	Learning about changing business, innovation, and development
Teachers think	Students need to be controlled	Students have potential to learn on their own if properly guided
Recognition	Teaches take credit for the success	Students take credit for success
Rewards	Extrinsic	Extrinsic and intrinsic
Information	Controlled information	Free flow of information
Problems	Teacher own the problem	Students own the problem

(*Contd.*)

(*Contd.*)

Criteria	*Existing Curriculum*		*Curriculum of 21st Century*
Communication	Often one way		Multi channels of communication are used
Creativity and innovation	Less scope Analytical thinking		Foster creativity in learning Promote thinking skills
Perspective for development	Limited scope		Life long learning
Learning methods	Teacher centered methods Input based		Students centered methods Output based
Use of media	Traditional		Multi-media
Way of learning	Formal		Formal and informal
Outcome of learning	Passing the examination		Learning for life
Curriculum Evaluation			
Method	No scientific method is used Based on formal and informal feedback Impact assessment is totally missing		Based on scientific method Impact assessment and tracer studies are carried out
Life cycle	Very long		As short as significant changes in corporate world

5. Model of Curriculum Management

Numbers of models of curriculum design and development have been evolved in the past based on the experiences and research studies. These models have been in vogue for a long time but now looking to continuous change in business and way of doing the business. There is a need to evolve a curriculum design and development model, which is user friendly and does not require much time and resources to revise, modify, refine and reengineer. To evolve such model a basic assumption of collaboration, cooperation, networking, coordination and linkage with employers, entrepreneurs, alumni, and society need to make. This tie up needs to be made at national level through formal and non-formal, statutory and obligatory mechanism. A system needs to be developed at national level to first design the curriculum once looking the needs of the employers, entrepreneurs, students and society and periodically review it once every year. This system needs to be in place to facilitate the curriculum management of all disciplines at all levels. This is a challenging task for the government and professional bodies but without it employers, students and public would continuously question the relevance of the curriculum. There would be wide variation in the curriculum documents of same discipline all over the country in terms of aim of the programme, competencies, content, approach, assessment procedure, certification procedure and so on. There is a need to design curriculum documents for all the discipline at national level. The curriculum document should have characteristics listed in Exhibit 1.4.

Exhibit No. 1.4: Characteristics of curriculum document

- It should clearly list the role the passouts can perform in the professional organisation.
- It should clearly mention the competency profile of the passouts stating their suitability in type of professional organisation.
- It should clearly separate out different types of competencies such as technical competencies, managerial competencies, entrepreneurial competencies, social competencies, research competencies, management of change competencies and so on and proficiency level in each competency.
- The competencies should be benchmarked with the best industrial practices in the world to make passouts internationally acceptable.
- It should define alternative approaches to achieve each competency of each type and time frame to achieve the same.
- It should indicate the competency relation diagram to move from elementary to advance, simple to complex and concrete to abstract competencies.
- It should state about availability of competency based learning material and hands on practices in the laboratory, workshop and world of work.
- If possible it should suggest alternative learning methods to be used to attain the competency effectively and efficiently.
- It should provide defined flexibility to students in terms of time, competency, learning approach, assessment and so on.
- It should suggest the method of assessment and certification at national level or state level.
- It should suggest procedure for establishing equivalence.

(Contd.)

(*Contd.*)

> - It should suggest about infrastructural and learning facility requirements if it is different than common facilities.
> - It should suggest the prerequisite qualification or competency if any.
> - It should state about the competence of the teacher if it is totally different than commonly found in teachers.

The curriculum development model is shown in Exhibit 1.5. This model is considered for developing the curriculum. Curriculum development is a research and interdisciplinary work. It requires inputs from various disciplines such as industrial practices, corporate culture, changes taking place in the environment on various dimensions such as economic, technical, political, social, educational and way of working. Initially the curriculum development cell should study the external environment of the corporate world to diagnose the present and future of the employer's organisation. The diagnosis of external and internal environment of the employer's organisation helps to understand the trends in development of corporate sector. The development trends in corporate sector guides the process of curriculum development. In fact it is a proactive approach to curriculum development in contrast to problem-based approach that is reactive approach. The proactive method of curriculum development keeps the institutions ahead all over the world. It enables the institutions to practice the things when their counter part thinks about it. Proactive approach always keeps the institutions in leadership positions. It develops the students in advance as professionals. To adopt proactive approaches of curriculum development institutions and curriculum development cell should work with corporate world in collaborative way. The national and international opportunities of human resources requirement can be identified using proactive approach and the institutions can grab the opportunity for competitive advantage.

The scanning of the external environment helps the institutions to diagnose the entrepreneurial opportunities in national and international market. The institutions can design the curriculum to produce entrepreneurs to capture business opportunities and help the country to develop economy. The country needs crores of entrepreneurs to grab and influence the economy at international level. The scanning of external environment of corporate sector helps to decide the present and future role of passouts of the institutions. These roles become the basis for curriculum design. The role should be analyzed to derive cluster of competencies or independent competencies.

Exhibit No. 1.5: Curriculum management model

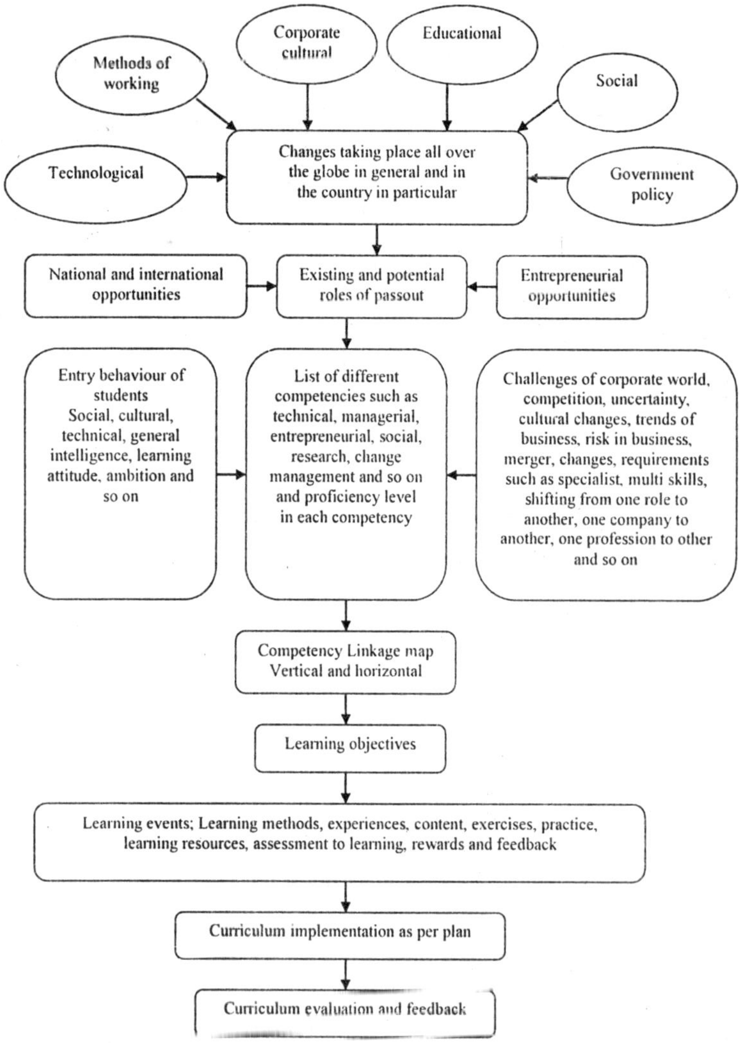

The competencies are further analyzed and classified such as technical, managerial, entrepreneurial, social, research, change management and so on. The proficiency level in each competency is defined as per prevailing proficiency level in professionals. The competencies and proficiency level is defined considering other factors such as entry behaviour of students; social, cultural, technical, general intelligence, learning attitude, ambition and so on. The industrial internal environment related to employment of passouts such as challenges of corporate world, competition, uncertainty, cultural changes, trends of business, risk in business, merger, changes, requirements such as specialist, multi skills, shifting from one role to another, one company to another, one profession to other and so on is also considered to identify the competencies. The identified competencies are prioritized and classified in various ways such as primary and supporting, essential and desirable, core and peripheral, must and want, hard and soft, technical and managerial, present and future and so on.

Once the competencies have been identified, finalized and validated by corporate world the curriculum design becomes very simple and easy. The competency map is prepared to establish horizontal, vertical and diagonal linkages in competencies. The complete horizontal, vertical and diagonal logic is established among competencies. So achieving a set of competencies in the competency map students become competent and proficient in performing the role. The logic among role, competencies and entry behaviour of students is shown in Exhibit 1.6.

Exhibit No. 1.6: Logic between role, competencies and entry behaviour of students

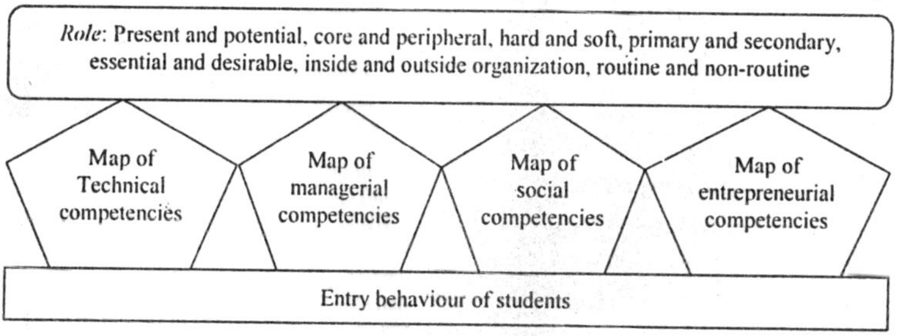

If the entry behaviour of the students is too low to develop competencies bridge courses are offered to students so they can start the competencies development in an easy way. Each competency is then divided in learning objectives in three domains of learning as shown in Exhibit 1.7. There may be some common denominators of objectives that may contribute for achieving more than one competency. The objectives are derived using concept map, flow chart, problem tree analysis diagram, and affinity diagram. The horizontal, vertical and diagonal links are established among objectives of various competencies.

Exhibit No. 1.7: Deriving learning objectives from competencies

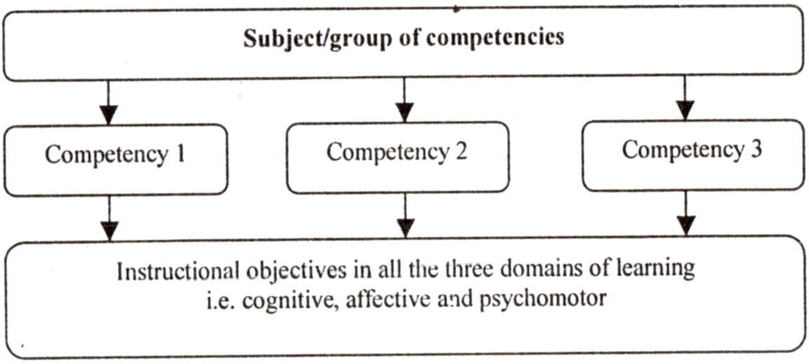

An objective map guides to decide learning events, methods, experiences, content, exercises, practice, resources, method of assessment of learning, rewards, and feedback. The curriculum designer would surprise to know that learning methods imbibe the development of associative competencies along with technical competencies. For example game playing on a particular technical competency imbibe the development of competencies such as facing the competition, accepting the challenge, designing win over strategy, working in a team, pooling talent and resources of team members, communicating and negotiating and so on. If lecture method is used for developing the technical competency other associated competencies cannot be developed. The selection of learning event should be perfectly aligned to learning objectives. The learning event should provide an opportunity to develop associative competencies.

The teachers prepare the curriculum implementation plan as per guidelines stated in the curriculum document. They use their creativity, innovativeness, experiences and expertise to prepare the implementation plan to create enjoyable and memorable learning experiences for the students. Initially a team of experts can suggest a curriculum implementation plan to guide the teachers. The team of experts should also provide critical learning resources, which may not be available to teachers of all the institutions. On the basis of curriculum implementation plan the teacher prepares the competency plan and lesson plan for effective and efficient implementation. The curriculum implementation strategy is suggested in subsequent chapters in more detail.

The impact of the curriculum is assessed after completion of one cycle that is one semester. This would be formative assessment to know the effectiveness and efficiency in implementation, impact of it on learning further competencies, implementation difficulties, opportunities of value addition, scope for modification, refinement and fine tuning. The formative assessment of curriculum would result in scope for incorporating new competencies and deleting redundant competencies. In emerging and new discipline the formative assessment is essential after every semester. In rest of the disciples it can be carried out after every four years or major changes in employers organisations. In all the disciplines the complete curriculum development process should be exercised using research approach. The impact of competency based curriculum should be assessed after every four years. The impact of curriculum can be assessed conducting tracer study and impact analysis study. The tracer study and impact study should aim at various objectives stated in Exhibit 1.8.

Exhibit No. 1.8: Objectives of tracer study

Impact of competency based curriculum: to identify the comparative professional contribution made by passouts in employers organisation in terms of expanding the business, improving productivity, improving quality of product and services, reducing wastage, accidents, losses, collaboration with other organisation for mutual benefit, corporate culture enhancement and so on.

Placement of students: comparative placement of students, enhancement in average salary, positions in industry, entrepreneurs, international placements, placements in international companies for the first time and so on.

Curriculum: gapes in curriculum, gaps in implementation, gaps in assessment, dropouts, coping problems, learning resources problems, infrastructure problems, teachers problems, work place learning problem and so on.

Institutions: governance and management problems, training problems, work culture problems, policy problems, systems problems, problems of specific groups such as physically challenged group, women, slow learners, training and placement problems, admission problem and so on.

6. Research Studies on Management of Curriculum

Numbers of research studies have been conducted on management of curriculum in technician education. Some of the significant research studies and their findings are noted in subsequent paragraphs.

Yasin & Jain (1993) measured the major entrepreneurial attitudes using four instruments namely who am I? Sentence completion test, achievement value and anxiety inventory and paired comparison test. They have summarized the entrepreneurial attitudes and their possession. The summarisation is shown in Exhibit 1.9.

Exhibit No. 1.9: Entrepreneurial attitudes of students

Sl. No.	*Entrepreneurial Attitudes*	*Level of Possession*
1.	Initiatives	Average to high
2.	Goal clarity	Average
3.	Problem solving	Low to average
4.	Internal resources awareness	Low
5.	Achievement motivation	Average
6.	Positive self concept	Average to high
7.	Risk taking	Average
8.	Level of aspiration	High
9.	Openness to feedback	Average
10.	Time-bound planning	Average
11.	Scanning environment	Average to high
12.	Need for influence	Low to average
13.	Reaction to failure	Low to average
14.	Sense of dissatisfaction	Low

They have reported that girl students have indicated following problems in high to low priority order; restrictions imposed by the society, permission required from the world be in laws regarding entrepreneurial career, change of location due to marriage, lack of suitable opportunities for women, parents do not have enough capital to invest, lack of knowledge in skills in producing quality products, society does not accept girls as entrepreneur or business women, parents discourage girls becoming entrepreneur, and lack of managerial and practical skills. They have reported that students have personal inadequacy such as lack of self-confidence, lack of motivation, lack of leadership qualities, lack of risk taking qualities, lack of goal setting ability and fear of failure. On the basis of research findings they have noted that the individual profile of students should be plotted by a trained trainer motivator, conducive environment should be created through planned and conducted curricular activities to develop entrepreneurial attitudes of students, intensive interaction with entrepreneurship development organisations should be promoted, and training of trainers programmes for teachers should be organized.

Khartri & Haider (1993) have reported that in mechanical engineering six types of courses are offered. They are foundation courses, hard-core courses, soft-core courses, basic technology courses, applied technology courses, and diversified courses. They have stated the formula for calculating the flexibility index. The flexibility index is number of courses available divided by number of courses required for diploma. They have stated that flexibility index can be calculated on the basis of the credits as well. Flexibility index on the basis of credits is equals to number of credits available in the curriculum divided by credits required for diploma. They have stated that 24 per cent students and 16 per cent teachers do not like the multipoint entry and credit system. They have reported that flexibility index for programme 10+ is 1.2, 12+ is 1.25, soft courses is 2, and diversified courses is 3. They have reported that those students completed diploma programme in minimum period who have not availed flexibility. The teachers work load increased because of multi point entry and credit system.

They have reported the student's opinion on multipoint entry and credit system. It is as follows; the students have selected courses as per directive of the head of the department. The difficult courses should be offered in each semester. They have faced difficulty in some subjects because less periods were engaged, inadequate equipment in the laboratory, strike by students and staff, inadequate guidance, less efforts of the teachers in the classroom, obsolete machines, transfer of staff, medium of instruction, no assistance from teachers to solve difficulty, no standard books in english are available, less time for reading during examination, poor attendance of students in classroom, no fear of detention and so on. They have reported reasons for suffering academic work. These are wastage of time in registration of courses, insufficient staff, short-term, delay in conducting examination, irregularity in engaging classes, careless students, strike, no reading time due to more term work, more facility for choices of course, less assistance from the teachers, poor taught by teachers and less instruction time. They have reported reasons for good academic work. These are good management by the head of the institution, no wastage of time in registration, guidance by staff for selection of courses, no fear for loosing the semester due to failure in the courses, no difficulty in match in timetable and computerized registration. They have reported that to improve the multipoint entry and credit system following concerted efforts should be made by the teachers; provision of sufficient human and physical resources, solving difficulties, new courses as per local needs, six months in plant training of students and effective functioning of guidance and counselling cell. They have suggested a map for improving multipoint entry and credit system. It is shown in Exhibit 1.10.

Exhibit No. 1.10: Suggestions for improving multipoint entry and credit system

Multipoint entry and credit system	Performance indicator	Suggestion
Entry qualification	Entry of students with different qualifications Completion of diploma in different duration Reduction in frustration among slow learners and promotion of competition among fast learners	Pattern of entry to polytechnic to be reviewed Entry of more and more 12+ students Entry of 10+ or 12+ students twice a year Opportunity to be provided for remedial learning to slow learners
Course selection and resources	Students demand for other courses Number of soft and diversified courses offered Expertise among staff and new equipment Catering the needs of industry Qualitative improvement due to passing of pre requisite courses	Recruitment of staff as per workload Purchase of equipment as per requirements Training of teachers and staff In plant training of students Review of condition of passing perquisite courses Revision of curriculum in three years Orientation programmes for students before starting the new term
Alternative roots	Courses provided, offered, selected Time required for conduction of examination and declaration of results Maintenance of record Difficulty in preparing timetable	Maximum possible courses to be offered Revision of rules for limiting number of courses for registration Prerequisite courses to be offered in each term Improving evaluation system Computerization of students record
Self pacing	Choice of courses as per their interest, need and abilities Catering for slow learners and gifted students Need for advice for course selection Time taken for completion of diploma	Courses to be offered as per student's requirement Proper guidance for course selection Orientation programme for becoming aware about guidance and counselling activities Recommendations for guidance and counselling unit

Dandoti, Mahashabde & Jain (1995) have reengineered curriculum development model and developed curriculum for diploma in textile engineering. The model is stated in Exhibit 1.11. They have developed the curriculum document on the basis of area of work in the industry, skills required for completing the work in a particular area. They have defined the technical terms used in curriculum, suggested the course structure along with theory and practical, and examination scheme. They have made the provision of in plant training, entrepreneurship and personality development in the curriculum. They have suggested for incorporating new technology area, multi skills and development of proper attitude. More opportunity should be provided to students to have hands on experiences during in plant training. They have suggested that diversified courses should be introduced in final semester.

Exhibit No. 1.11: Reengineered curriculum development model

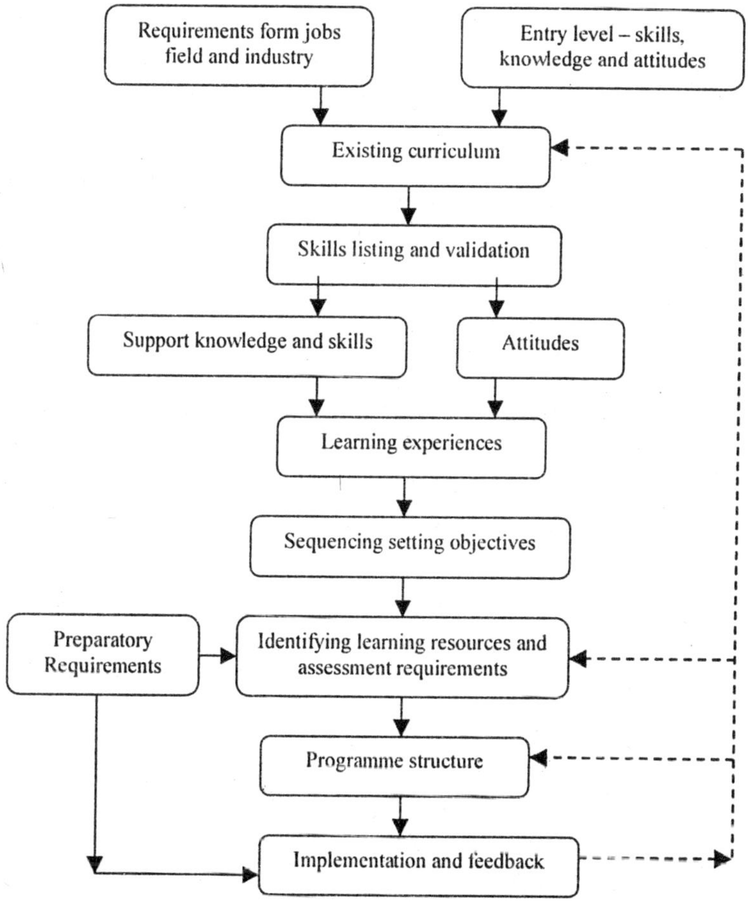

Shrivastva, Tegar, & Lahiri (1998) have suggested a modular approach to achieve competencies. They have suggested that in first stage concentration is given on achieving academic objectives in detail including acquisition of knowledge, psychomotor skills and certain essential skills

within the institute to the extent possible and attainable. Second stage deals with the training cycle on developing competencies essential for the industry. Evaluation of competencies is carried out during this cycle with the standards set down by industries. The two-stage model is shown in Exhibit 1.12

Exhibit No. 1.12: Composite model for developing manpower

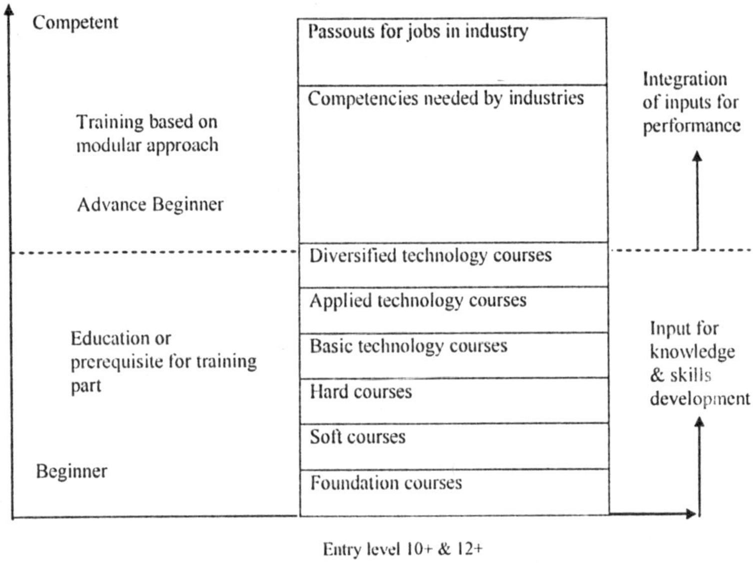

Chondhikar & Lahiri (1999) have developed the competency based curriculum for three courses and designed assessment scheme. They have used a model to design curriculum and assessment scheme shown in Exhibit 1.13.

They have derived competencies from the job and then they have identified broad supporting skills. Teachers and industry experts validated all the competencies and broad supporting skills. They arranged the competencies in sequence and detailed out the curriculum. They have validated the practical experiences. They have noted that more emphasis is given to skills development, provision of flexibility is made, provision of industrial training is made as extended laboratory, more emphasis is given on use of professional softwares and weaknesses of students have been considered in designing the curriculum. They have noted that assessment of competency is a process of collecting evidence by one or

Exhibit No. 1.13: Model of competency based curriculum design and assessment scheme

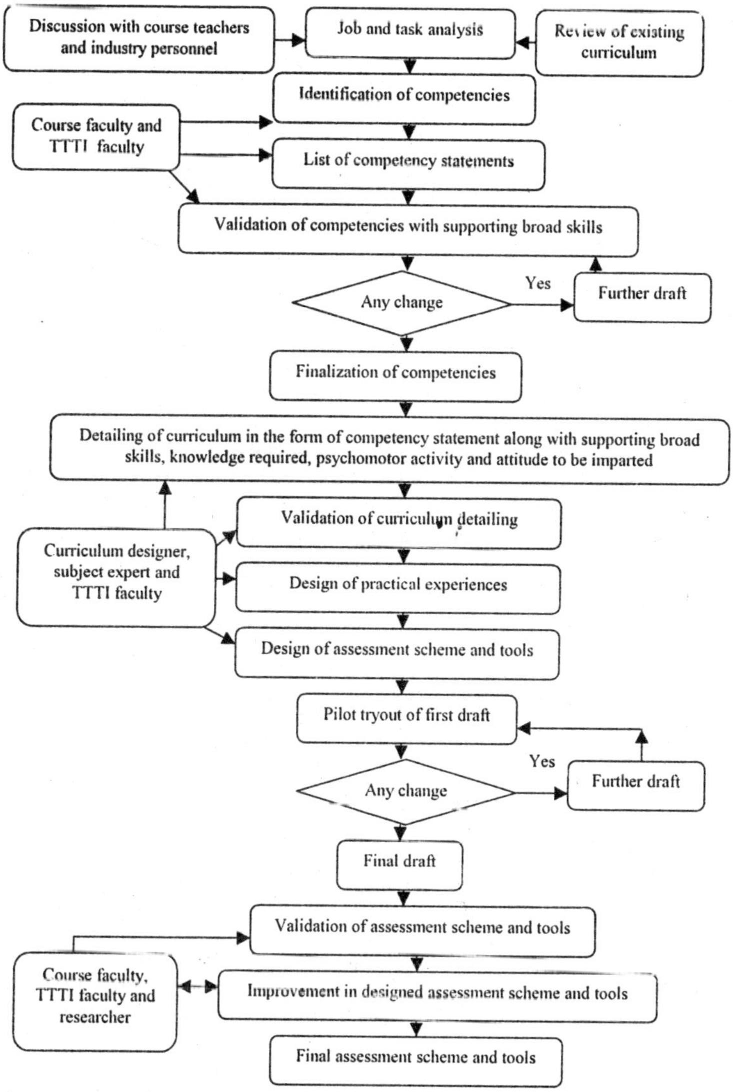

more means and making judgment to see whether competency is achieved or not. They have noted some basic features of assessment of competency. These are stated in Exhibit 1.14.

Exhibit No. 1.14: Features of competency assessment

- There should be continuous assessment of knowledge, skills and attitudes.
- Desired level of attainment of competency is important.
- The competency attainment is assessed against standards/criteria and students know these in advance. These standards and criteria serve the purpose of feedback to students.
- Certification of competencies is based on two-point scale. However marks can also be allotted for each competency for comparison among students.
- Competency statements are performance oriented hence assessment becomes easy by observation or evidences.
- Standard/criteria are to be set by employers.
- Competency should always be linked with time and should have ethical value.
- Competency is achieved through practice so more weightage should be given to practice.
- There should be continuous assessment to provide constructive feedback to students.
- Separate tools for continuous assessment and practice should be used.
- Cognitive competencies need to be assessed through assignments.
- 75 per cent weightage should be given for continuous assessment and 25 per cent weightage should be given for end of term assessment.
- 75 per cent weightage to practical experiences and 25 per cent weightage to cognitive skills is given.
- Passing criteria for end of term examination and oral examination is kept 50 per cent. Similarly passing criteria for assignments and progressive test is kept 50 per cent.
- Passing criteria for practical experiences is kept 80%.
- If students fail to achieve prerequisite competency s/he is not allowed to take advanced competency.
- Students can take up any independent competency.
- Student if fail in continuous assessment is not allowed to appear in end of term examination.
- Profile reporting is essential in continuous assessment.
- Progressive assessment is to be integrated with teaching learning process.

They have noted significant suggestions for implementing competency based curriculum and assessment scheme. These suggestions are;

- To introduce competency-based curriculum prior orientation is necessary

- Teachers should be motivated, devoted and committed to make competency based curriculum feasible
- There has to be teachers with industrial experiences
- Minimum facilities should be created to implement the competency based curriculum
- The students record should be computerized

Pagare & Rawlley (2000) reported on curriculum document, curriculum implementation and performance of passouts as follows.

Curriculum Document: they have reported that the curriculum document contains all essential and desirable components such as title of the programme, rationale of the programme, aims of the programme, minimum entry qualification, programme duration, intake capacity, job descriptions, procedure of writing job description, procedure of validating the job description, relation of job function and curriculum objectives, programme structure and scheme of examination, and examination rules. They have reported that details of course such as course title, and code, teaching scheme of the course, rationale/objectives of each course, detailed contents of each course, contents of each topic provided with time duration, marks allotted for assessment, instructional strategy suggested for each topic, list of demonstrations, list of experiments, and number of industrial visits, assessment plan of a course and total programme, reference books/codes, specifications, handouts, details of each course, the probable vacation duration, preparation time and examination time, sample path of the programme, number of courses to be taken from each level, credit points for each level of courses and total programme and prerequisite courses at different levels are mentioned. They have reported that some desirable components such as table of specification, sample question paper, meaning of different terms used in autonomy, information regarding institute and list of equipment were not included in the curriculum document. The ratio of theory and practice ranges between 60-40 to 50-50. The flexibility ratio ranges from 1.5 to 1.63. They have reported that most of the teachers agree with overall structure of the curriculum. They have mentioned that topics are relevant and in logical sequence. The curriculum document is user friendly.

Curriculum Implementation: they have reported that most of the trained teachers are involved in implementing the curriculum. Teachers prepare well before engaging the classes and practical. Teachers use variety of teaching methods. The most popular method is assignment and question answer. They use media in the classroom. The library and other facilities are adequate. Teachers engage extra classes and complete the curriculum. Industry experts are also invited to deliver the lectures. The attendance, punctuality, interest and performance on progressive tests are reported good. They have reported that the teachers and students are satisfied with laboratory work. Teachers use demonstration and practical assignment methods in laboratory. They check the journals and laboratory sheets and assign the grades. Teachers provide feedback for improvement and solve problems. The facilities available in laboratory are sufficient. The record of students' progress is maintained in the laboratory. All the students are taken to industrial visits to get exposure of machinery and techniques. Students prepare a report on visit. It helps in understanding the theory and practice. However students do not select projects from industry. The students get benefit from industrial visits and lectures from experts. They get exposure to production, technical, management, entrepreneurship, personality development and general knowledge. They have reported that the progressive assessment is carried out that helps in developing habit of continuous study. The students are confident in taking progressive tests. They find sufficient time to respond to questions. Teachers organize progressive tests, library assignment and mini project for progressive assessment. In laboratory progressive and summative assessment mode is used and immediate knowledge of results is provided. Teachers analyze the results of progressive work and improve the teaching learning method. All results are declared within fifteen days.

Performance of Passouts: the significant increase in result of student is reported after grant of autonomy. The percentage of marks of students has also increased. The institute is providing placement services to students through placement cell and guidance and counselling cell. The industries are approaching the institution and institution is also approaching to industry for providing employment. The employment is as high as 100 per cent. The number of students opting for higher education has increased after autonomy.

Joshua and Soni (2001) have evolved a model of competency based curriculum design and named it TTTI-Xavier Model of curriculum development. The model is based on the significant logical steps starting in the sequence of occupation analysis, on the basis of job-role analysis and deriving competencies for each job-role. Then each competency is spelled out on broad skills and sub skills. Each sub skill is analyzed to derive practical skills, cognitive skills, attitudes and social skills. On the basis previous analysis, subject-matter is derived and it is cluster/re-organize into course and programme structure is decided.

They have collected responses of industries on technical competencies and generic competencies. They have collected responses on perception of passouts on same competencies and decided the priority of the competencies to be addressed in the curriculum. They classified the competencies as core and desirable and developed the curriculum following the model. They designed the credit-based curriculum allocating separate credits for theory and practice. The competencies are arranged in logical manner to assure the development of prerequisite competency before developing the higher competency. They have suggested implementation guide for each course in which they have described credits for practical and cognitive skills, duration, competency map, resources required, instructional strategy for classroom and laboratory, industrial visit and training, assessment scheme of learning process and learning outcome, skills assessment tools and competency certification. Researchers have scientifically designed competency based curriculum, implemented in St. Xavier's Technical Institute Mumbai with industry partnership and evaluated the impact. This is a latest tested and practical model of competency-based curriculum design.

Researchers have noted that every competency has cognitive, practical and social skills. So to make the assessment valid and reliable assessment at progressive assessment at micro level and competency assessment at macro level should be carried out. They have suggested an assessment design that describes the assessment of practical skills and attitudes and cognitive skills and attitudes. They have suggested that 50 per cent weightage should be given to each practical and cognitive skill. They have suggested that 50 per cent weightage should be given to progressive and end of term assessment for both the skills. They have suggested that practical skills and attitudes should be used using portfolio assessment, mini project, viva voce, and end term assessment. They have suggested that cognitive skills and attitudes should be assessed using progressive and end of term tests.

They have enumerated new findings of their research study in the area of competency based curriculum development. These are; the evolved model is dynamic, implementation guide ensures effective implementation, the concept of core and desirable and partial competencies, sub skills and thinking skills, wholesome curriculum, standard assessment procedure, competency certification, innovations in classroom instructions, laboratory instructions and industrial training, accreditation of prior learning, modular instruction, flexibility in learning, and transparent and open process of educational programmes.

Armarkar & Saksena (2002) have identified key aspects influencing effectiveness of curriculum implantation. These are industry institution interaction, faculty development, guidance and counselling, continuous assessment, internal monitoring, instructional resources and teaching learning process. They have further detailed out these areas in indicators. The present status on curriculum implementation is studied on these indicators and reported that different polytechnics are using different practices for implementing the curriculum. They have reported significant difficulties faced by polytechnics in implementing the curriculum in key aspects. And finally they have suggested strategies for effective implementation of curriculum.

7. Summary

Curriculum is a written well-designed educational plan prepared to produce competent and professional passouts from engineering institutions. Policy-makers, administrators, teachers, students, certifying agencies and employers use this document for various purposes but it is prepared in such a way so that it is objectively interpreted by every one. Competency based curriculum design has picked up very fast in technical education system but it is at infancy stage. The promoters of competency based curriculum are still following traditional approaches of curriculum design, implementation and evaluation. The one strong reason for this practice is that most of the teachers are not familiar and comfortable with the competency based curriculum design approach. They want to implement the change in incremental fashion that is not going to serve the competency based curriculum development, implementation and evaluation purpose. There is a need to totally reengineer the whole process of competency development. There is a strong need to rethink on various elements of curriculum design, implementation and evaluation process. There is a need to design strategy to deliberately drop the old methods and invent new methods aligned to manage competency based curriculum, which are effective and efficient. The competency based curriculum should have competency development approach which may require total shift on number of parameters of educational programmes such as duration of the programme, approach of detailing the curriculum, design of learning methods, flexibility in the curriculum, role of the governing body, principal, teachers, and supporting staff, role of the students, responsibility of learning, certification of learning/competency, cost of the education, role of the stakeholders including industry and employers, facilities in the institution and so on. The shift should be total or no shift, the partial shift confuses curriculum designers, implementers, evaluators and employers. There should only one formula followed that is development of competency and proficiency in curriculum design, implementation and evaluation rest of the things should be totally flexible and support the competency and proficiency development. So, for different disciplines and for different levels of technical educational programmes variety of appropriate models, approaches, procedures, resources, networking, collaboration, cooperation, duration, strategy, learning resources etc should be used which are effective and efficient.

8. Activity

Please go through curriculum document and identify the weaknesses, gaps and develop a model to make it competency based/refine the competencies/modify the competencies, add competencies/identify competencies which are essentials to take up professional positions or establish an enterprise. Discuss the model with the faculty of your discipline and related disciplines and design strategies to take steps at your level to modify and implement the curriculum.

2

Management of Learning

Objectives: The readers will be able to:

1. Define the concept of learning
2. Explain the characteristics of the learner
3. Describe the learning process
4. List the dimensions of learning process
5. List the domains of learning
6. Describe the hierarchy of learning in each domain of learning
7. Explain learning methods
8. Compare learning methods on given parameters
9. Explain the process of learning through teaching
10. Describe the role of a teacher for producing learning
11. Describe the guidelines for a teacher to produce effective learning.

1. Introduction

Over the years the main focus of technical educational was to teach students for learning. It is not necessary that the students will learn what the teachers are teaching. They may not give attention to the teaching and mis the learning links in the process of teaching. In fact the teachers learn a lot teaching students. They may learn wrong things about learning of students during the process of teaching. Teachers often adopt a particular teaching style throughout the life. They practice the same style of teaching irrespective of the subject they are teaching and students they are teaching. The main players of teaching process are teachers so they have to bear the responsibility of performing teaching process. They have to struggle during the process of teaching for every thing including bringing students in the classroom.

Learning of students depends on numbers of factors including teaching by teachers. It is necessary to shift the focus from teaching to learning. The shift requires extra efforts on the part of the teachers outside the classroom. They have to plan the complete learning process of students in the classroom, laboratory, industry, library, students' home and learning resources utilisation center. They are required to shift in their role from teaching to learning. The shift in role from teaching to producing desired level of learning in students requires professional and innovative skills.

2. Concept of Learning

Concept of learning in technical students is altogether different than general learning. Technical students are required to exhibit their competency to perform the role professionally. Their contribution to society and economy can do miracle for achieving social and economical objectives. At the same time their small mistake can lead to disaster and take lives of thousands of people within no time. The learning of technical students cannot be left to the chance. They have to be competent and proficient to do the job and perform changing role in their employer's organisation. Technical institutions lay sound foundation for developing competencies and attaining proficiency level. But this is not enough. They have to be prepared for present and future for changing world of work. They need to develop habit of self learning, learning to learn, learning for positive learning, learning for better cause, learning to harness their full potential and potential of others in a joyful manner for making the life more comfortable and satisfactory. They are expected to save, conserve and nurture the gift of the god for future generations as their gift. The learning has to be with a purpose and ambition.

Students joining technical institutions are matured and are having potential for learning at enormous level. It is the teacher who has to shape the behaviour of the students to create better world to live. The students come with different ambitions, interest, preferences, determination and vision. It is the teacher who shows them path to their vision. S/he removes obstructions, barriers and problems to their vision. S/he creates healthy climate to traverse the path in a joyful manner. S/he creates memorable experiences for students to carry throughout life.

3. The Learner

The engineering students are quite different than their predecessor so for learning maturity is concerned. In some areas they are far ahead from their teachers because of access to television, computers and internet connecting the whole world with access to all types of latest information within no time. They have wide variety of expectations from teachers and technical institutions. The characteristics of engineering students are listed in Exhibit 2.1.

Exhibit No. 2.1: Characteristics of engineering students

- They are more conscious to their career and want to enjoy the life. They want to learn career related competencies and not outdated theory.
- They have interest in purposeful learning rather than copy of the old book on green board or on power point.
- They want experiential learning through challenging learning projects. They want to learn learning. They want to have a deeper feel of it.
- They want respect and recognition at the same time want to open up the hidden portion of the self.
- Their needs of the learning are varied and strong. They want to satisfy their learning needs so want flexibility in learning process.
- They are ready to learn skills of their interest at any time and at any cost. They want an expert who can make them learn joyfully.
- They have different styles of learning. They want flexibility in learning process and learning methods.
- They explore opportunities for learning and not for getting bored listening for hours and hours without relevance.
- They want psychological, emotional and social support during the process of learning. They want to share the learning, feelings and learning problems openly with their true friends may be teacher.
- They want to spend their precious time for fruitful activities may be learning activities. They want to become mover of the learning process. They want to do concrete and significant things. They do not want to kill their time in irrelevant activities.
- They want to develop their personality. They want to develop competencies related to personality, entrepreneurship, software development and use, pursuing hobbies, and career.
- They want to develop competencies such as facing competition and crisis.
- They learn uniquely. There are differences in individuals that affect the learning process. They want that individual differences should be recognized by the teacher and design the learning process to suit them.

4. Learning Process

Learning is a dynamic process. The learner, the teacher, learning resources, learning environment and learning objectives go as input to learning process. The interaction takes place among learning inputs and the output is produced in the form of learning outcome. The learning outcome is development of competence of students and experienced teachers. The output of the learning process provides feedback to learning inputs and learning process for improvement in terms of leaning, time saving, effort saving, improving quality of learning resources, improving the learning environment and competence of the teacher. It makes the learner competent to perform the role competently and proficiently. The learner performs the process of learning and s/he is the immediate beneficiary of the process. In the long run employers and whole society is the beneficiary. Learning process is a complex process of change in behaviour of the learners. The process has various dimensions listed in Exhibit 2.2.

Exhibit No. 2.2: Dimensions of learning process

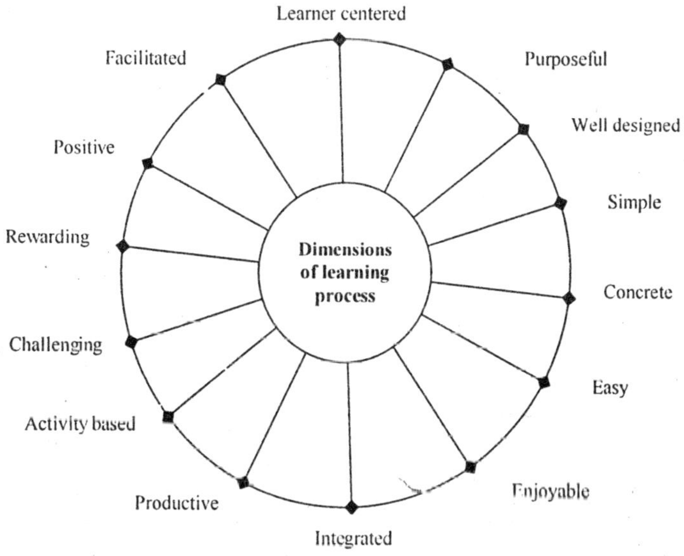

4.1 Learner Centered

The learning process should concentrate on the learner. It should satisfy the learning needs of the students. It should match with the entry behaviour of the students. It should prepare the students for the profession. The planning of different learning events in learning process should be carefully designed. The learning events and activities should be based on previous knowledge, skills and attitudes of the students. The learning events should fit with learning capabilities of the students.

4.2 Purposeful

The learning should be with a purpose meaning there by it should develop the competency required to perform the role in the employers organisation or in self-enterprise. Students should realize in the beginning of the learning process the purpose and importance of learning. The purpose of learning should create sort of urgency for learning. It should create inner urge for learning. Learning with a purpose gets stored in the permanent memory. It is easy to retrieve the purposeful information from permanent memory to workable memory.

4.3 Well Designed

The learning process should be well designed. A teacher on the basis of curriculum and entry level of the students designs the learning process. The teacher keeps in mind the principles of learning while designing the learning process and learning events. S/he designs the learning process and learning events in a way that students learn naturally. As they learn while playing and interacting with nature.

4.4 Simple

The learning process should be as simple as possible. To make it simple it should be very close to nature, practice and reality. It should create learning environment that foster automatic learning. It should require minimum efforts on the part of the learner and produce maximum learning. All the learning resources should be well organized to facilitate the learning process. It does not mean that learning process should not create opportunity for struggle for learning.

4.5 Concrete

The learning process should incorporate concrete concepts, ideas and experiences. These concepts, ideas and experiences should provide rich stimulus for learning. Provision of concrete concepts, ideas and experiences can be made using laboratory, workshop and real life situations. It is worth to explore the real world first than thinking about imaginary world. Concrete experiences produce unforgettable learning. It creates intense interest in learning process.

4.6 Easy

The learning process should be as easy as possible. An analogy of staircase, lift, and elevator can be cited here. One can climb to all heights with comfortable heights of stairs with appropriate landings to regain the energy. One can use lift, elevator, escalators (technology) to climb with ease and comfort to do business at any story. One should not consume all energy in climbing the heights but it needs to be saved for performing the task. Similarly students should not exhaust their all energy to learn and then no energy for performing the jobs. The learning process should be as easy as play.

4.7 Enjoyable

Every learning event, activity and experience should create joy and fun. The students should come forward on their own to participate in learning process. The learning process should create an opportunity for human processes such as open interaction, expressing, proposing, sharing, criticizing, supplementing, complementing, appreciating, recognizing, encouraging, accepting, rejecting, collaborating, cooperating, influencing, winning, losing, evaluating, celebrating and so on.

4.8. Integrated

The learning events, activities and experiences should be integrated and interwoven to produce whole or complete learning to develop competencies to perform the role. The learning experiences should act as colourful flowers woven in a thread to make a beautiful garland. Each flower in the garland has its importance and beauty at the same time it adds to beauty of the garland. All the learning activities, events and experiences should be logically arranged with creativity to make the complete process of learning enjoyable.

4.9. Productive

The learning process should produce desired competency and proficiency in the learner to perform the role. It should bring the desired change in the behaviour of the learner. It should be effective and efficient to produce productive learning. There should not be wastage of time, money and efforts of the students. The output of learning should be visible and measurable in concrete terms.

4.10 Activity Based

The meaningful learning would take place when learner performs the meaningful learning activities. S/he feels the joy of learning when s/he drives the learning process and feels the excitement of climbing and rolling down, enjoying the turns and curbs of learning and fascinating with climate and culture along the learning journey. S/he should be responsible for taking initiative to learn. S/he should get an opportunity to experience, experiment, innovate, evaluate, modify and feel the learning activities. True learning is caused by enrichment of experiences on significant activities.

4.11 Challenging

The learning process should create enough challenges to motivate the learners to apply previously learnt competencies to learn further. It should provide an opportunity to learners to integrate the learning of various subjects and to complete the learning event successfully. The challenge may be in the form of a difficulty, complexity, competition and crisis. The learning challenge should invite students to conceptualize, think. analyze, experiment, synthesize, and review previous learning for further learning.

4.12 Rewarding

Learning should be rewarding. Each learning event should create some significant rewards for the learners. It should satisfy their inner need to learn or they should be able to see the result of the learning in the form of a solution of a problem or decision in a situation or a plan to accomplish or design of a production process or some thing concrete. These intrinsic rewards should be inbuilt part of the learning process. If these rewards are not possible in learning process provision should be made for extrinsic rewards.

4.13 Positive

The learning should be desired learning and not the unwanted learning from the environment. The negative learning is difficult to forget and it may create destructive thinking in the minds of the students. The learning form the environment may be negative and hazardous to the students as well as to the society. Perhaps it is the affective part of the learning and it has to be controlled right from the beginning.

4.14 Facilitated

Learning is a process and each process requires to be facilitated by a competent person. In case of learning teacher is a facilitator to the process. S/he facilitates the process in many ways such as planning the learning process, providing learning resources, providing encouragement during the process of learning, creating healthy environment for learning, solving learning problems, assessing the learning outcomes, providing constructive feedback for improving learning, counselling for various purposes and so on.

5. Domains of Learning

Learning can be classified in three broad categories called domains of learning. These categories are related to thinking, doing and feeling. Thinking takes place in our brain, doing is related to hands and feet and feeling is relates to heart. Learning in these categories is briefly described in following paragraphs:

5.1 Cognitive Domain

Brain is the storehouse of all the information it receives from different senses. Basically the brain controls all the parts and functions of the body. The stored information is processed in the brain with reference to a particular purpose. The cognitive domain is primarily related to thinking skills. It is related to acquiring, storing, processing, and retrieval of the information. It helps people to do mental work such as recalling the information, identifying, defining, analyzing and solving the problem, designing strategy, designing a product or service, evaluating the effectiveness and efficiency of a process, planning, providing information with reference to query, questioning the issue, reasoning, rationalizing, justifying, decision-making, report writing, convincing, counselling, communicating, resolving, concluding, comparing, influencing and so on. The greater part of the job of the engineers is related to cognitive domain. In twenty first century more emphasis is given on variety of cognitive skills such as thinking to think, thinking strategically, thinking to visualize whole on the basis of available information, creative thinking, seeing details, predicting, analyzing the issues, learning fast, learning to learn, learning for life and so on. In undergraduate programmes and postgraduate programmes these cognitive skills should be developed with reference to profession instead of rote learning, appearing in examination, passing examination and forgetting. In fact these cognitive skills will help the students to stand in global market.

5.2 Psychomotor Domain

Brain controls the functions of each and every part of the body. It controls the action part as well. So there are two aspects of performing any task that is what is to be done and how it is to be done. Knowing part is related to cognitive domain and doing part is related to movements of muscles. There are some jobs that are physically performed by engineers for these jobs they are required to learn control of movements of muscles and integrate physical activities to perform professionally. In performing activities more than one senses act in order to perform the task. The performance results from two processes. The receptor process senses the information through senses and takes it to brain. The effectors process directs the body parts to do movements in order to perform the task. Both the process are interlinked and controlled by the brain. The brain takes the decision on the basis of information received. The movements of parts of the body perform a task naturally after practice and experience. The integration of movements of parts of the body gets controlled and refined through training, learning, practice and feedback. The proficiency is developed in five stages that is planning the activity, initiating it, controlling it, terminating it, and checking that it has been done correctly.

5.3 Affective Domain

There is one more aspect of doing side and that is related to attitude of the person performing the task. There are numerous tasks that are hazardous for the performer and mankind. A small ignorance of attitude may create crisis, conflict, disaster and chaos. These tasks are very important from quality, service, and cost point of view. Apart from the task professionals work together to perform a task. They are expected to work in a healthy atmosphere. It all requires good attitudes. So the performance of the task is important but it is more important that it should be safely performed. It should be performed with joy and fun in correct way. The task related behaviour is dealt with affective domain.

6. Learning Methods

There are various methods of learning that can be used during the process of learning by learners and teacher. An indicative list of learning methods is given in Exhibit 2.3. The strengths, limitations and use of these methods are briefly described in subsequent paragraphs.

Exhibit No. 2.3: Learning methods

➢ Learning by practice ➢ Learning from actions ➢ Learning by projects ➢ Learning through problem solving ➢ Learning thorough assignments ➢ Learning from discussions and interactions ➢ Learning from introspections ➢ Learning from struggle ➢ Learning collectively ➢ Action learning ➢ Learning from opportunities ➢ Learning through reading ➢ Learning from observation ➢ Learning by listening ➢ Learning from mistakes ➢ Learning through copying ➢ Learning under guidance	➢ Learning from feedback ➢ Learning by discovery ➢ Learning by thinking ➢ Learning by role playing ➢ Learning from games ➢ Learning from seminars, conferences and symposium ➢ Learning from Internet ➢ Learning from researches ➢ Learning through imitation ➢ Learning from creativity ➢ Learning through assessment ➢ Learning from simulation ➢ Learning through experimentation ➢ Learning through experiences ➢ Learning from competitions ➢ Learning from technology

6.1 Learning by Practice

Practice makes the man perfect. In general all skills whether cognitive, or psychomotor or attitudinal requires practice. More you practice the skills more you refine it. Especially the psychomotor skills requires good amount of practice. Practice involves the learners' whole in the learning process. Learners get immediate and continuous feedback on the quality of performance thereby enriching the learning in every subsequent practice. During initial phases of learning skills practice is always done under the guidance of a teacher. The teacher is required to provide socio emotional support to learners. S/he provides the constructive and immediate feedback for refining the skills. The skills learning are a chain of practice—feedback-practice and use skills in new situation—feedback—practice.

6.2 Learning from Actions

Actions provide an opportunity to be active and be part of the learning process. In many situations real life practice is not possible under such situations students are asked to participate in simulated conditions. These simulated conditions provide them an opportunity to learn the skills in correct way. Actions are also simulated to teach attitudes. It is said that attitudes are caught. Actions enrich the learning and learning process.

6.3 Learning from Projects

Projects provide an opportunity to learn in all the three domains of learning. They provide the scope for integrating the learning of different competencies and complete the project activities. Projects are based on principles of struggle for learning, application of learning, bearing responsibility for learning, collective learning, dynamic learning and transfer of learning. Projects create challenge and urgency for performance. They are considered to be good means of testing the competencies of students.

6.4 Learning through Problem Solving

Problem solving situations create scope for applying the learning in real life situation. It is good way to practice and apply the learning in classroom situation. Problem solving can be done individually or in a group. It can be related to single concept or many concepts. It can be done in the classroom or at home. Problems can be provided to students in many forms such as; case study, puzzle, game, mini project and even real life problem. Problem solving develops defining, analytical, creative and reporting skills.

6.5 Learning through Assignments

Assignments are considered to be the good means of shifting responsibility of learning to students. Assignments make students active, participative and performing. They stimulate the thinking process. Assignments create challenges and demonstrate the purpose of learning. They are good means of intrinsic feedback on learning progress. There is a wide range of assignments such as classroom assignments, library assignments, laboratory assignments, internet assignment, and industry assignments. Assignments create enough scope for practicing learning and refining the learning outcome. It helps to increase the proficiency.

6.6 Learning from Discussions and Interactions

Students have variety of needs including need for recognition and belongingness. The discussion and interaction provide them to express and share their views and feelings. The principle of peer learning holds good in interaction and discussions. Variety of skills such as influencing, convincing, thinking creativity, communication, listening, respecting, trusting, designing, collaborating, cooperating, criticizing, leading, resolving, judging, encouraging and so on are developed through interactions and discussions. Apart from technical skills these skills are essential for working internationally in empowered teams.

6.7 Learning from Introspection

Students should be encouraged to do introspection and analysis of their performance. They should be asked to note down their strengths and weaknesses related to learning. They should be asked to find out ways and means to use their strengths and remove their weaknesses. Students should be encouraged to analyze all aspects of their learning styles, preferences and modes. Students should be encouraged to use self-checks to measure learning outcomes and difficulties. They should be asked to maintain a log of their learning strengths and learning difficulties.

6.8 Learning from Struggle

Students should be exposed to step-by-step difficult situations to learn through struggle. The struggle should encourage the students to move further and farther in the process of learning. There has to be inbuilt rewards for learning achievements in learning process. Learning through struggle is used in self-learning instructional materials, games, puzzles, cases studies, action learning and series of assignments. Continuously increasing difficulty level in the learning process motivates the learners to complete learning process and achieve the learning objectives. They can be put in teams to learn and come out from unfamiliar situation. Students will use their creativity and mobilize their resources to come out from the situation. They will develop confidence for resolving uncertain and unfamiliar situations because they have learnt skills of struggling and learning. The difficulty level should not be beyond the capacity and ability of students otherwise it might turn learning situation in frustration.

6.9 Learning Collectively

The power of synergy is boosted in collective learning. Students learn collectively to set learning objectives and achieve them. They learn to live collectively and collaborate, cooperate, network, and share the learning objectives. They find the creative ways of learning. There are numerous learning methods available for collective learning in the institution such as action learning, creativity techniques, group discussions, case method, U method, force field analysis, fish bowl, fish bone, tree analysis, role analysis, stakeholders analysis, multiple role play, relationship mapping, business process reengineering, meetings, quality circles, seminars, projects etc.

6.10 Action Learning

It is a process of collective learning from the real life situation. Situation may be related to problem solving, decision-making, planning, implementing plans, resolving conflict, developing something new and so on. During the process of dealing with the situation students learn collectively from the interaction, discussion and reflection on actions taken. During performing they seek intrinsic feedback from action and receive extrinsic feedback from fellow team members. Students learn through solving real life problems as well as dealing with uncertainties and risks. It produces learning in all the three domains of learning that is cognitive, affective and psychomotor. It prepares students to accept and meet challenges. Students learn skills of thinking to think and challenge their own learning through action learning.

6.11 Learning from Opportunities

Institutions work in an external open environment. They have linkages with variety of organisations and institutions. Many learning opportunities are available in the external environment for the unique and different learning of the students. The potential opportunities include participation in special workshops, seminars, debate, case study, meet, competitions, social activities etc. Professional bodies and organisations sponsor these opportunities to achieve specific purpose.

6.12 Learning through Reading

Technical institutions are having well equipped library and learning utilisation center. They have latest literature and information related to business and culture. They are networked with sister institutions, research institutions and industries. Students have a choice to select one or two hobbies or areas of their interest and read literature and take notes. They can develop a habit of writing on the topic of their interest and publish it in newspapers and professional journals. Doing so they can have specialisation in area of their interest. Apart from this they can do general reading of books, journals, and research studies and learn many new and latest things.

6.13 Learning from Observations

Learning from observation facilitates the process of concept formation. Learning through observation is concrete and long lasting because it uses the strongest sense that is sight. Observation helps to understand the whole as well as part. Students learn to describe minute things in real life situation. They learn to explore the real world of work. They can easily understand the interrelationship among the parts of a machine, various process, technologies, human beings and machine etc. Observation arouses interest of the students for learning particular technology and technique. Observation is a first step in the process of skills and attitudes development.

6.14 Learning by Listening

Traditional students were forced to listen and learn. Listening is a method to learn from lectures, interactions, discussions, interviews and similar interpersonal communications Listening helps to learn empathy, gather new information, validate information, know the intension of communicator, understanding feelings of others and so on. It stops the students to jump to conclusions, form wrong concept, prejudice opinion about any person or process or thing. Good listening develops the skills of clarifying, encouraging, reflecting and concluding. Listening is a key to interpersonal skills development.

6.15 Learning from Mistakes

Mistakes are good teacher of students in learning process. Students have a long list of mistakes they commit generally. They analyze these mistakes individually and collectively to find solution. They learn during the process of identifying, analyzing and correcting mistakes. Students use trial and error method to correct mistake. They learn from success and failures. Students should be encouraged to prepare a list of mistakes at the end of the sessions such mistakes should be discussed to find the solution and not to commit them in future. After all prevention is better than cure. The strong punishment for students could be ask them to analyze their mistakes and tell others how they can avoid committing such mistakes.

6.16 Learning through Copying

There are many students and teachers in the campus possessing distinct and different skills and talent. Some are more influential than others, some are creative, some are analytical, some are visionary and some are humorous and so on. Different types of learning skills are required to learn various competencies. Considering the type of learning one can copy the style and skills of the person best suiting in that situation. One can use his/her wisdom in copying the behaviour or style of role models. It boosts confidence to learn new competencies. One should assure that s/he has selected right person and right style for copying otherwise it may lead to disaster.

6.17 Learning under Guidance

Learning under the guidance of experienced and expert teacher or senior students reduces time of learning. It minimizes the repetition of learning mistakes. One can develop confidence that s/he has chosen a right path of learning and right way of learning. Learning under the guidance helps to receive constructive feedback on the quality of learning and progress of learning. Right guidance on right time is provided by the guide that acts as a source of motivation for the performance. Learning under guidance prepares the students to take up higher level learning experiences. The system of teacher, guardian, mentor and learning facilitator is being used to provide proper learning guidance to students.

6.18 Learning from Feedback

Students receive internal and external feedback on their progress on learning. They get internal feedback from the progress on assignments, projects, and performance in group learning, individual learning, role-play, game, test and similar activities. Internal feedback is a very strong source of motivation, encouragement and reward. Internal feedback enhances motivation to learn more and faster. Teachers, peers and coach offer positive, constructive and purposeful feedback on progress of learning and performance on the assignment, project, game, role-play and similar tasks. The feedback offered by them is rewarding and encouraging to do better.

6.19 Learning by Discovery

Students form their own concepts and learn the world of work in their own way. They learn skills such as exploring, reasoning, judgmental and drawing conclusion from discovery. They learn about real life situation and concept, principles and theory underlying it. They develop imagination and hypothesizing skills in discovery situations. It creates anxiety to know unknown and do adventure that is the human tendency. They learn to do experimentation, take risk and work in unfamiliar situations.

6.20 Learning by Thinking

Thinking promotes learning in cognitive domain. It develops learning to recall of previously learnt concepts and apply them to learning situation. It also helps to generate new, different, and original ideas. Thinking promotes reasoning and imagination. It helps to visualize the unfamiliar situation and resolve the situation. Thinking skills are required for planning, decision-making, problem solving, conducting scientific inquiry and strategy design. Teachers use various methods to develop thinking skills such as problem solving, role-play, game, creativity techniques and case methods.

6.21 Learning by Role-playing

Role-playing method of learning is widely used to develop professional attitudes along with professional competence. It develops interpersonal skills, values, ethics and norms required to productively work with people and satisfy the needs of the customers, clients and beneficiaries. It is helpful to develop empathy and sympathy for the people. It is a live experience to know the self and others with relation to a situation. It is a method to approach the situation in different ways and come out with non-traditional views on the situation. The role-playing is a replication of real life situation in the classroom or laboratory. It is a risk free method of learning. It is based on principles of learning and psychology such as close to real life, experiential learning, feeling the excitement of the situation and its objectives, thinking to perform better, design strategy as per requirements of the situation, feedback on progress, involvement in the learning process, introspection of performance and continuous improvement. Development of interpersonal and professional skills is significant to immediate productivity. Role-playing provides an opportunity to exhibit the behaviour on the task.

6.22 Learning from Games

Educational games provide an opportunity to accept the challenges inbuilt in the game and use previously learnt concepts and principles in new and different situation to learn more and refine previously learnt skills. The educational games are based on competitive spirit. They provide opportunities for learning in natural and joyful way. Students learn to design approaches to win the game, apply them while playing and evaluate the effectiveness of their approaches. At the same time they guess and evaluate the strategy of opponents also. Educational games provide an opportunity to learn spontaneously.

6.23 Learning from Seminars, Conferences and Symposium

Seminar is a method of learning in which a particular student or group of students explore the assigned topic or problem or issue or principle or process in detail. They get to explore real life situations as well. They explore the problem from various aspects such as its negative effect on the quality, wastage, unnecessary time consumed, amount of efforts required, lead time, safety and so on. In fact seminar provides an opportunity to do a piece of research on given topic or theme or issue. The research may be related to review of literature to find solution of real life problem or design something new or add value to existing practices.

6.24 Learning from Internet

Internet facilities are available everywhere. The teacher can design assignments related to latest technology and techniques and ask students to work on assignments. Students review the material available and achieve learning objectives. They learn associated and related things. The internet assignments create learning interest in wide areas of disciplines. Students search and study latest and significant information. Self-learning packages on various topics are available on internet that can be used by them whenever they wish. Practice related information is also available on internet that helps students to relate theory with practice. Students can see the diagrams, photographs, power point slides and video on internet that enriches the learning process.

6.25 Learning from Researches

The students are required to develop research skills for solving the complex problems, developing new technology and techniques, developing new products and services, meeting the competition, entering in new business, resolving crisis and introducing big changes in the organisation and so on. These are called professional and generic skills related to any business. These skills cannot be learnt in isolation. The students are put under research conditions. They identify the problem or explore the new needs of the customers, define the problem or needs, frame hypothesis, gather information in a systematic way to test the hypothesis and apply the results in real life situation. During the process of conducting research they learn research skills and essential business skills. Each student should under go at least one major research to have a feeling of research skills and generic skills.

6.26 Learning through Imitation

Students learn motor skills and attitudes through imitation. They minutely observe the behaviour of teachers, instructors and their colleagues. They try to copy the behaviour and perform the task. This is the initial method to learn motor skills and attitude. Gradually students develop complex skills through practice and feedback. Students completing this stage of learning successfully develop complex skills and attitudes without much of difficulty. Students have very little scope for using their creativity at this stage of learning. The principle of trial and error, practice and feedback works during the process of imitation.

6.27 Learning form Creativity

Creativity means coming out with new, different and unique idea. Creativity is seeing or expressing new relationship. Creativity is required everywhere in life activities in familiar and unfamiliar situations. Creativity is required in learning process. Creativity fosters thinking process without evaluating the ideas being generated. Creativity is essential to make adjustments in new and different learning environment. The learning is considered to be dull without creativity. Individual and group creativity techniques are used to develop thinking skills. New and different learning produced by creativity helps to apply it in real life situation to learn new things. Teacher plays a very important role to foster creativity in students. S/he can create conducive climate to produce variety, diversity and difference in learning outputs. S/he can use creativity techniques to stimulate creative learning in subjects such as marketing, design, problem solving, and customer needs analysis.

6.28 Learning through Assessment

Every semester the performance of the students is assessed and teacher provides positive feedback to them. Analysis of the assessment results at the end of the semester provides sense of achievement and motivates to think to improve performance in next semester. Formative assessment on assignments, group work and projects helps students to take a stock of learning and design strategies to bring improvements in performance. Self-feedback increases confidence and causes self-learning.

6.29 Learning from Simulation

Students learn many skills in simulated conditions. Learning through simulation is risk free and provide feelings of real life situation. Simulated situations can be created in the classrooms and laboratories to develop particular skills in individuals and groups. Simulation adds the purpose to learning process and ensures participation of the students. There are numbers of simulation techniques available for producing various types of skills to name a few action learning, game, role-play, mechanical simulator, electronic simulator, and computer simulator. Apart from learning application, analysis, synthesis, visualisation skills one can develop right kind of attitudes.

6.30 Learning through Experimentation

Experimentation is a technique that promotes thinking, applying and testing the ideas in a new and different situation. It promotes the habit of exploring, trying, changing and learning. Experimentation fosters learning in higher level of cognitive domain and psychomotor domain. It develops attitudes of discovering new concepts, processes, and technologies. It promotes attitudes for risk taking, careful working, and changing. Experimentation is promoted in the classroom to promote cognitive skills such as development of new product, design of new strategy, exploring better ways of marketing etc. It is promoted in the laboratories and workshops to transfer the skills in newer and different situation. Various management techniques are also used to promote experimentation. The popularly used techniques are survey, process analysis and process design, fish bone diagram, relationship analysis, U process, SWOT analysis, customer supplier charting, projects etc.

6.31 Learning through Experiences

Experiences provide an opportunity to learner to use all the senses of learning that is see, hear, feel, touch and test to explore the real world. Learning comes through experiences. A learner should go through purposeful variety of experiences. Learning experiences make the learner motivated to identify learning needs and satisfy the same. Learners learn differently from the same learning situation because they have different learning needs and experience the learning situation differently. Learners learn from all experiences but if they are consciously exposed to learning situation and they know that they have to learn with reference to something they learn fast and retain it for a longer time. The teacher should design the learning situation to make the students conscious about learning and learning outcome. The learners should feel the energy of learning. Learning experiences are designed for producing learning in all the three domains of learning. In this learning process many learning activities such as micro study of the process, known to unknown, specific to general, simple to difficult concepts of learning are adopted. The refined process is collectively understood and anticipated results are analyzed. In the process of learning capabilities such as risk taking, accepting the challenges and continuous improvement are developed. Work related skills are generally learnt through experiences. Students should be conscious for learning while working. The process of learning through experiences is lengthy and may be costly in some situations. There are numbers of methods such as action learning, project, case, assignment, game, simulation, practice on machine, role play, discussions, problem solving etc. that provide a good opportunity to undergo learning experiences.

6.32 Learning from Competition

Competition is a good way to create self-responsibility for learning. Competition is created among individuals and groups to make them learn significant and important competencies. Students prepare to face the competition using their capacity. They learn deeply and comprehensively from competition. Competitions create sense of urgency and challenge for learning. It provides an opportunity to learners to learn consciously and unconsciously in a natural way. Learners explore all learning difficulties and sort out their learning problems on their own. Competitions imply various principles of learning such as; readiness to learn, responsibility for learning, struggle for learning, complete learning, collective learning, learning with a purpose etc.

6.33 Learning from Technology

Media plays a significant role in creating learning. Use of computer in learning has created added advantage and created lot of flexibility and scope in learning process. Computer aided instructions, simulations and games have changed the entire process of learning. The video films, multimedia packages and internet have added colours to the process of learning. At the same time it has helped to bring the industry in the classroom. The latest technology and techniques are available through internet. The technology has made the job of the teacher easier at the same time enriched the learning process of students. They can see the whole variety of industrial world related to their discipline within no time.

7. Learning Styles

Kolb has proposed a learning model based on the assumption that learning takes place through thinking and doing. He has classified his model in four stages. These are activist, reflector, theorist and pragmatist. Rosenberg defined learning styles of students in four categories that are rigid inhibited, undisciplined, acceptance anxious and creative. Kagan has described two types of styles of learning that is impulsive and reflective. These styles of learning help a teacher to select a method of learning to develop an appropriate competency. Piaget proposed that there are four processes basic to intellectual organisation and development. These are schema, assimilation, accommodation and equilibrium. One psychologist defined kinds of learning such as verbal learning, conceptual learning, perceptual learning, motor learning, problem solving and emotional learning.

8. Promoting Learning through Teaching

Learners are a key to learning process. They enjoy the privilege of learning in and outside the campus of the institution. The characteristics of the learners are described in Exhibit 2.1, dimensions of learning process are described in Exhibit 2.2 and learning methods are listed in Exhibit 2.3. Considering the requirements of learning, learning process and learning methods a teacher should plan to guide and facilitate the learning of students. The teacher should develop core competence to facilitate the process of learning professionally. That means to make the learning meaningful, relevant and purposeful a teacher should design a curriculum meeting the needs of the employers and matching the level of students. The curriculum document clearly spells out the expected learning outcomes in the form of well-defined competencies or in the form of knowledge, skills and attitudes. The teacher should develop the competency plan on the basis of curriculum document. The competency plan should be translated to lesson plans to bring clarity in learning tasks. The teacher should be able to design learning events to develop competencies in students. S/he should be able to motivate the students to participate in learning events and activities to develop competencies. S/he should be able to mobilize the physical as well as learning resources to facilitate the learning process. S/he should evaluate the learning outcomes frequently and if necessary modify the learning process. So a teacher is considered in a different sense than a traditional teacher. Teaching should not be considered as preaching. Teaching should be taken in a broader sense to facilitate the learning.

Teaching is a process and should be considered supporting and guiding the learning process. It is designed on the basis of expected learning outcomes, learning style of students, level of students, availability of time and availability of physical and learning resources. Teaching in engineering institutions should take students towards learning maturity. Learning maturity of students is developed through providing them enough opportunities to learn, practice and learn new concepts and principles. Before they leave institution they should demonstrate professional skills such as self reliance, self confidence, self responsibility, accepting challenges, visualizing the future, influencing the future of others and so on. The teaching process should empower the students in learning over a period of time. The students cannot depend on a teacher and college campus throughout their life. Teaching should create life long interest in learning.

9. Role of a Teacher to Produce Learning

The role of a teacher in technical institution is very simple and easy going if s/he professionally plans the teaching learning process. There is no need to struggle for organizing the classes and preparing for reproducing the matter written in books. There is no need to threaten students to learn and remember the lesson at any cost. But there is certainly a need to develop professionals for future. Professional teachers can only develop professionals. That means a teacher should be a professional as well a professional teacher. S/he can make or break the career of students. A teacher is a person that promotes to develop competencies and proficiency in all the students using principles of learning and of course taking the benefit of information technology. A teacher is a chief architect of producing learning in students at a cheaper, faster, natural and enjoyable way. A teacher has to perform variety of roles to produce learning in effective and efficient way. The various role dimensions of a technical teacher are listed in Exhibit 2.4.

Exhibit No. 2.4: Role dimensions of a teacher to produce learning

- ➢ Designing effective and efficient learning plans.
- ➢ Designing learning experiences such as learning material, learning activities, learning experiments, learning problems, learning projects,

(Contd.)

(*Contd.*)

learning assignments and so on in order to develop competency and proficiency. ➢ Organizing learning interactions, practices, competitions, games, seminars, conferences, symposium, role-playing, creativity sessions to develop professional and associated competencies. ➢ Implementing, controlling and evaluating various learning events as per learning plan. ➢ Guiding, supporting, helping and encouraging students to put efforts to learn. ➢ Recognizing the learning problems of individuals and solving them using appropriate methods. ➢ Creating healthy environment for learning, organizing learning and physical resources. ➢ Ensuring through continuous assessment that all students attain a predefined level of learning. ➢ Enhancing learning maturity of students through shifting the responsibility of learning to them. ➢ Introducing flexibility in learning process to match individual needs. ➢ Arranging learning, resources such as self learning packages, manuals, models, video films, computer aided instructions, and internet facility to facilitate learning process. ➢ Exploring and assigning issues for research studies and encouraging the students to do so. ➢ Organizing excursion tours, field visits, hands on experiences in industry or research organisation to develop and refine professional competence. ➢ Organizing equipments and machines in laboratories and workshops to learn, practice and use skills. ➢ Recognize the learning achievements of students. ➢ Providing constructive, positive and encouraging feedback to students based on learning outcomes. ➢ Creating challenges in learning process. ➢ Observing the behaviour and learning attitude of students and putting them on learning task of their interest. ➢ Identifying and harnessing the potential of students for learning process. ➢ Creating scope for struggle for learning in learning process. ➢ Stimulate the creativity of students in learning process.

One author describes five types of teachers employed in educational institutions. These are; the rebel is always found to be against the system having no constructive suggestion for change. The retreatist always thinks to leave the system. The ritualist always repeats the same lessons with the same notes and tests year after year. The conformist always goes along with the popular fad of the moment. The innovator is a proactive person s/he predicts the needs of the future, plans the change and bring it. S/he is rewarded in existing system for innovation by denying promotion and departmental inquiry.

A teacher devotes the cream part of her/his life that is youth life and cream time of the day that is effective working hours for producing learning in the institution. S/he should do some miracle through professionalism otherwise s/he is a cog in a wheel. It is wastage of life of the self and spoiling the life of thousands of potential young professional. Thereby they contribute meager to the growth and economy of the country. As a teacher one should enjoy the noble profession and grab the opportunity to serve the youth of the country. As a teacher one should live the profession with pride and dignity. S/he should demonstrate example of high level of professionalism. An inventory to check the level of professionalism is given as an activity for you at the end of this chapter.

10. Guidelines for Performing the Role of a Teacher

The role of the teacher is vivid and challenging so for learning of students is concerned. Some indicative guidelines are noted in Exhibit 2.5 for performing the role effectively and efficiently to produce desired level of learning in all students.

Exhibit No. 2.5: Guidelines for performing the teaching-learning role effectively and efficiently

- Design the competency plan and lesson plan to effectively and efficiently carry out the process of learning to develop desired level of competencies.
- Design learning resources specially the learning assignments and learner centered activities using principles of educational psychology and educational technology.
- Identify and consider individual differences in competency plan and lesson plan. Plan and organize separate session to solve problem of individual differences using tutorial, bridge courses and remedial classes.
- Introduce the learning difficulty level in learning events starting from simple and progressing towards complex creating fairly reasonable challenges for learning.
- Always try to work on concrete concepts and ideas in the beginning. Use creativity and thinking skills for developing abstract concepts and ideas. Or use application examples of abstract concepts.
- Introduce enough flexibility in learning process to satisfy the requirements of learning style, interest and pace. This is possible by shifting the responsibility of learning to students.

(Contd.)

(*Contd.*)

- Introduce self evaluation and concept of formative and summative evaluation immediately followed by constructive feedback for improvement.
- Built up learning events, activities and processes on each other like a staircase with a provision of gaining energy for another set of learning.
- Organize learning resources in a way to make them easily accessible to students at any time and if possible anywhere.
- Make provision to use creativity and talent of students in learning process throughout the course of study.
- Show empathy for learning problems of students. It is always better to prevent learning problems by pointing out, highlighting and addressing them.
- Always create friendly environment during the process of learning. Join the students and become an element of learning process. Have positive attitude for learners and learning process. Encourage positive and rewarding thinking throughout the learning process.
- Recognize the learning of students and reward it. They need recognition and appreciation after all they are learners. They are not experts like you.
- Encourage students to be proactive in learning events. Ask students to drive the learning process.
- Use variety of learning events, learning experiences and learning methods to create enough interest, joy, challenge and competition in learning process. The variety is also required to use the potential of all senses of learning. The variety in learning process makes the process dynamic and demanding. The variety should not be introduced at the cost of learning.
- Ensure that attitudinal aspects of the competency are inbuilt element of learning process. Ensure that peripheral, associated and connected competencies are developed simultaneously and linked properly in the learning process itself.
- Organize the learning events in a way to make the students feel and experience real life situation. Tape the potential of learning at work place, industrial training, exposure visit, project method and action learning.
- Use law of association and put connected and interrelated things together.
- Give examples and non-examples of the concept that is being developed in order to develop competency.
- Club the concepts belonging to same category to learn and at the same time use the concepts of opposite category also. Use the law of similarity and contrast in the learning processes.
- Create situations to make the students see, feel and experience the joy and anxiety of learning.

(*Contd.*)

(*Contd.*)

- Organize the learning events to develop higher level of knowledge, skills, and attitudes in order of difficulty. Students should feel that they are climbing the steps of difficulty but each step is requiring same time and energy. There is no difference in steps whether it is at lower or higher elevation.

11. Paradigm Shift—Traditional Teaching to Producing Competency based Learning

It is little bit difficult to convert traditionally teaching institutions to competency development institutions but it is the need of the day. The technical institutions should shift their practices to produce learning in effective and efficient way to develop professionals. The governors, director and key faculty members of the institution should promote the culture of promoting competency based learning and not teaching. They should create necessary facilities to practice learning oriented methods in the institution. A learning resources development and utilisation center should be created in the institution to support learning processes. The teachers should be encouraged to procure and develop learning resources to enrich the learning resource center. The shift required from teaching to competency based learning on various parameters listed in Exhibit 2.6.

Exhibit No. 2.6: Paradigm shift from teaching to competency based learning

Criteria	*Teaching*		*Learning*
Focus	Teacher	⇒	Students
Learning	Passive learning		Active learning
Philosophy	Principles of teaching		Principles of learning
Responsibility for learning	Teacher		Students
Role of teacher	Directive		Participative
Motivation	Teacher influences the behaviour of the students		Promote self motivation for learning
Power	Enjoy expert power and authority to award marks or grades		Empower students for learning Learning to learn concept is promoted

(*Contd.*)

(*Contd.*)

Criteria	*Teaching*		*Learning*
Emphasis	Curriculum completion		Learning about changing business, innovation, and development
Teachers think	Students need to be controlled		Students have potential to learn on their own if properly guided
Recognition	Teachers take credit for the success		Students take credit for success
Rewards	Extrinsic		Extrinsic and intrinsic
Information	Controlled information		Free flow of information
Problems	Teacher own the problem		Students own the problem
Communication	Often one way		Multi channels of communication are used
Creativity and innovation	Less scope Analytical thinking		Foster creativity in learning
Perspective for development	Limited scope		Life long learning
Approach	Teacher centered methods		Students centered methods
Use of media	Traditional		Multimedia
Effect	Passing the examination		Learning for life
Force	Supply driven		Demand driven
Way of learning	Formal		Formal and informal
Focus of teaching	Input		Output
Approach	Generic		Specific and generic both

12. Summary

In technical institutions the concept of management of learning should be promoted. The learning should lead to professional competence in students. Students have variety of characteristics some are common and some are different. Similarly the learning process should have variety of learning events and dimensions to cater the learning needs of the students. There are varieties of learning methods having immense potential to produce learning in interesting and joyful manner. The potential of these learning methods need to be harnessed in learning process. The teacher is expected to be professional and need to perform variety of roles to produce proficient learning in students. S/he has to use the science, art and technology for producing joyful learning. To make the learning process memorable s/he should use the principles of education psychology, educational technology and androgogy. S/he should use systematic and professional approach for producing learning.

13. Activity

Check Level of Your Professionalism

The characteristics of professional teachers are stated in the inventory given below in table. As a teacher you can check your level of professional approach. Please respond to each parameter stated in the inventory without deceiving yourself. The percentage of marks would decide the level of your professional approach. In the inventory 5 indicates very high degree of professionalism, 4 indicates high level, 3 indicates moderate, 2 indicates low and 1 indicates very low level of professionalism.

Sl. No.	*Indicators of Professionalism*	*Extent of Professional Approach*				
		5	4	3	2	1
A.	*Self Concept*					
1.	I have full respect for my job as a teacher					
2.	I know my strengths as a teacher					
3.	I know my weaknesses as a teacher					
4.	I have a vision to achieve as a teacher					
5.	I know and explore opportunities for self development					
6.	I explore alternative ways to refine professional competence and approach					
7.	I enjoy the job of managing learning					

(*Contd.*)

(*Contd.*)

Sl. No.	*Indicators of Professionalism*	*Extent of Professional Approach*				
		5	4	3	2	1
8.	I feel accountability for my role					
9.	I am confident to produce joyful learning					
B.	*Technical Competence*					
10.	I regularly attend training programmes, workshops, conferences, seminars, discussions and meetings on areas of my specialisation					
11.	I do visit industries and receive training on latest technology					
12.	I read international journals					
13.	I read reference books					
14.	I do research work in technology					
15.	I undertake consultancy projects to solve industrial problems and design innovations					
16.	I write books on technical subjects					
17.	I frequently update content related knowledge and skills					
18.	I am quality conscious					
C.	*Professional Competence*					
19.	I set challenging goals to achieve					
20.	I have sense for purpose					
21.	I am loyal to my profession					
22.	I prepare competency plans and lesson plans to achieve the goals					
23.	I design effective and efficient strategies to achieve the goals					
24.	I design alternative strategies to achieve the goal					
25.	I design effective learning resources such as self learning material, handouts, guidelines, manuals, power point presentations, multimedia, work books, video films, computer aided instructions and so on					

(*Contd.*)

(Contd.)

Sl. No.	*Indicators of Professionalism*	*Extent of Professional Approach*				
		5	4	3	2	1
26.	I regularly attend training programmes, workshops, conferences, seminars, discussions and meetings on education technology, educational psychology, technical education, educational research, curriculum design and implementation and similar topics					
D.	*Approach*					
27.	I clearly know the learning needs of students and curricular requirements					
28.	I encourage students to take self responsibility for learning					
29.	I promote right learning habits					
30.	I provide freedom to learn to students					
31.	I establish healthy relationship with students					
32.	I use student centered, humorous, interesting and joyful learning methods					
33.	I design and use learning methods such as discussions, case studies, simulations, games, role play, action learning, seminars, conferences, symposium, problem solving sessions, assignments for students to create challenging and involving learning environment					
34.	I have concern for learning problems of students					
35.	I provide socio emotional support to students for effective learning through guidance, counselling, problem solving, encouraging, recognizing, coaching, and resources providing					
36.	I work in learning teams of students					
37.	I communicate effectively					

(Contd.)

(*Contd.*)

Sl. No.	*Indicators of Professionalism*	*Extent of Professional Approach*				
		5	4	3	2	1
38.	I promote higher level of thinking skills during the learning process using stimulating questions, discussing current issues and creating challenges for learning					
39.	I promote flexibility in learning with respect to time, mode of learning, style of learning, place of learning and duration of learning					
40.	I promote creativity in the learning process					
41.	I ensure the full utilisation of time, resources and money for producing learning					
42.	I use holistic and systems approach for academics					
E.	*Attitudes*					
43.	I am punctual to my duties					
44.	I dedicate myself for producing learning					
45.	I am self disciplined so far my work is concerned					
46.	I am eager to learn new things					
47.	I have respect for professional norms and observe them					
48.	I have concern for effective learning of students without tension, anxiety and stress					
49.	I appreciate the individual differences and design learning approaches accordingly					
50.	I take self initiatives					
F.	*Innovation*					
51.	I often think on not to take lecture					
52.	I experiment, research and innovate for producing effective and efficient learning					

(*Contd.*)

(Contd.)

Sl. No.	*Indicators of Professionalism*	*Extent of Professional Approach*				
		5	4	3	2	1
53.	I create new ways and means for improving learning					
54.	I take risk for grabbing any opportunity for producing effective learning					
55.	I challenge my own competence and ways of performing the role					
56.	I share the experiences of managing learning with fellow teachers					
57.	I adopt innovative methods in learning					
58.	I take lead to develop facilities of the institution to make the learning easy					
59.	I am open to change					
G.	*Evaluation*					
60.	I evaluate my performance periodically in terms of quality of learning of the students					
61.	I feel the results of evaluation is self rewarding					
62.	I learn to refine my technical as well as professional skills through self evaluation and feedback from others					
63.	I feel positive change in attitude to produce learning through evaluation					

3

Management of Learning in Classroom

Objectives: The readers will be able to:

1. Concept of management of learning in classroom
2. Explain the various dimensions of learning environment
3. Prepare curriculum implementation plan on the basis of analysis of curriculum
4. State types of learning produced in classroom
5. Design learning events on the basis of learners psychology and entry behaviour
6. Prepare lesson plan
7. Design various layouts for sitting arrangement to produce effective learning
8. Select appropriate learning resources
9. Explain strengths, weaknesses and use of various learning methods to achieve predefined objectives
10. List the criteria to select the learning method
11. Select learning method to develop desired competency and proficiency level
12. Carryout learning process to develop competency and achieve proficiency
13. Assess the learning outcomes
14. Design remedial learning opportunities to assist the students to achieve the competency
15. Design learning opportunities for physically challenged students

1. Introduction

Traditionally classrooms have been used as major places of learning for all the students. Classrooms have their importance and strengths to produce learning. This will continue till the responsibility of learning is totally shifted to students. The environment of the classroom plays a significant role in the process of learning. The management of learning is a prime focus of classroom. The problem of discipline, disinterest and bunking in classroom arises because of poor management of learning process in the classroom. A professional teacher can produce effective and efficient learning with joy and pleasure. S/he can prevent all types of distractions, problems, barriers and indiscipline using proper methods of learning and planning. Classrooms provide a very good opportunity for learning in social setting. The teachers should harness the potential of learning in social setting. At the same time s/he should avoid the evils of undesired learning in social setting. The teacher should study the learning behaviour of students and design the learning events that psychologically and physically involve them in learning process. The teacher should initiate the involvement and it should gradually shift from him/her to students. Lesson plans are considered to be helpful in achieving the learning objectives successfully.

2. The Learning Environment

The learning environment in the classroom is governed and influenced by numerous factors listed in Exhibit 3.1.

Exhibit No. 3.1: Factors influencing learning environment

➢ Topic of learning and learning objectives ➢ Entry behaviour of students ➢ Use of learning method ➢ Sitting arrangement ➢ Size of classroom ➢ Location of classroom	➢ Learning resources ➢ Educational technology ➢ Competence of the teacher ➢ Availability of time ➢ Learning culture in the institute ➢ Willingness of students and teachers

2.1 Topic of Learning and Learning Objectives

The topic of learning and learning objectives play a crucial role in managing learning in classroom. The teacher is required to plan the learning events to achieve learning objectives. The learning events should be designed observing the principles of learning and styles of learning. Instead of spoon feeding in the classroom students should be made active in performing learning activities. Here the question is not related to expertise of the teacher but it is related to expertise in seeking full participation of students. A teacher creates interest in the process of learning using different learning methods. The objectives should create enough learning challenges to invite participation of students.

2.2 Entry Behaviour of Students

A teacher should assess entry behaviour of students before selecting learning methods. Selection of right learning method helps the students to participate in the learning process. There are many prerequisite to learning of a particular concept, principle or theory. If students do not know this they will loose the focus and will not be able to assimilate the learning points. In such a case the teacher should plan the learning events matching to their entry behaviour. In some situation the entry behaviour of the students may be high and low level of learning events may create boredom for them. They may lose the interest and may get involve in distracting activities in the classroom.

2.3 Use of Learning Methods

Considering the learning objectives and entry behaviour the teacher should plan the learning methods and learning events aligned to achieve learning objectives. A wide range of learning methods is available to be used in the classroom. To name a few lecture, improved lecture, question answer, demonstration, role play, game, simulation, action learning, learning in groups, quality circle, classroom presentation, quiz, and so on. These methods can be used in a combined way one after other. In one session of an hour a teacher should use at least combination of four methods.

2.4 Sitting Arrangement

Sitting arrangement facilitates the learning process tremendously. The sitting arrangement depends on the method of learning being used by the teacher and size of the class. Brief description of sitting arrangement along with learning methods and their strengths is stated in Exhibit 3.2.

Exhibit No. 3.2: Sitting arrangement with method of learning

Sl. No.	*Sitting Arrangement*	*Learning Method*	*Strengths*
1.	Semi-circular or circular	Group discussion Case method Buzz group	➢ Face to face communication ➢ Understanding the verbal message and body language ➢ Maximum participation of students in learning process ➢ Very good for 10 to 15 students ➢ Cross communication can be controlled ➢ Socio-gram can be drawn
2.	U shape	Action learning	➢ Easy to create learning situation ➢ Facilitate interaction between different groups ➢ Easy to observe learning process
3.	Row curvilinear sitting arrangement	Seminar, conference, symposium, demonstration, lecture	➢ Easy to see the presentation ➢ Individual interaction with the presenter ➢ No cross communication among participants
4.	Face to face, triangular or circular	Buzz group Case method	➢ Face to face communication ➢ Consensus and agreement among learners ➢ Exploring truth and facts
5.	Inner and outer circle	Group discussion Observation	➢ Facilitates learning through observation and feedback ➢ Suitable for developing observational skills ➢ Specific feedback is possible
6.	Teacher sitting inside the circle	Question answer Interview	➢ Seeking controlled participation of students

2.5 Size of Classroom

The size of the classroom affects the learning process significantly. Number of students for learning process should be decided on the basis of learning method being used by the teacher and not on other trivial factors that can be managed easily. The teacher can control the number of students in the classroom provided the institution is having adequate number of faculty members and support staff. Generally the student teacher ratio is kept 8:1 to facilitate the use of variety of learning methods. The teachers should be deployed for academic activities only to obtain excellent learning results. The size of learning group depends on number of factors such as learning objectives, learning method, physical facilities available, faculty and staff members available, learning resources available, professional skills of the teacher, relation between teacher and students, relation between students, entry behaviour of the students, students familiarity with learning method, availability of time and difficulty level of the topic.

2.6 Location of Classroom

The classroom should be situated at a calm and quite place away from the disturbance area. The classroom should be either air conditioned or well illuminated and free from outside distractions. It should be attached with other rooms suitably furnished for facilitating other methods of learning.

2.7 Learning Resources

The teacher should provide the learning resources to students at right time as per need of the learning method. All the learning resources such as handout, assignment, references, manuals, standards, codes, diagrams, charts, situation descriptions, games, simulation scripts, case studies, quiz, puzzles, manuals, workbooks, power point presentations, photographic albums, video films, computer aided instructions, should be ready to use at right time in right quantity. The teacher should organize all the resources well in advance to run the learning process smoothly. Learning resources can reduce the learning time and create interest in the learning process. All the learning resources should be professionally used to seek highest degree of participation of students in the learning process.

2.8 Educational Technology

Different types of hardwares are required to use the learning resources in the classroom. Generally the classrooms are furnished by variety of equipments such as green board, magnetic board, white board, overhead projector, LCD, computer, flip chart, past it slips, video cassette recorder, compact disc player, television, and web camera. The teacher should plan and use these technologies professionally to facilitate the learning process. Use of media is necessary to change the stimulus to break the monotony during the process of learning. It helps to bring the world of work in the classroom. The process of learning attitudes such as observing safety rules, proper use of tools and machines, concern for others should be video recorded to provide specific feedback for refining attitudes.

2.9 Competence of the Teacher

Modern teachers are different than traditional teachers. They are different in the sense that they focus on learning of the students and not on teaching. They professionally implement the learning process using learning resources and learning technology. Competent teachers significantly reduce the learning time and efforts of students. At the same time they make the whole process of learning joyful. The joyful learning process creates interest in the students to get fully involved in the learning process. Competent teachers shift the responsibility of learning to students. They are expert in the contents as well as in producing learning. They create natural environment for learning as if it is a part of the life.

2.10 Availability of Time

Time is very important factor in the process of learning. The teacher designs the learning process in a way to take minimum time. Teacher explores alternative ways to use the student's time optimally for producing learning. Students should feel that they are devoting time for purposeful and gainful learning activity. Experience of students on time utilisation motivates them to participate in subsequent learning process. All the learning sessions should be properly conducted to produce learning in purposeful and joyful way. The students must feel that they are learning something worth that will be useful in their professional life. This feeling will compel them to attend learning sessions without wasting time in political activities.

2.11 Learning Culture in the Institution

The learning culture in the institution helps to enhance the effectiveness of learning process. All the learning events going smoothly in the institution keeps students close to academic activities. The dedication of previous batches of students for learning process and their experiences of learning processes matters much to transfer learning culture. Their experiences get transferred in the form of stories and anecdotes to junior students and they behave accordingly. The good learning practices and norms promoted by institution motivate the students to strengthen the learning culture. Good learning culture automatically avoids and prevents many problems of the campus. The learning culture is based on various factors such as competence of the teachers, training of the teachers, expectations of teachers from students, interest of students in learning, cohesiveness of the group, responsibility of learning and so on.

2.12 Willingness of Students and Teachers

Willingness of students and teachers plays a very important role in the process of teaching learning. A teacher should elevate the mood of the students for learning. In absence of willingness the teacher can do formality of teaching but it would produce no learning. The teacher should assess the mood of the students for learning and accordingly select the learning event. There may be important events happening in the world such as cricket match, launching of space shuttle, political ceremony, important festival and so on. Students may be more interested in the events and less in learning during that time. The teacher must appreciate the importance of such events and declare off hours during the important event.

The teacher may not be prepared to introduce a new learning event or take up a complex problem for learning in the classroom. The teacher may get more important work or assignment than producing learning in the classroom. The teacher should inform the students about importance and urgency of the work but at the same time s/he should plan for self-learning of students and take off time to complete the assignment honestly. S/he may plan purposeful alternative arrangement for classroom. In the competency plan a teacher should plan for such contingencies so that the time of students is not wasted. There are various alternatives that can be used by a teacher such as library assignment, review of research article, handout for general reading, laboratory work, viewing a film, working on a problem, reading textbook in the classroom, bright students solving the problems of slow learners and so on.

The theories of motivation suggest various strategies to motivate students for learning. These strategies are creating challenge in the learning, providing opportunities for applying variety of previous learning for further learning, establishing the importance of the learning relating it with the profession, providing autonomy and flexibility for learning, providing constructive feedback, setting higher level of expectations, assign different roles to students in group learning as per their needs such as assigning leadership role to student having need for power, relationship role to student having need for affiliation and problem solving role to student having need for accomplishment. Make the process of learning rewarding and self-motivating. Provide opportunities for pursuing hobby and career.

3. Learning in Classroom

Learning in classroom has been prominent in education system. It has contributed significantly for the development of children and human being. Over the years the discipline of education psychology, education technology, education research and related disciplines emerged to guide the process of learning. At the same time developments in science and technology created challenge for learning many things in a shorter span of time. The society is creating increased amount of pressure and demand for professional services at cheaper, faster and better way. This pressure is encouraging organisations to offer quality products and services. The quality products and services are created by professionals using technical, professional and interpersonal competence. The engineering institutions are assigned the responsibility of developing professionals to assume roles in professional organisations. This challenge of developing professionals for variety of organisations with wide spectrum of competence has enforced technical institutions to be more professional in producing learning. The whole concept of learning in classroom has changed over the years. Now the teachers are expected to develop higher level of competencies than merely transferring the information. The modern professional teachers are expected to develop competencies listed in Exhibit 3.3.

Exhibit No. 3.3: Types of competencies developed in classroom

➢ Comprehension ➢ Application ➢ Comparative ➢ Analytical ➢ Synthesis ➢ Evaluation ➢ Planning ➢ Decision-making ➢ Visualizing	➢ Critical study ➢ Observation ➢ Interpersonal ➢ Communication ➢ Conceptualizing ➢ Relating various disciplines ➢ Influencing ➢ Learning

In the changing world if competencies are to be developed in the classroom in order to prepare the students to become professionals. The responsibility of learning should be shifted to students. The teacher has to become a learning planner, designer, environment creator, learning initiator, and learning partner in the learning process. Initially, the teacher as a leader should show the destination of learning and importance of the destination with respect to profession and career to students. This destination should create attraction, interest, and responsibility for learning in the students. The teacher should remove the barriers from the path of the learning and make it easy through simple learning process. The teacher should build environment for learning so that students organize themselves for individual and collective learning. They get involved in the learning process and achieve the learning goals. In subsequent part of this chapter the learning methods have been described right from traditional teaching to fully empowering methods of learning. You should try these methods and enjoy the benefits as a teacher and as a learner.

3.1 LECTURE METHOD

1. Introduction

Lecture method is most commonly used method in teaching learning process. Every teacher uses this method very often. Teachers have learnt this method from their teachers because they have been taught by this method. Teachers obviously use this method for any type of learning such as transforming information, informing about skills and attitudes. Teachers think that this is a very simple method that requires almost no special preparation. Teachers think that whatever they know that has to be reproduced in the classroom. Teachers think that whatever they teach to students they learn it. If students do not learn atleast they know what has been taught so they read from books and learn. Teachers think that whatever they are teaching is important from examination point of view and help the students in passing the examination.

On the other hand experienced and trained teachers have also realized during their career of teaching that lecture method is ineffective and inefficient. It is ineffective because it cannot produce all types of learning in students. One-way communication cannot produce higher level of skills such as application, analysis, synthesis and evaluation. Students cannot develop desired level of professional attitudes listening a teacher in a classroom. A teacher using lecture method can teach about skills but students will get awareness. The main character of the lecture method is teacher so the onus of teaching lies with teacher. Students may not share responsibility of learning. Even if they share the responsibility the level of responsibility may be low. The students may enjoy teaching because personal characteristics of a teacher but they may not enjoy the learning. Moreover entire class of students may not find it interesting and as per their needs, interest and level of understanding. So lecture method is ineffective because it does not satisfy the learning needs of the students.

Lecture method is considered inefficient from learning point of view. Students are required to learn the things on their own or taking tuition or discussing with their colleagues who have learnt. The duplication of time, effort and energy in learning process is wastage on the part of the students. It creates anxiety, tension and stress because they have fixed time in one semester. If students opt the option of taking tuition they have to pay for it. It is inefficient from teachers' point of view because s/he devotes her/his maximum time in the classroom and it is not contributing for effective and efficient learning. The time of teacher in preparing for the lecture, lecturing and evaluation of learning is not appropriately utilized. The impact of teaching is also low so teacher get frustrated and draw wrong conclusions such as students are not interested in learning, their intelligence level is low, the subject is difficult, and so on.

The educational psychology, educational technology, educational research, information technology, and sociology have helped the teachers to understand the learning process. Now they can better plan and implement educational programmes to develop desired level of competencies in students. They can use variety of methods of learning with lecture method. Now they are trained not to copy the book on black board or green board or on power point presentations but to provide something new which is not available to students or that is difficult to learn by them on their own. Keeping this thing in mind the teacher prepares a competency development plan, implement it and evaluate it.

2. Strengths of Lecture Method

Over the years teachers and researchers have worked with an objective to improve the effectiveness and efficiency of lecture method. They have tried to remove its weaknesses and harness its strengths. The weaknesses of lecture method are removed using concepts, theories and models of education psychology, education technology, androgogy, and sociology. The lecture methods has numerous and variety of strengths if used by a trained teacher. The strengths of lecture methods are listed in Exhibit 3.4.

Exhibit No. 3.4: Strengths of lecture method

- It can be used for a larger group of students to transfer new information that is required to learn higher level of knowledge, skills and attitudes.
- It is a flexible method of learning that can be combined with other methods of learning to develop complex skills.
- It does not require special physical and learning resources. It can be conducted at any time at any place.
- It helps to arouse the interest of the students for learning. Teacher can make the learning process interesting.
- It prevents the students to come out from learning process because of learning difficulty. The learning problems of students are immediately solved.
- It provides an opportunity for immediate rewards for learning to students. The teacher immediately fills up the learning gaps.
- It provides an opportunity to use all the senses in learning process. The teacher can use variety of modes of transferring information such as showing transparencies, showing power point slide, showing a film, asking students to observe an equipment, inviting students to touch the material, asking students to test the material and so on.
- It provides an opportunity to teacher to test the progress and level of learning spontaneously.
- It provide an opportunity to use the bright students for transferring learning to slow learners thereby providing recognition to them at the same time encouraging slow learners to become like bright students.
- It provides an opportunity to jointly learn difficult and complex matter. The students can move with teacher in learning process. Gradually the teacher can transfer responsibility for learning to students.
- It provides an opportunity for social interaction thereby satisfying social needs of students. Students can verify the learning with teacher.

3. Preparation for Lecture Method

The teachers need to be trained formally to harness the full potential of lecture method. They are required to plan their lecture before going for delivering the lecture. They need to procure learning and physical resources to deliver the lecture effectively and efficiently. The teacher should do holistic planning to produce learning to achieve predefined level of competency. The major steps of lecture are stated in Exhibit 3.5.

Exhibit No. 3.5: Steps of lecture method

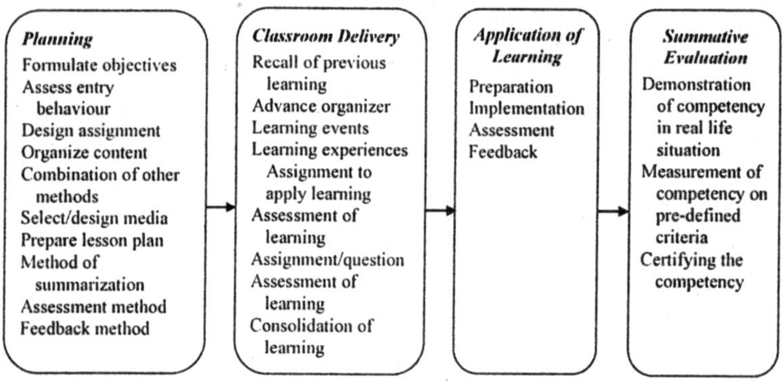

3.1 Planning

Planning is the first major step to assure the effectiveness and efficiency in a lecture method. The effectiveness of the plan depends on the competence of the teacher in contents, educational psychology, educational technology, androgogy, information technology, and hands on experiences.

Formulate Instructional Objectives: Teacher should prepare a cluster of competency plan at the beginning of the semester. The competency plan should be derived from the subject plan or it could be based on the cluster of competencies. The curriculum document is the source for subject plan or cluster of competencies plan. Each competency is divided in instructional objectives. The subject plan, competency plan and lesson plan provides continuity in learning process to achieve cluster of competencies to perform a particular job or a role dimension. The process of formulating instructional objectives is shown in Exhibit 3.6.

Exhibit No. 3.6: Instructional objectives for lesson plan

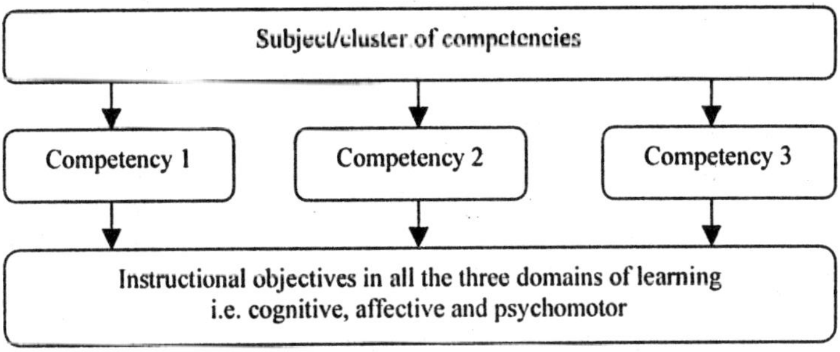

It is always better to list the objectives in all the three domains of learning that are cognitive, psychomotor and affective. The plan should be prepared for the competency and not for a session or group of objectives. The lesson plan should emanate from the competency plan. Lesson plan for achieving objectives in different domains of learning may be different.

Assess the Entry Behaviour of Students: The entry behaviour of students is deciding factor for designing the learning events to achieve the objectives. A teacher should test the level of knowledge, skills and attitude possessed by students. In engineering most of the knowledge, skills and attitudes are interrelated and logically linked. There may be possibility that students have qualified in the prerequisite subjects or competencies but their level may not be appropriate to learn the intended objectives. In such cases the teacher should incorporate remedial treatment or preparatory lessons to make the students ready to acquire desired competencies. There may be other possibility that students already possess knowledge, skills and attitude related to competency in that case there is no need to plan from basics. If the group is mixed and possessing varied levels of knowledge, skills and attitudes in such situation a teacher should bring all the students at same level. This can be done through planned interactions among students. In such situation a teacher should use the strengths of higher-level entry behaviour students to remove the weaknesses of lower level entry behaviour students.

Organize Contents: The content should be logically organized to achieve the desired level of competency. The contents should be organized observing principles of learning, education psychology and educational technology. The newly appointed teachers should do content mapping and content analysis exercise to organize the content. The teacher should follow the guidelines stated in Exhibit 3.7.

Exhibit No. 3.7: Guidelines for organizing contents to achieve competency

- List the importance of learning the competency through the contents. Establish the relevance of learning competency with the role in professional life.
- Establish the linkages of contents with other competencies already achieved and expected to be achieved in future.
- Organize the content considering the entry behaviour and desired level of competency. The teacher should not list what s/he knows it may not lead to achievement of the competency.
- Organize the contents in simple to difficult order. This order should be from students' point of view because it is new to them.
- Arrange contents from known to unknown order. Students are exposed to contents in an unfolding manner so that they know the next when receiving the particular information.
- Arrange the contents in concrete to abstract order. Students should know concrete things first to appreciate abstract information. The abstract information should be provided in more than one way to make a correct picture in the minds of the students.
- Pack the contents in one learning unit. So after each set of contents or learning events a pause can be given and level of learning can be assessed or an opportunity to clarify the doubts can be given to the students.
- Do cognitive mapping to understand interrelationship in contents. This relationship would help to organize contents for other competencies.

Design Assignments: The assignments after each learning event helps to apply the learning in real life situation. The teacher should design assignments to provide opportunity to students to apply the knowledge and appreciate the importance and purpose of learning. The students derive satisfaction completing the assignments. It is a good method to involve students in learning process. The output of assignments is the direct evidence of learning of students. The teacher can take spontaneous remedial instructions to fill up the learning gaps. The assignments can be in the form of set of questions to be answered individually, issues/themes to be discussed in small groups, response sheet on some predefined items, physical activity in the form of performing a role or completing small task, reciting important points with teacher and so on. The students get involved in learning process and they take the responsibility of learning in subsequent learning units. Assignments are designed keeping in mind the output of learning event.

Select/Design Media: A teacher can use wide variety and range of media to communicate the message. The content should be converted in the form of media to minimize the lecturing by a teacher and save time. Students use more than one sense to learn effectively. Media provide added advantage to teachers to convert abstract learning in concrete, complex learning in simple, and disinteresting learning in interesting. The real life world can be brought in the classroom and can be imbibed with lecture method. The teacher should prepare a list of media to be used to develop a particular competency. The learning resource center of the institution should help teacher to use media.

Prepare Lesson Plan: The preparation of the lesson plan starts with preparation of the cluster of competency and competency plans. The hierarchy of various plans is shown in Exhibit 3.8.

Exhibit No. 3.8: Hierarchy of plans

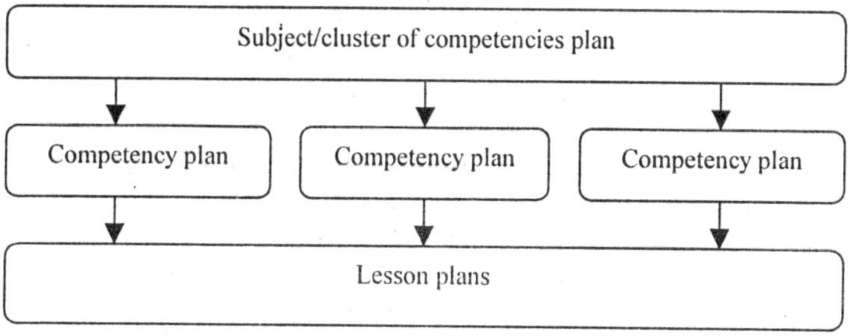

The subject cluster of competencies plan is achieved through numbers of competency plans. The subject plan is broad and it is based on blue print approach meaning thereby the broad framework of the subject is decided at the beginning of the semester. The subject plan is a curriculum document if it is scientifically designed and documented. It contains the cluster of competencies, objectives, contents, time available, broad methods, media, and assessment scheme. The competency plan emanates from the subject plan. It is a more detailed plan to achieve the competency The competency plan contains, competency statement, learning objectives, contents, methods, media, assignments, time, method of assessment, criteria of assessment, place of instruction, number of lesson plans, resources required and method of learning and so on. Each lesson plan emanates from competency plan. It is a detailed and flexible plan. In this plan there is a provision of alternative course of action. It is a plan that is implemented by the teacher and students. The lesson plan is prepared on headings listed in Exhibit 3.9.

Exhibit No. 3.9: Headings for lesson plan

➢ Name of the subject ➢ Name of the competency ➢ Instructional objectives ➢ Advance organizer ➢ Learning event ➢ Contents ➢ Assignments ➢ Method	➢ Media ➢ Learning resources for students ➢ Teacher activity ➢ Students activity ➢ Time available ➢ Physical setting required if any ➢ Sitting arrangement ➢ Summarization ➢ Assessment scheme

Method of Summarisation: The summarisation of learning is very important to consolidate the learning and link it with next lesson or practical or problem or learning at work place or project work and so on. A teacher or a student or a group of students can do the summarisation of learning. The teacher can use power point presentation for summarisation, or a transparency or flip chart or a photographic album. Summarisation should always be done using a media. The teacher should systematically note down points for summarisation.

Assessment Method: The learning outcomes should be tested at the end of accomplishment of each competency. This is called formative assessment. The testing of competency should be carried out against the predefined criteria. If the competency is related to learning in cognitive domain the final outcome of the competency should be tested. It can be on preparing the plan, or design of something, or solving a problem, or taking a decision, or evaluating the outcomes of a strategy or analysis of a failure and so on. The teacher should design the method of assessment of the competency during the stage of preparation of lesson plan. If the assessment is related to affective domain competency the teacher should create a situation in which the students are required to exhibit the attitudinal competence. If the competency is related to learning in psychomotor domain the teacher should provide necessary material, tools and machine to students to exhibit the competency. The competency assessment plan helps to assess the proficiency level and provide constructive feedback before it is too late.

Feedback Method: Feedback plays a very important role in the process of learning. The right behaviour should be reinforced and undesired behaviour should be discouraged. The positive and constructive feedback for improvement in learning is essential. It gives confidence to learners to move ahead in the process of learning. The teacher should continuously provide the feedback. It can be provided even after every learning event. The teacher should learn skills of providing feedback. S/he should use these skills in natural way. The teacher should note down the feedback points in the lesson plan.

3.2 Classroom Delivery

The classroom is the place where the teacher gets an opportunity to deliver the information to students and make them proficient in particular competencies. The lesson plan provides an immense level of confidence to stand in the classroom and transfer the learning. An unprepared teacher will definitely deliver the information in disorganized, confusing, and causal way. The information will go above the head of the students. After some time students will find it boring and they will get frustrated. They will try to do mischief. If they find it informative, purposeful and meaningful they will participate in the process of learning. The teacher should ensure the desired physical setting in the classroom before starting the class.

Recall of Previous Learning: The very first step the teacher should perform in any class is recall of previous learning. The previous learning may be related to the subject s/he is teaching or it may be any related thing. Recall of previous learning provides hint on entry behaviour of students at the same time it makes the students ready for learning new competencies based on previous learning. The previous learning may be related to concepts or principles or it may be related to previously performed competencies.

Advance Organizer: The next step is informing students about what they are going to learn, why they are going to learn, how they are going to learn and how their learning will be assessed. It is a very important step in the process of learning. It is related to informing students what they will learn in the present class and how it is related to real life situation or accomplishing other competencies. The teacher establishes the importance of the learning with negative examples as well. If you do not learn this lesson it may harm you in professional life in this way or you may not be able to demonstrate competence in the examination. The use of advance organizer helps to arouse the interest of the students for learning. It makes them appreciate the level of efforts required to learn and raise their expectations for learning. A teacher can make her/his expectations clear to them in terms of commitment to learning. The advance organizer can be presented through overhead projector or power point slide or flip chart.

Learning Events: The next step is providing contents to students in the form of information or chart or graph or photograph or power point slide or model or handout or in any other form. The teacher introduces new terms defining them and built up the communication logically and sequentially. Teacher uses effective communication skills along with correct body gestures and postures. S/he reveals the new things to the students in an interesting manner. At the same time s/he reads the faces of the students to ensure the effective transfer of the message. To be firm on transfer of learning s/he asks questions randomly to students after significant learning events. Teachers should observe guidelines listed in Exhibit 3.10 to make the learning effective.

Exhibit No. 3.10: Guidelines to make the learning events effective

- Keep the learning event as short as possible but it should be complete in itself. The learning event should be purposeful and meaningful to students.
- Use more media to make the students attentive to the new information. This helps in changing the stimulus and breaking monotony in learning process.
- Use concrete examples to reinforce the concepts and principles. Associate examples with learning points so that students can recall the concepts easily. Use number of illustrations for abstract concept. If possible give analogy or comparison.
- Use real life case studies, anecdotes and incidents to provide purposeful shape to learning.
- Ask questions very often to seek the attention of students and involve them in the process of learning.
- Gradually unfold the learning points and learning process to increase anxiety of students in the classroom.
- Involve students in the learning process in variety of ways such as invite them on dais to share experiences related to topic, read handout, interpret graph, draw conclusion on the basis of data, guess exercise, recall previous learning, discuss the issue in a very small group in three to five minutes, encourage to raise questions and so on.
- Use principles of learning such as general to specific, whole to part, part to whole, simple to complex, known to unknown, concrete to abstract, real to imaginary and so on.
- Use other methods of learning with lecture to bring variety, change, and energy to grasp more information
- Emphasize and repeat major learning points and invite students to repeat the learning points.

(Contd.)

(*Contd.*)

- Use examples and non-examples to differentiate the learning about a particular concept.
- Search opportunities to seek participation of students. The teacher can divide the time in units of 15 minutes and after every fifteen minutes s/he should change the method of learning.
- Provide socio-psychological support during the process of learning. Students should learn freely and frankly in the classroom. They should be treated as friends and permitted to ask any question related to learning.
- Clearly pronounce the sentences and give sufficient pauses during the process of providing information to students.
- Inform students about important points and provide sufficient time to take notes in their language.

Assignment to Apply Learning: Each learning event should be followed by an assignment or exercise so that students get an opportunity to apply the learning to complete the assignment. The assignments could be any thing ranging from a simple question to complex problem or visualisation. The assignment or exercise should be pre-designed and should be organized systematically to test the level of learning of students. The enthusiasm of the students for learning can be tested during the process of completing exercise. The group exercises/assignments produce social skills. The teacher should acknowledge the efforts of students and provide constructive feedback on weak learning or learning gap or wrong learning. Then s/he moves to next learning event. The next learning event may be in classroom or in laboratory or in the field. It all depends on the lesson plan. This process goes on till all the students attain desired competency and level of proficiency.

Assessment of Learning: A teacher carries out assessment of learning after each learning unit to ensure effectiveness of learning. The assessment method could be formal paper and pencil test or randomly asking questions or providing a situation to apply the learning. The questions could be right wrong type or multiple-choice type or fill in the blank type. At the end of the learning unit short answer type or matching type or comparison type or puzzle or different type of questions can be asked. The teacher observes the behaviour of the students and provides them specific feedback related to learning or learning process. This is an informal method of providing the feedback. This method reduces the test anxiety and tension. The assessment of learning is carried out on the basis of the instructional objectives. The formative assessment helps to make students attentive and on right track throughout the process of learning. It helps the teacher to design remedial measures and provide recognition to well performers. During the process of learning event also the teacher reads the faces of the students and assess the progress of learning. Accordingly s/he decides the further course of study.

Consolidation of Learning: At the end of each learning competency the learning should be consolidated by the teacher. The teacher should follow guidelines listed in Exhibit 3.11 for consolidating the learning.

Exhibit No. 3.11: Guidelines for consolidating the learning

- Use pictures, models, charts, graphs, diagrams, power point slides, actual machine for consolidation of learning.
- Associate learnt concepts, principles and theory with real life situation.
- Repeat the significant learning points and ask students to recite them.
- Keep learning points as simple as possible.
- Link the learning points with previous learning and subsequent learning
- Point out common mistakes committed by students and precautions to be taken.
- Name the student who has informed any new and important learning point and repeat the learning point.
- Give handouts to students. The handouts should be simple, easy to read, precise, short, logical, legible, full of diagrams and in colours if possible. The handouts should not be a copy from the book. It should be based on real life situation and provide additional and interesting information to students. The students prefer soft copy as well.

3.3 Application of Learning

The teacher should provide an opportunity to students to apply the concepts and principles learnt in real life situation after accomplishing each competency and accomplishing cluster of competencies. The teacher can design case studies, games, role-plays, simulation, practice exercises, action learning, product development etc. to apply learnt competencies and sharpen competence. The teacher should again use the sequence of learning events. The teacher should inform the students about importance of practice and provide challenging real life situations for learning purpose. These situations create challenge for learning for students. Students work on these situations as an individual and in teams. The teacher should design the methodology to work on the situation. The teacher should inform her/his expectations to the students and guide them during the process of completing the exercises. The exercises may be home assignment, laboratory assignment, industrial assignment, library assignment or learning in classroom. The teacher should incorporate practice exercises in the competency plan. S/he should do field work and research work to prepare the exercises. S/he should implement the exercises in systematic and planned way. S/he should assess the learning outcomes and provide specific feedback to students for improvement.

3.4 Summative Evaluation

At the end of attainment of each competency the teacher should formally assess the competency of all the students using pre-designed criteria. It should not be a paper and pencil test only. The assessment method is decided on the basis of nature and type of competency. It should be performance based in real life situation and not theoretical testing. The competency assessment procedure should be simple feasible and less time taking. The students should be well informed at the beginning of the process of learning the competency that they would be tested against pre-declared set of criteria. The test of the competency should be objective, reliable and valid. The test results should be declared immediately to provide recognition or constructive feedback for improvement. Summative evaluation of competency is used for certification purpose. The examination body on the basis of criteria laid down in the curriculum should carry out the summative evaluation. The summative evaluation certificate is used for granting license, providing recognition for higher study, providing recognition of prior learning, establishing equivalence and so on.

4. Use of Lecture Method with Other Methods of Learning

Lecture is a versatile method of transferring learning to students. Learners want variety and change in learning process. Change in methods of learning is also necessary for producing learning in different domains of learning and higher levels of learning. Change is necessary to overcome the limitations of lecture methods as well. Change in methods of learning breaks monotony and sustain interest of students in learning process. The teacher should plan change in methods of learning. The change depends on factors such as learning objectives, size of the class, type of the content, physical setting of the class, resources available in the class, availability of time, learning resources, competence and experience of the teacher and so on. The combination of various methods of learning should lead to accomplishment of competency. The various combinations of lecture method with other methods of learning are shown in Exhibit 3.12.

Exhibit No. 3.12: Use of lecture method with other methods of teaching learning

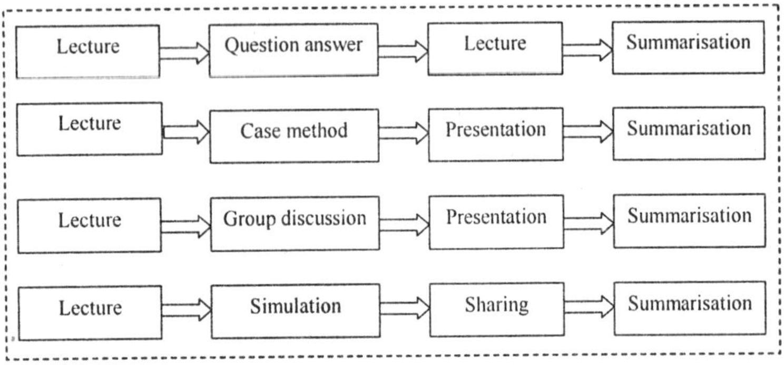

5. Summary

Traditional lecture method is commonly used for teaching all types of subjects in educational institutions. Over the years the lecture method is refined. Teachers and researchers have removed its limitations. The information technology has added significantly to enhance its effectiveness. The trained teachers in education psychology, education technology, information technology and their own discipline can transfer learning effectively and efficiently. The refined lecture method has got much strength over traditional methods of teaching. The teacher should prepare a plan to produce competent students. S/he is required to prepare subject/cluster of competencies plan, competency plan and lesson plan to produce learning in all the students at acceptable level of proficiency. The subject plan is prepared on the basis of curriculum document. The competency plan emanates from subject plan and lesson plan emanates from the competency plan. Lesson plan is prepared to achieve set of learning objectives. It is prepared in detail covering various aspects such as learning objectives, entry behaviour of students, contents, learning events, media, assignments, methods of assessment, time for each learning unit, teacher activities, students activities and so on. A teacher in the classroom confidently implements the lesson plan. S/he arranges the physical setting of the classroom, ensure proper sitting arrangement of students, recall previous learning, provides advance organizer, tells importance of learning relating it with professional life, make presentation, use media, ask questions, give learning assignments, test outcomes of learning, provide opportunities to practice learnt concepts and principles, varies stimulus to sustain interest of students, involve students in learning process, provide constructive and positive feedback to students, provide remedial treatment, assess the final learning outcomes and use another method of learning for next learning unit. In this way s/he completes the learning process and helps the students to achieve pre-defined competency.

6. Activity

Assess your Effectiveness on Lecture

As a teacher you should refine your skills to produce learning in students. You can self evaluate the effectiveness of your lecture and take measures to make it more effective and efficient in future. Your conscious effort will help you to refine and fine tune the skills. You can ask your colleagues to attend your lecture and observe your overall behaviour and provide you feedback for improvement. A list of criteria is given in following table. These criteria are generic and indicative. There may be some criteria, which may not be relevant in a particular context. You may omit assessment on such criteria. If you consider all the lectures engaged in a semester in that case most of the criteria should be considered for assessment.

Sl. No.	*Criteria*	*Extent of effectiveness*		
		High	*Medium*	*Low*
A.	*Planning*			
1.	Appropriateness of objectives			
2.	Entry behaviour of students			
3.	Sitting arrangement			
4.	Size of the class			
5.	Organisation of physical resources			
6.	Organisation of learning resources			
7.	Design of media			
8.	Design of learning resources			
9.	Selection of examples, anecdotes and incidents			

(*Contd.*)

(*Contd.*)

Sl. No.	*Criteria*	*Extent of effectiveness*		
		High	*Medium*	*Low*
10.	Design of learning events			
11.	Design of assignments			
12.	Allocation of time to each learning event			
13.	Method of assessment of learning			
14.	Rehearsal			
B.	*Delivering the lecture*			
15.	Recall of previous learning			
16.	Advance organizer			
17.	Importance of learning relating to professional life and further learning			
18.	Presentation of new information			
19.	Voice during the presentation			
20.	Pitch during the presentation			
21.	Body expression during the presentation			
22.	Reading the faces and actions of students and receiving feedback			
23.	Involvement of students in learning process by asking questions, inviting them to share experiences, involving them in group discussion, reading handout etc.			
24.	Providing opportunity to students to seek clarification, ask questions and share experiences			
25.	Use of media			
26.	Use of description of incidents and anecdotes and relating them with contents of the lecture			
27.	Use of examples and non-examples			
28.	Definition of new terminology			
29.	Sequence of presentation			

(*Contd.*)

(*Contd.*)

Sl. No.	*Criteria*	*Extent of effectiveness*		
		High	*Medium*	*Low*
30.	Richness of contents			
31.	Thought provoking/stimulating questions asked			
32.	Command on language			
33.	Establishing linkages between theory and practice			
34.	Handling of equipment and material during presentation			
35.	Humour during presentation			
36.	Movement during the presentation			
37.	Mannerism			
38.	Socio-emotional support provided to students			
39.	Use of time			
40.	Use of senses of learning			
41.	Assignments			
42.	Consolidation of learning			
43.	Supportive and positive attitude for transferring learning			
44.	Time provided for notes taking			
45.	Assessment of learning			
46.	Providing feedback			
47.	Distribution of learning resources			
48.	Ensuring learning of all the students			
C.	*Application of Learning in Real Life Situations*			
49.	Games			
50.	Simulation			
51.	Role play			

(*Contd.*)

(Contd.)

Sl. No.	*Criteria*	*Extent of effectiveness*		
		High	*Medium*	*Low*
52.	Demonstration			
53.	Practice exercise			
54.	Action learning			
55.	Assignment			
56.	Design			
57.	Development			
58.	Visualisation			
59.	Assessment of impact of learning			
60.	Providing constructive feedback			
D.	*Summative Assessment*			
61.	Selection of situation for demonstration of competency			
62.	Criteria for assessing competency			
63.	Validity and reliability of assessment			
64.	Time taken to declare assessment results			
65.	Certification of competency			
66.	Feedback for refining the subject plan, competency plan and lesson plan			
67.	Feedback for refining the curriculum			

3.2 TEAM TEACHING

1. Introduction

This is the world of professionalism. Every one wants satisfaction from products and services at a cheaper rate, in less time and without much of efforts. Every one is interested to complete most of the work without putting much of the energy for learning. The professionals provide solutions to make the life easy and enjoyable. This is the era of interdisciplinary approaches and fast change. Every one is changing so as the need of the technical institutions. They should revise curriculum every batch. This is happening in the field of computer science and information technology. Numbers of new disciplines are emerging every year. There is a huge demand for teachers and teachers are not available to institutions. Team teaching is a way for developing professional teachers.

2. Need of Team Teaching

The team teaching is one of the solutions to many problems, challenges, crisis and opportunities of technical institutions. The need of team teaching is stated in Exhibit 3.13.

Exhibit No. 3.13: Need of team teaching

- It is a solution to meet the fast changing requirements of professions and emerging professions.
- One teacher cannot impart instructions to fulfill the varied needs of the students to develop competency at pre-defined proficiency level in emerging, new and interdisciplinary areas.
- There may be a requirement of developing different levels of competencies ranging from manual skills to design and evaluation skills. To fulfil these learning requirements a team of teachers is required.
- The class size is large with an intake of 60 to 90. It is difficult to ensure equal amount of learning by single teacher.
- There are various aspects of learning such as need identification, curriculum design, planning to transfer learning, instructional resources design and evaluation of learning. These aspects are inter-related, varied and cannot be professionally performed by a single person. This requires a team approach.
- There is more demand for developing competencies at pre-defined level of proficiency.
- There is a greater need for variety of experiences in new and emerging disciplines. Single teacher may not have varied experiences.
- There is a greater pool of resources available to students for discussion, sharing information, clarifying doubts and so on.
- There is a need to foster creativity, flexibility and variety in learning process. The team of teachers is supposed to be creative.
- There is a possibility for fulfilling the learning gaps and satisfy the individual needs.
- More diversified competencies, learning options, flexibility to work on live problems can be provided to students.
- Teachers for emerging and new disciplines can be developed.

(*Contd.*)

(*Contd.*)

- Teachers are equally loaded for teaching learning process.
- Second line of command is required to take up new challenges.
- The teaching learning process is affected in the absence of expert teacher. Team members take care of the learning in absence of expert teacher.
- There is a high need to develop learning culture in technical institutions that can be developed through team teaching.
- Bring innovations in teaching learning process.

3. Definition of Team Teaching

Team teaching is a method of producing interdisciplinary learning in students in new and emerging disciplines, or producing hierarchy of learning in one discipline using a team formed of experienced teachers, content experts, industry experts, researchers, new teachers and instructors. This team is made responsible for curriculum design, subject planning, competency planning, lesson planning, implementing the plans and assessing the competency of students. This team is also responsible for preparing instructional resources and providing feedback for improving the process of curriculum design, curriculum implementation and evaluating the impact of the curriculum. There could be one core team supported by many teams and individuals. The team teaching should be seen in broader perspective. It is not only teaching but it is in fact facilitating learning to achieve desired level of competence in a flexible way. The team uses all modes of learning for producing learning. The team inculcates the habit of learning, inquiry, experimentation, problem solving, accepting challenges, confrontation, effective communication, coping with situation and risk taking. The team of teachers demonstrates and promote above habits that are the demand of the corporate sector.

4. Characteristics of Team Teaching

Team teaching has many distinct characteristics. It is a most powerful approach to make the educational institutions as learning, innovative and professional institutions. It matches with the teams' structure of the institution where governing body, governing teams and management teams work effectively and efficiently. Institutions having teams structure can easily promote team teaching. The significant characteristics of team teaching are stated in Exhibit 3.14.

Exhibit No. 3.14: Characteristics of team teaching

- Team teaching matches with teams' structure in the institution. Therefore it requires fewer efforts to undergo team-building exercises.
- Team teaching is based on the principles of commitment, coordination, cooperation and collaboration to achieve common goal that is developing competencies in all the students to perform professionally on new and different jobs.
- Team teaching develops team members on the job to take up the responsibility of developing continuously changing competencies.
- Team teaching promotes holistic thinking about the job and then develop competencies accordingly.
- Team teaching involves people from different strata so it produces integrated learning from the point of view of skills, disciplines, professional competence and associated competence.
- Teams are formed with a purpose that is according to needs of the learning requirements and after achieving the purpose they disperse. So people get an opportunity to work and learn in variety of teams.
- Team members address the needs of the individuals through forming and reforming the teams of students according to their needs. It appreciates the fact that individual differences are there in students and incorporates strategies for the same.
- Team teaching has inherent distinct characteristics for learning that are synergy, creativity and innovation. That is naturally learnt by students.
- Team teaching is a vehicle to bring continuous improvement in education programmes. The improvement is observed in contents as well as methodology.
- Team teaching promotes simultaneous learning activities in different teams to explore various aspects of learning.
- Team teaching addresses many academic and non-academic problems pooling all types of its members for common purpose.
- Team teaching improves communication in the classroom and institution.
- Teams developed during the process of team teaching can easily work on challenging research projects, consultancy projects and real life problems.

5. Organizing for Team Teaching

It is easy to promote team teaching in institutions having teams structure. Institutional teams have experienced the thrill of working in a team. They have experienced the benefits of working in a team such as synergy, creativity, covering up the weaknesses of each other, accepting and meeting the challenges, working in uncertainty for mutual gain, sharing the work and experiences, learning together about the business, sharing the risk, sharing the culture, pooling the resources and so on. They already have experiences of team building and team development, working in a team and achieving goals.

5.1 Formation of a Team

Team for teaching is formed considering numbers of criteria such as number of students in the class, demand of the subject, requirement of competency, experience of the team members, expertise of the team members, interest of the team members to develop in a particular area, resources availability, learning resources, newness of the subject or competency, teaching experience on the subject or competency, level of skills required and so on. The team formation exercise can be jointly undertaken within the department and then adjustments are made to include members of other departments and outside consultants and experts. The size of the team may vary between 2 to 5. External and internal faculty members can form a team. Very experienced and content expert teacher, a learner teacher and instructors can form a team. Faculty members from various disciplines can form a team. The team should be formed to develop at least one competency in students. There could be different teams for different competencies. The teams are formally developed to take up specific assignments of producing learning and developing competencies. Teams are developed conducting seminars, team building exercises, meetings and training programmes on various aspects of educational programmes. Teams are developed on the job under the guidance of an expert teacher.

5.2 Planning in a Team

The team prepares a subject plan, competency plan and lesson plan, as it is prepared in the lecture method. The plan is prepared holistically considering the views of all the members of a team. The team may use same format for preparing the lesson plan. In team teaching the size of the class is large so apart from lesson plan the team members decide their roles. They perform these roles under the leadership of content expert. They commit to share their roles, responsibilities and resources. It is obvious that they share their expertise and experience. The team teaching plan may have simultaneous team activities for students. One team of students may go to laboratory for practice, second team may surf the internet, third team may solve a problem, fourth team may go to workshop for product development and fifth team may go for field visit. The size of the group of students is decided on the basis of learning requirements, mode of learning and resources available with the teacher. The formation of students' team also depends on the learning purpose. It may be homogeneous, mixed and heterogeneous. A teacher or instructor or resource person leads each team of students. After completion of the assignments all the students teams and teachers team join together to share the learning experiences. The detailed planning is carried out for each team of students. An indicative example of team teaching is shown in Exhibit 3.15.

Exhibit No. 3.15: Plan of team teaching

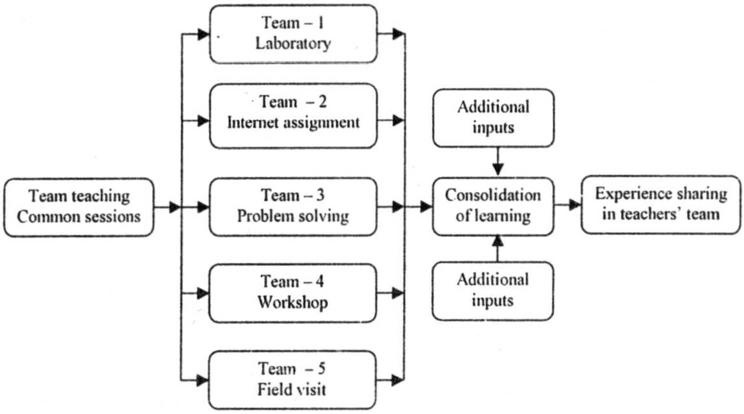

5.3 Implementation of a Plan

Team members implement the plan as per their commitment. In the beginning of the competency initiation process the content expert may take the lead and provide information to the whole group of students. Then area specific members also provide inputs to the students. They can use variety of methods and media to provide information. They can provide handouts and other learning resources to students. It could be series of sessions conducted by a teacher's team. The teachers team has an option to use methods such as presentation of information, question answer technique, discussion, panel discussion, demonstration, role-play and so on. Once teachers transfer the information they make their expectations clear to students to participate in subsequent sessions conducted by individual teacher as per plan. The teams of students disperse for different exercises. They follow the instructions of team leader and organize the sessions and assignments. They guide the students and note down the learning points. They note down the issues to be discussed during the consolidation session. They also note down the observations on behaviour of students. Generally an inventory is prepared by teachers to produce learning during working in small team. Teachers use this inventory during consolidation phase of learning.

5.4 Consolidation of Learning

Once the groups have undergone different learning exercises under the guidance of different teachers they assemble and share the learning outcomes and learning experiences. They raise the issues, questions, and doubts that are not clear to them. The team of teachers first reinforces the learning and then takes up the issues for clarifying. All the teachers in a team participate in this process of sharing and clarifying the learning issues. If necessary the team provides additional inputs to fill up the learning gap and unlearn the wrong concepts. The students are encouraged by teachers to explore issues further for the benefit of the self and others. In some cases teachers provide issues for further exploration that are the concern of the industry. The next plan of learning is informed to students and the session ends with thanks. Another sequence and team of teachers may take the next competency.

5.5 Experience Sharing in Teachers Team

The teachers' team shares the experiences of working in a team. They share the experiences of transferring learning in a team. They reinforce the positive behaviour of each other. They provide constructive feedback for improving the performance of the team and individual members. They assess the effectiveness of the team on parameters listed in Exhibit 3.16.

6. Summary

Team teaching is a method of producing interdisciplinary learning in students in new and emerging disciplines, or producing hierarchy of learning in one discipline using a team formed of experienced teachers, content experts, industry experts, researchers, new teachers and instructors. This team is made responsible for curriculum design, subject

Exhibit No. 3.16: Parameters to evaluate effectiveness of a team

Sl. No.	*Parameters*	*Extent of Achievement*			
		VH	*H*	*M*	*L*
A.	*Learning of Students*				
1.	Achievement of competency by all students				
2.	Fulfilment of individual needs				
3.	Interest and joy in learning				
4.	Learning associated skills to competency such as interpersonal relationship, effective communication, leadership and so on				
B.	*Use of Resources*				
5.	Effectiveness of learning methods				
6.	Efficiency of learning methods				
7.	Effectiveness of media				
8.	Effectiveness of utilisation of time				
9.	Effectiveness of utilisation of physical resources				
10.	Effectiveness of utilisation of learning resources				
C.	*Effectiveness of Working in a Team*				
11.	Learning of team members				
12.	Commitment, coordination, cooperation and collaboration among team members				
13.	Effectiveness of team leader				
14.	Level of creativity, innovation and synergy in team working				
15.	Settlement of problems and conflict				
D.	*Impact*				
16.	Commitment to work in a team				
17.	Interest to take up new assignments				
18.	Willingness to assume leadership				
19.	Desire to work on challenging project				
20.	Corporate climate				

VH — Very high, H — High, M — Medium, L — Low

planning, competency planning, lesson planning, implementing the plans and assessing the competency of students. This team is also responsible for preparing instructional resources and providing feedback for improving the process of curriculum design, curriculum implementation and evaluating the impact of the curriculum. There could be one core team supported by many Teams. Team teaching need to be practiced in technical institutions because of many reasons such as inter disciplinary competencies, individual differences, demand for developing creative, innovative, risk taking, presentation and visualisation skills, need to pool resources, new and emerging disciplines. The team teaching addresses the needs of learning. It has got many advantages over other methods of teaching such as holistic approach to learning, fostering creativity, stimulating thinking, training of existing faculty in new and emerging discipline, use of variety of modes of learning, and greater pool of resources. The team is formed as per need of the competency and it is developed to produce learning effectively. The team prepares a plan for developing competencies and implements it. The initial session is planned as input session in which all the members of the team participate to produce learning. Varieties of methods are used in input session such as lecture, demonstration, question answer, panel discussion and role-play. These methods are used considering the requirements of learning. After input session teams of students are formed to work on different aspects of learning. Teachers guide the teamwork. During the team learning process students and teachers note learning points and difficulties. Then consolidation of learning session is organized in which all the teams participate and share their experiences. Teachers also share the experiences and provide constructive feedback to students. Learning gaps are fulfilled by remedial inputs by teachers. Teachers also evaluate the effectiveness of working in a team. The team teaching is used for developing other competencies.

7. Activity

Identify inter disciplinary competency that can be developed by a team of resource persons. Identify the resource persons, contact them and prepare a plan to develop the competency through team teaching. Think about the formation of teams of students to learn in a team. Run the team teaching and assess its effectiveness on criteria such as competency development of the students, creativity, innovativeness, attitude development of students, relating disciplines, time consumed, interest of students in learning, and learning of resource persons.

3.3 QUESTION ANSWER

1. Introduction

Students are curious about the discipline they have chosen and they have many questions to ask to teachers about the career, programme and learning. They come to college to satisfy their learning needs, desires and ambitions. It is human tendency to ask questions. It is said that more you learn more questions you have about a topic or subject or profession. The instinct of learning can only be satisfied asking questions to self and others. Questions come from within so students try to find the answers to questions on their own. They take initiative and explore all sources to find the answer. It means it is also a natural tendency to find the answers of questions. Teachers should harness the opportunity of instinct to learn and explore through questioning and answering. Teacher should design the lesson plan to put the students in process of learning.

Question answer technique is easy to practice because everyone is familiar to it. Question answer technique is considered vary strong method for purposeful and need based learning. It initiates the problem solving skills development process. It develops the confidence of students to communicate the answer in effective way. It develops maturity for learning. It develops the habit of taking initiatives. It is a powerful method to produce learning and test outcomes of learning.

2. Learning from Question Answer

Question answer is a powerful method to learn new and different information. This method helps to develop skills in cognitive domain. The list of indicative skills developed by question answer method is stated in Exhibit 3.17.

3. Use of Question Answer Method

The question answer method has many versions. The use of different versions of the question answer method depends on creativity of the teacher, her/his preparedness for the method, interest in changing stimulus during the process of learning, competence of using various methods of learning and so on. A brief description of various versions of question answer method is given in subsequent paragraphs.

Exhibit No. 3.17: Learning from question answer method

➢ Develop confidence to seek and provide information ➢ Organize information logically and serially with reference to an issue or problem or context ➢ Stimulate thinking process to formulate hypothesis and test it ➢ Recall and apply information in given situation ➢ Develop testing and verification skills ➢ Develop attitude of inquiry ➢ Review the learning	➢ Develop analytical skills with reference to a particular context or problem or issues ➢ Develop comparing skills ➢ Develop judgmental skills ➢ Develop interpretation skills ➢ Develop problem solving and decision-making skills ➢ Develop thinking skills ➢ Develop written and oral communication skills ➢ Develop assessment skills ➢ Develop appreciating skills ➢ Develop observation skills

First version of question answer techniques is that a teacher presents information to achieve learning objectives and asks a set of questions to randomly selected students. This method helps to keep the students psychologically and physically attentive during the lecture. This method helps a teacher to assess the level of learning and provide recognition to students for learning. The teacher finds learning gaps using this version of question answer method. S/he fulfils learning gaps using remedial inputs. Most of the teachers use this version of question answer technique. This is not a powerful version of question answer method but it can be enriched using variety of questions such introductory questions, developmental questions and testing questions. Students should feel that the questions are obvious and part of the learning and not a part of testing. Various steps of this version of question answer method are listed in Exhibit 3.18.

Second version is related to ask students to read handouts, text book, reference book, see video film, study a particular machine, observe a particular technique, observe a process and so on. The students study in detail the assignment given by the teacher. Then they assemble on pre-defined date and place after completing the study. The teacher asks them questions on random basis. Each student answers the question asked by a teacher. If s/he fails to answer or partially answers, the teacher asks the same question to another student. If s/he answers the question up to satisfaction level of the teacher then teacher moves to next question that is logically connected to previous question but difficult than

Exhibit No. 3.18: Steps of first version of question answer method

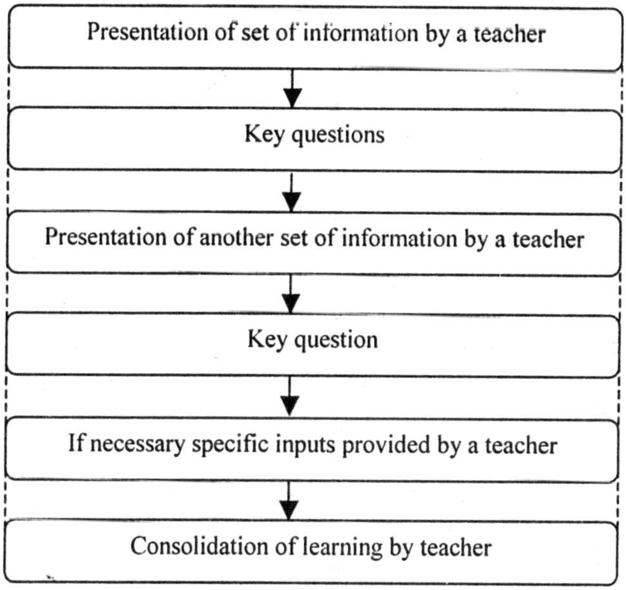

previous one. A teacher repeats the same process till learning objectives are accomplished. The questions are asked randomly to students and they should be encouraged to answer. Teacher should ensure that a particular student or group of students should not answer all the questions. Every student should have a turn to answer the question. In case students fail to answer question, the teacher should give cue to answer the question, s/he should help the students in answering the question. In such situation teacher should become a part of the learning process and should lead the learning process. If necessary s/he can provide necessary inputs in between to fill up the learning gaps. At the end of the question answer method teacher consolidates the learning in an interesting way. Steps of second version of question answer method are stated in Exhibit 3.19.

This method of conducting question answer may save large amount of time of a teacher. S/he does not require preparing lessons that are easily learnt by students on their own. S/he can save time that ranges between 4 to 8 sessions. S/he can use saved time for developmental activities. S/he also inculcates the habit of self-learning and transfers the responsibility of learning to students. It is interesting to note that students

Exhibit No. 3.19: Steps of second version of question answer method

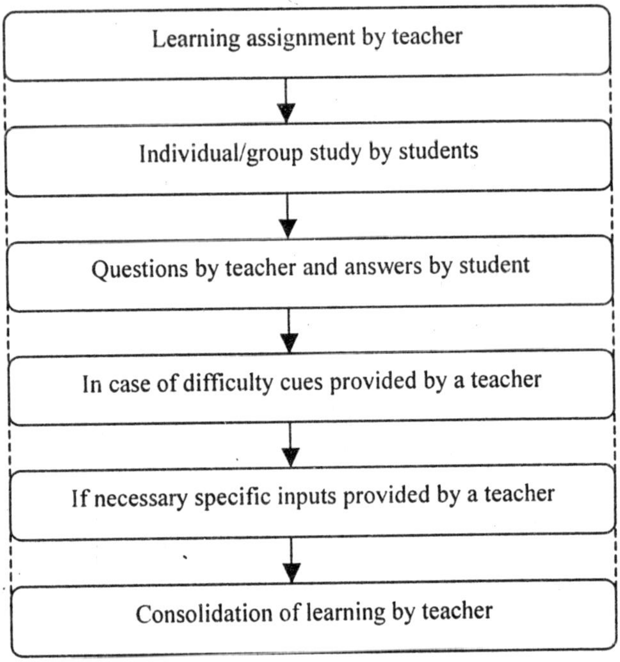

learn much more than expected because they know that teacher may ask any question that has to be replied by them. Students bring more and latest information to answer the question that is even not known to teacher. Teachers know new things related to topic and they also become proficient in using appropriate method of transferring learning.

Third version of question answer is teacher informs the students about learning objectives, provides them appropriate learning material, tells them about the sources of learning resources and asks students to go through it thoroughly. S/he asks students to frame questions on the basis of information. S/he asks each student to frame at least one question the answer of which is not clear to her/him. The students are invited to share the learning and they get an opportunity to ask answer of the difficult question from the teacher. Other students are also invited to answer the difficult question. The teacher keeps some questions ready to be asked to test/ensure the learning. This version of question answer can also be converted in the form of a question game between the two teams of students and teacher becomes the judge. At the end of question answer session the teacher consolidates the learning. The steps of question answer method conducted by students are stated in Exhibit 3.20.

Exhibit No. 3.20: Steps of third version of question answer method conducted by students

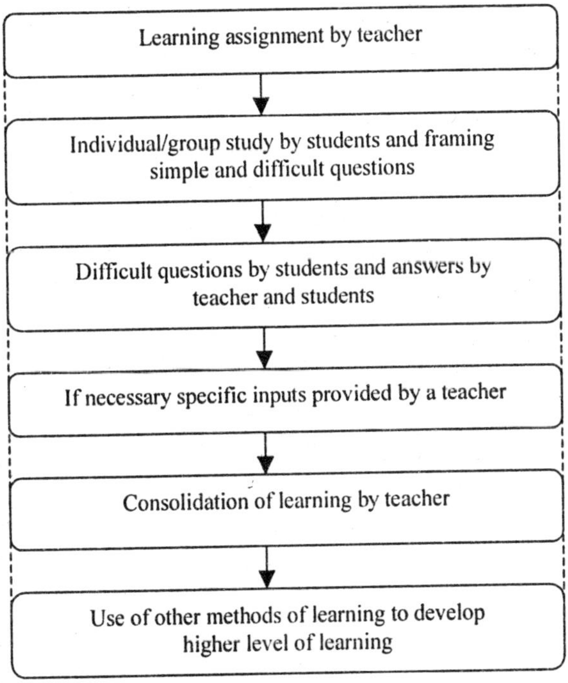

Student led question answer method saves more time of teachers. This version of question answer should be used after five rounds of first and second version. The third version would be effective with matured students may be third and final year students of undergraduate programmes. The third version takes students to higher level of skills. Students become more confident in communication and organizing the content with reference to a question.

Fourth version of question answer method is recording video programme on a particular subject. A person asks the questions and subject specialist gives answers. The sequence, logic and difficulty level is maintained in asking the questions and answering the questions. The expert can use power point slides, models, charts, graphs, pre-recorded process, and simulated practice, role-play, for answering the question. The theoretical answer is related to practice and practice can be shown in pre-recorded form. It changes stimulus and brings interest in watching and learning process. Whole process of question answer is video recorded. The video programmes can be disseminated to hundreds of institutions and it can be watched by thousands of students collectively or individually. The sequence and logic in the questions are unfolded as per progress of the question answer session. The difficulty level of the questions is increased gradually and continuously in the programme. The video-cassettes can substitute the input sessions. The teacher organizes a session in which s/he tests the learning and provides necessary inputs if necessary. From this point of learning the teacher can start facilitating learning process for higher levels of learning. The steps of this version of question answer method are stated in Exhibit 3.21.

Exhibit No. 3.21: Steps of fourth version of question answer method

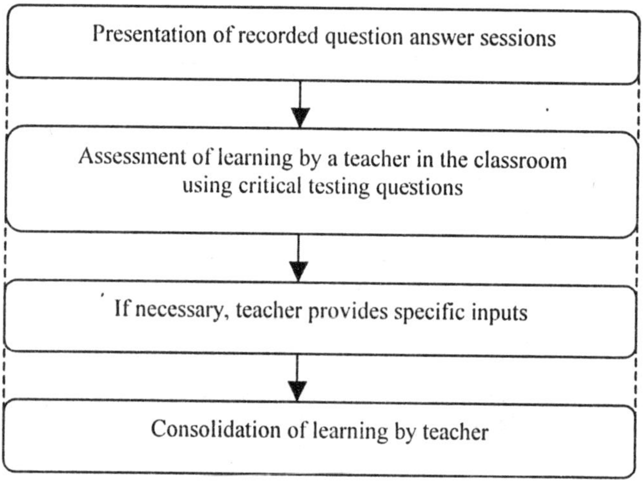

Fifth version of question answer method is a teacher uses photographs, sketches, diagrams and charts and asks appropriate questions related to learning. The students study the picture and answer the questions. The teacher provides cues to students in case they find it difficult to answer. Students develop observation skills, interpretation skills and concluding skills. They receive the information on their own and accumulate it in their previous learning. This method is useful to bring real world in the classroom and making students to learn through observation and interpretation. The students are taken to observe a particular process in industry for one to three hours and then a teacher organizes question answer session to assess the level of learning and understanding the relationship between theory and practice. This version of question answer method creates immense amount of interest in learning process. Students associate their learning with the picture so the retention time is high. The teacher uses another method of learning for developing higher level of competency. The steps of this version of question answer method are stated in Exhibit 3.22.

Exhibit No. 3.22: Steps of fifth version of question answer method conducted through photographs

Presentation of sequence of photographs by a teacher

↓

Individual/group study of photographs by students

↓

Questions by teacher and answers by students

↓

If necessary, teacher provides specific inputs

↓

Consolidation of learning by teacher

↓

Use of other methods of learning to develop higher level of learning

4. Framing Questions

In question answer method framing of questions is the first step. The questions should motivate students to find answers. The teacher can use what, why, where, when, whom, how words in framing the questions. The question should lead to learning and not assessment of students. These questions should motivate students to review the literature, search new literature, think upon the topic, discover the unknown world, experiment, discuss with peer and seniors, apply logic, use guess, recall previous learning, search for analogy, compare with something, and so on. If a teacher frames the question s/he should know the answer of it. The teacher should exhibit supportive, encouraging, guiding, helping, motivating, appreciating, and friendly behaviour. In no case the teacher should exhibit negative, evaluative, punishing, criticizing, hostile, discouraging, unsympathetic behaviour. The teacher should follow the guidelines mentioned in Exhibit 3.23.

Exhibit 3.23: Guidelines for framing the questions

The question should

- be related to learning objectives
- match with entry behaviour of the students
- specific and clear to students
- have single and short answer
- produce learning
- be framed in order of increased level of difficulty
- stimulate learning
- be challenging
- not be a puzzle
- not be confusing
- have variety
- not be duplicated in other form
- conversational

An indicative list of questions on learning is shown in Exhibit 3.24.

Exhibit No. 3.24: List of questions on learning

1. What is learning?
2. How learning takes place?
3. Where learning takes place?
4. Who causes learning?
5. Who is responsible for learning?
6. When learning takes place?
7. When learning does not take place?
8. What are the characteristics of a good learner?
9. What are the characteristics of learning?
10. What are the modes of learning?
11. What are the limits of learning?

(*Contd.*)

(*Contd.*)

12. How important are drives and incentives, and rewards and punishment in the process of learning?
13. Does learning one thing help to learn something else?
14. What is the role of practice in learning?
15. What is the difference between temporary learning and permanent learning?
16. What is wrong learning?
17. What is the difference between right learning and wrong learning?
18. What is the meaning of effective learning?
19. Why learning is necessary in life?
20. How does brain learn?
21. What is learning?
22. What are the domains of learning?
23. What are the main factors affecting learning?
24. How does environment contribute to learning process?
25. How do you know that there is a learning problem?
26. How do we learn attitudes?
27. How do we learn manual skills?
28. What is the role of teaching in learning process?
29. What is the difference between formal learning and non-formal learning?
30. What do you mean by learning to learn?
31. Why learning to learn skills are necessary?
32. What are the barriers to learning?
33. What is natural learning?
34. How does natural learning take place?
35. How do adults learn?
36. What are the characteristics of adult learners?
37. How do we learn attitudes?
38. Why people fail to learn a particular thing?
39. What do you mean by meaningful learning?
40. Is it necessary to learn each and everything related to particular discipline?
41. What do you mean by problem-based learning?
42. What is the role of the perception in learning?
43. What is the role of stimulus in learning?
44. How does rewards contribute to learning?
45. What Is the role of punishment in learning?
46. What is collaborative learning?
47. what is the relation between teaching and learning?

5. Guidelines for Conducting Question Answer Sessions

The teacher is required to do lot of preparatory work for producing learning through question answer sessions. The teacher should follow the guidelines listed in Exhibit 2.25.

Exhibit No. 3.25: Guidelines for conducting question answer sessions

Planning Stage

- Ensure that question answer method would be the most effective and efficient method to produce desired level of learning.
- Check the quality, sequence, difficulty and logic of the questions considering learning objectives and entry behaviour of the students. Frame the questions assuming you are a student and question is coming in your mind obviously and naturally.
- Prepare the answers of all the questions to be shared with students during the question answer session and after the session. Note down the sources of answers.
- Inform the students about learning objectives and expected outcomes along with time of having question answer session.
- Distribute the learning resources and inform about additional sources of learning resources to students.
- Organize the visit of industry or workshop or laboratory if students are expected to learn through observation.
- Arrange necessary resources before conducting the question answer sessions.

Organizing Stage

- Conduct introductory session to inform students about learning objectives, importance of the learning, and process of learning. Explain the way of learning to students and your expectations in terms of terminal behaviour of students. Inform about the next schedule of class and method and time of approaching to you in case they find individual difficulty in learning.
- Handover the learning resources and inform about sources of additional information to students. Give instructions on how to use the learning resources.
- Create conducive, encouraging and rewarding atmosphere in the classroom for full participation and involvement of students.
- Provide equal opportunity to all the students to ask and answer the questions. The bright students or a group of students should not lead the complete session.
- Appreciate, reward and acknowledge the answers of students and supplement them with additional, new, and different learning information
- Handle controversy, conflict and unnecessary discussion through appropriate interventions.

(*Contd.*)

(*Contd.*)

- Respect the curiosity, eagerness, anxiety and interest of students for asking the question or answering the question.
- Supplement and complement the learning process with additional brief inputs to enrich learning, boost up interest and further explore the issue, if necessary.
- Consolidate the learning summarizing main learning points.
- Appreciate the efforts made by students for learning through question answer method.
- Inform about next learning event to students.

6. Summary

Question answer method provides an opportunity to learn in natural way. Teachers shift the responsibility of learning to students. This method is a powerful method to develop lower level cognitive skills. Question answer method has many versions. The most common version used by traditional teachers is lecturing and in between asking questions to students. This is the weakest version of question answer method. It ensures attentiveness of students in learning process. It is a sort of testing of learning that is generally not liked by students. The other versions are powerful versions for producing learning effectively and efficiently.

The teacher and students both learn using remaining versions such as teachers provide the learning resources and sources of information of learning resources for self-study. The students study the learning material. The teacher frames questions and prepares answers and question answer sessions are organized for collective learning on predefined time and dates. The third version of this method entrust more responsibility for learning on students. The students study the learning resources and they prepare the questions and answers. A teacher organizes the question answer session, in which students ask questions, and their colleagues give answers in organized way. Students and teacher answer the difficult questions jointly. In fourth version the recorded question answers provided to students they learn it on their own and then a teacher organizes difficulty solving session and consolidation of learning session. Fifth version is based on observation method. Teacher provides the photographs, diagrams, sketches and video films. Students learn from the photographs and film and a question answer session is organized by a teacher to test the level of learning. Teacher provides additional information if necessary and consolidates the learning.

The questions for learning should be set carefully and cautiously to avoid confusion, multiple interpretation and complexity. The questions should create interest to learn more and more on the topic. The questions are framed following set of guidelines such as it should be related to learning objectives, match with the entry behaviour of the students, simple, challenging, specific and so on. The teacher should thoroughly plan for using the method of question answer. The question answer session should be conducted in conducive, positive, encouraging environment for producing learning and providing recognition for learning. At the end of the question answer session the teacher should consolidate the learning outcomes and appreciate the efforts of the students.

7. Activity

Select a subject/cluster of competencies/set of instructional objectives from your discipline in which various versions of question answer method can be used. Prepare learning resources to achieve set of objective and give to students for learning with brief guidelines. Prepare a list of questions following the guidelines stated in this chapter. Organize a question answer session on predefined date and time and note down your experiences on criteria listed in table.

Criteria for Evaluating the Effectiveness and Efficiency of Question Answer Session

Sl. No.	*Parameters*	*Extent of Achievement*			
		VH	*H*	*M*	*L*
A.	*Learning of Students*				
1.	Achievement of competency by all students				
2.	Fulfilment of individual needs				
3.	Interest and joy in learning				
4.	Flexibility in learning				
B.	*Your Learning*				
5.	Enrichment of contents				
6.	Competence of conducting question answer method				
7.	Time saved				
8.	Improvement in quality of learning resources				
9.	Flexibility in working				
10.	Difficulties faced by you				

(Contd.)

(Contd.)

Sl. No.	*Parameters*	*Extent of Achievement*			
		VH	*H*	*M*	*L*
C.	*Use of Resources*				
11.	Effectiveness of media				
12.	Effectiveness of utilisation of time				
13.	Effectiveness of utilisation of physical resources				
14.	Effectiveness of utilisation of learning resources				
15.	Learning environment in the classroom				

VH – Very high, H – High, M – Medium, L – Low.

3.4 DEMONSTRATION

1. Introduction

Learning through observation plays a vital role in the process of learning. Students learn more when they use more than one sense. It creates intense and deep learning. Use of all the senses of students in learning processes creates desire to learn. It psychologically involves them in learning preprocess. Proper planning of learning process can enrich learning to a greater extent.

2. Demonstration

It is a method to produce learning using all the senses of students about a concept, process, parts of machine and their functions, connections to be made, steps of finding fault, method of performance, attitudes to be observed, precautions to be taken, skills to be used, resources to be organized, sequence to be performed in completing the task, elements of operation, correct procedure of use of tools, and so on. It is a powerful method of producing learning when the real life experiences are dangerous, difficult, unapproachable, inaccessible and costly. This is a good method to initiate the skills development process in all the three domains of learning. Demonstration method of learning incorporates various principles of learning such as simple to complex, concrete to abstract, examples and non examples, use of all senses of learning, learning close to reality, involvement of students in the learning process, formative assessment of learning outcomes.

3. Types of Demonstrations

Demonstrations are classified on the basis of place of demonstration such as classroom, laboratory, workshop, computer center, industry and field situation. It is classified on the basis of mode of presentation such as teacher led, industry person led and video film led. It is also classified on the basis of purpose of learning such as learning of concepts and principles, learning of psychomotor skills and learning of attitudes or combination of all the three. The demonstration can be educational and promotional as well. The students observe the technique of observation and learn about it. Later on they can use it in their professional life.

4. Use of Demonstration with Other Methods of Learning

Demonstration can be used with many methods of learning. It is a good vehicle to involve students in learning process. The demonstration should bring continuity in learning. After demonstration students should be asked to practice the skills or attitudes in right way. The use of demonstration depends on number of factors such as topic, learning objectives, competence of a teacher, availability of time, level of students, preparedness of a teacher, size of the group, availability of the resources etc. General combinations of teaching learning methods are listed in Exhibit 3.26 for ready reference.

Exhibit No. 3.26: Use of demonstration with other methods of teaching learning

Presentation → Demonstration → Question answer → Summarization

Demonstration → Question answer → Practice → Reporting

Demonstration → Simulation → Sharing experiences → Summarization

Lecture → Question answer → Assignment → Demonstration

5. Guidelines to Use Demonstration Method for Producing Learning

The guidelines for effectively and efficiently using demonstration method are listed in Exhibit 3.27. These guidelines are indicative and noted for the teachers.

Exhibit No 3.27: Guidelines for conducting demonstration

Before Demonstration

- Analyze the learning objectives to be achieved and inform the students about them.
- Plan the process of demonstration on activities, resources, time, learning resources and learning methods.
- Define the role of the persons involved in the process of demonstration. Make sure that they have understood the role and perform it in integrated manner with ease.
- Inform the students in advance about the demonstration, place of demonstration and time of demonstration.
- Inform them to do preparation such as reading a particular topic, referring a manual, listing the questions to be asked, sequence of notes taking etc.
- Arrange the resources in order before demonstration time.
- Rehearse the significant steps of demonstration.

During Demonstration

- Inform the students to recall the theory they have learnt related to demonstration.
- State the importance of demonstration and relate it with theory and practice.
- Inform about the demonstration and points to be observed and noted during demonstration.
- Distribute the diagram or sketch of the equipment.
- Distribute the points of observation and observation to be noted by students.
- Start demonstration as per plan. Explain and demonstrate the things in sequential and logical way as they happen in real life situation. Teacher should also explain why s/he is performing things in a particular order and implications of the same.
- Arrange the information in sequence giving actions, learning points, clarifications to ensure learning.
- Ask questions to seek attention after each stage or learning event.
- Involve students asking any student randomly to come forward and repeat the event or touch the equipment or name the parts of the equipment or tell the functions of different parts of the equipment or tell the steps carried out to use the equipment and purpose of each step.
- Complete the demonstration as planned and repeat the complete process to summarize the learning.
- Keep the voice tone and action in tune with the explanation of the procedure, parts or attitudes. Have confidence during the process of demonstration.

(Contd.)

(*Contd.*)

After Demonstration
➢ Ask students to recite the process along with demonstration. Actions are carried out by teacher and explanation is given by students.
➢ Students come forward and carryout the demonstration.
➢ Students share their observation on given criteria.
➢ Teacher relates the concept, theory, and process with real life situation.

6. Use of Technology in Demonstration

Simple equipments, machines, procedures and technology can be explained using demonstration method. There are complex technology, machines, equipments, processes and operations that cannot be accessed by all students and teachers. The accessibility is limited because they are very costly, dangerous, risky to operate, requires precious skills, difficult to bring in campus and permission is not provided because of security reasons. There are other reasons also to record the demonstrations such as machine makes very high noise or spread of dust or very high illumination, or spark, or high temperature, or high or slow speed. In such a case the demonstration can be recorded and distributed to institutions. The compact disc or the cassette can be purchased and used by institutions. It brings colour to the process of learning and saves time of the teacher and students. To avoid the repetition of efforts professional body or statutory body should take initiative to develop recorded demonstrations. A manual on use of demonstration can endorse guidelines for use. The manual can contain the guidelines listed in Exhibit 3.27.

7. Summary

Learning through observation is an initial stage in the process of learning skills and attitudes. Demonstration is a method controlled by a teacher to initiate learning in students. It is a strong method to initiate development of right types of skills and attitudes in right ways. The trained teacher uses all the senses of learning during the process of learning. S/he involves students in the demonstration process to create interest and anxiousness in the learning process. The teacher can organize trial practice after each significant stage of demonstration. Demonstrations are classified on the basis of place where they are conducted such as classroom, laboratory and field. Video recorded demonstrations are very useful in the process of learning. These demonstrations are carefully recorded by professional teachers and disseminated to all the institutions where it can be used.

Demonstration is a flexible method of producing learning and can be combined with any method of learning to maintain continuity in learning process. The demonstration should be properly planned, performed and evaluated by a teacher. S/he should assess the learning outcomes at the end of the demonstration process.

8. Activity

The effectiveness of demonstration process is assessed against well-defined criteria. These criteria depend on the type of demonstration performed by the teacher. An indicative list of criteria is given below to measure effectiveness of the demonstration. You can ask your colleague to measure your effectiveness and provide constructive feedback for improvement.

Assess Your Effectiveness on Demonstration

Sl. No.	*Criteria*	*Extent of Effectiveness*		
		High	*Medium*	*Low*
1.	Selection of the method			
2.	Organisation of equipment, machines and material			
3.	Size of the group			
4.	Appropriateness of place of demonstration			
5.	Planning of the demonstration			
6.	Rehearsal			
7.	Advance information to students			
8.	Information on points to be observed			
9.	Sitting arrangement of students			
10.	Distribution of learning resources			
11.	Steps of demonstration			
12.	Connectivity of demonstration steps, narration of learning points and theory			
13.	Ensuring learning of all the students			
14.	Involvement of students in learning process			
15.	Question answer during demonstration			

(*Contd.*)

(Contd.)

Sl. No.	Criteria	Extent of Effectiveness		
		High	Medium	Low
16.	Handling of equipment and material			
17.	Cleanliness and clarity in demonstration			
18.	Progress of demonstration			
19.	Creating anxiety to learn			
20.	Voice, confidence and handling demonstration activities			
21.	Opportunity to students to repeat the action			
22.	Feedback and learning points for all students			
23.	Opportunity to ask questions			
24.	Use of time			
25.	Skills demonstrated			
26.	Attitudes demonstrated			
27.	Command on subject			
28.	Command on language			
29.	Summarisation of learning			
30.	Establishing linkages with theory and practice			

3.5 LEARNING IN GROUPS

1. Introduction

Students come with different strengths, weaknesses, background, need, interest and ambitions to learn technical and professional competencies. There strengths can be used to remove weaknesses. They can be put in a situation in which they satisfy social needs and learn professional skills. In such situations they get an opportunity to learn different culture, habits and values that are necessary for doing work in different locations with different people. Learning in a group is a powerful method to develop cognitive and affective skills. They enjoy leaning in group and from the group. Learning in-group provides a powerful means to develop people skills, interpersonal skills, social skills, managerial skills and entrepreneurial skills. They learn skills of working in real life situation such as effective communication, negotiation, bargaining, collaborating, working in teams and collective learning. The group exerts pressure on members to conform to group norms.

2. Types of Learning Groups

Learning groups can be formed and put in a learning situation by a teacher in a formal setting. Apart from this students also form groups to learn different subjects informally. Formal groups are formed using criteria such as learning requirements, time available, requirement of the learning task, availability of the resources, and competence of the teacher. The classification of learning groups is shown in Exhibit 3.28.

Exhibit No. 3.28: Classification of learning groups

Formal	Dyads, Triads, small groups and large groups.
Informal groups	Quality Circles, interest groups, hobby groups and sports groups.

2.1 Formal Groups

A teacher forms formal groups or they are formed voluntarily on the basis of certain criteria. The main purpose of the groups is to achieve the learning objectives in effective and efficient ways. The purpose of formal group is listed in Exhibit 3.29.

Exhibit No. 3.29: Purpose of formal groups

Type of Group	*Purpose*
Dyads	To develop skills such as rapport building, information seeking, communicating message, obtaining commitment, making complaint, handling complaint, interacting with a purpose, encouraging with each other to learn, influencing with a purpose, solving learning problems, sharing experiences, developing reasoning, seeking consensus, careful listening etc.
Triads	In addition to skills mentioned in dyads students develop skills such as judgmental, decision making, conflict management, consensus seeking, feedback giving and receiving, concluding etc.

(Contd.)

(*Contd.*)

Type of Group	*Purpose*
Small group	In addition to skills mentioned in dyads and triads students develop skills such as taking initiatives, planning, thinking, visualizing, forecasting, summarizing, observation, reporting, information giving and seeking, appreciating the feelings of other, creativity, working in a team and inferring.
Large group	In addition to skills mentioned in dyads, triads and small groups students develop skills such as leadership, team building strategy design, complex problem solving, accepting challenges, taking risk, facing competition, designing major change, crisis management and negotiations.

2.2 Informal Groups

Students form informal groups on their own initiatives to achieve specific purpose. The purpose may be related to academic or non-academic issues. The teacher can ask students to ask to form a voluntary group to solve academic problems. Teacher and students join the group to solve problems related to teaching learning process. This group meets weekly or fortnightly to discuss and solve the learning problem or to learn advance skills, technology and techniques. The group is provided all necessary resources by the institution to facilitate learning process. The purpose of the group may be learning new competencies or software or interdisciplinary competencies. It all depends on the collective decision of the group. In last decades some institutions have introduced quality circle approach in their institutions. They have introduced homogeneous and heterogeneous approach of forming quality circle. Quality circles have been formed in academic and non-academic areas of functioning of the institutions. The results are encouraging.

3. Advantages of Learning in Groups

There are numbers of advantages of using learning in-group in technical institutions. Some of the indicative advantages are listed in Exhibit 3.30.

Exhibit No. 3.30: Advantages of learning in groups

It Develops	*It Reduces*
➢ Discussional attitudes ➢ Reflective thinking ➢ Socio-emotional support ➢ Foster creativity and synergy ➢ Desirable attitudes for collective learning ➢ Greater energy to learn ➢ Adjustments with individual differences ➢ Opportunity for fun and joy ➢ Trust building	➢ The feeling of loneness ➢ Anxiety and tension for learning ➢ Problems of learning ➢ Negative thinking ➢ Frustration ➢ Feeling of exhaustion and withdrawal ➢ Dominance ➢ Fear of failure

4. Use of Groups in Learning Methods

The learning in-group is a versatile method. It enriches the process of learning. It is used with other methods of teaching learning to get added advantage and change the stimulus and mode of learning. It has wide variation and provides the scope for flexibility in the process of learning. The teacher can use any method of group learning independently or with other methods to facilitate and enrich learning. The power of learning in groups is used in methods listed in Exhibit 3.31.

Exhibit No. 3.31: Use of group in learning methods

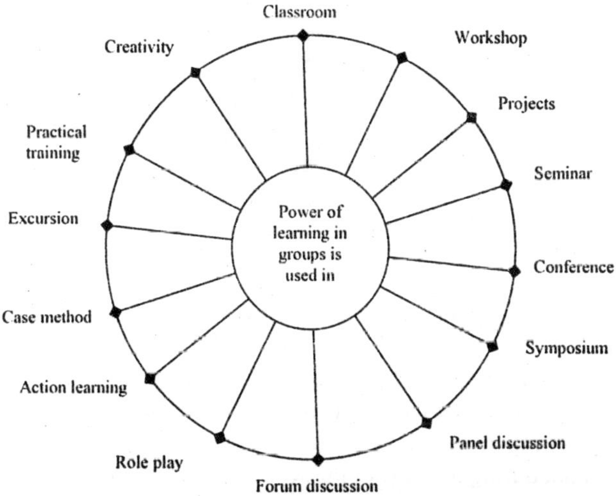

5. Role of the Teacher

The teacher has to perform variety of roles to produce productive, purposeful and intense learning during the process of learning in groups. At different stages of learning the role of the teacher changes significantly. Teacher should note that s/he should not dominate the process of learning in a group. S/he should fuel the process of learning at various stages. The teacher should withdraw gradually from the process of learning in groups and till final year of the programme s/he should totally withdraw from the learning process. The students should develop ability and capability to learn on their own with this method of learning. The role of the teacher is listed in Exhibit 3.32.

Exhibit No. 3.32: Process of learning in group

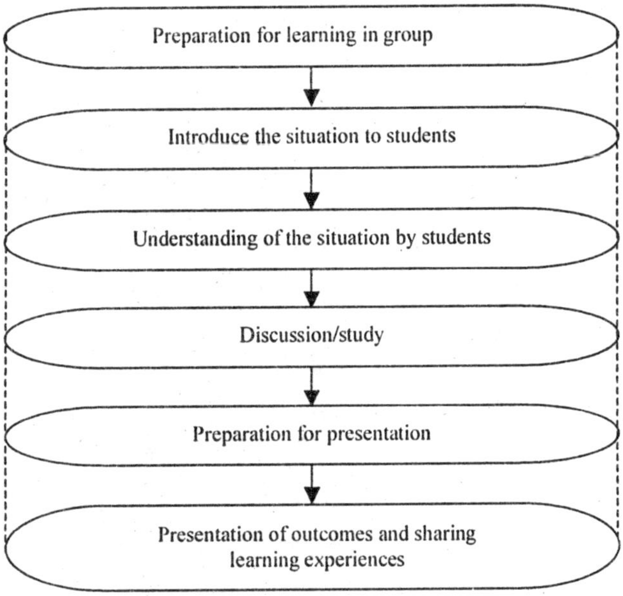

5.1 Preparation for Learning in Groups

The teacher analyses the curriculum and competencies to identify the learning objectives that can be accomplished effectively and efficiently through learning in groups. The analysis of the curriculum and objective is carried out during the start of the semester and put in the subject plan/

lesson plan. If the major part of the learning is related to the cognitive domain or affective domain and learning through discussion is most appropriate and feasible method. Then the teacher selects the situation from the world of work and describe it in writing in the form of issues, problems, decision requirement, planning requirement, strategy design and so on. The problem or issues can also be video recorded from the world of work to better comprehend the situation. If the learning objectives are related to affective domain and that to related to safety, cleanliness, sanitation, systematic working, observing set steps or rules or norms the teacher simulates the situation in the classroom/laboratory/workshop/field/ computer center with the specific behaviour to be observed.

5.2 Introduce the Situation to the Students

The teacher introduces real life situation to the students and provides them written description of the situation or shows them the recording. S/he asks the students to visualize the situation and come out with alternative solutions. S/he informs them about the group procedure such as what they are supposed to do with situation, how much time is available to them, how they are going to make the presentations.

5.3 Understanding the Situation by Students

The students go in their respective groups and try to comprehend the situation to arrive at issue. If they are unable to visualize the situation they note down the points that require clarification from the teacher. The teacher visits all groups and provides clarification of situation and not on issues or problem. If more than three groups are working on a problem in that case more than one teacher are required to monitor the progress of the work.

5.4 Discussion on the Situation

The students select their leader and reporter and start working on the situation. During the process of discussion they perform activities such as; developing common understanding of the problem, clarifying the process of working, deciding the issues involved in the situation, keeping focused discussion on the issue, noting down the outcome of the discussion, encouraging the group members to participate in the discussion, accepting the ideas, rejecting the ideas, arrive at conclusions, reflecting on learning and so on.

Use of sociogram: During the group process the teacher observes the whole process of discussion and note down her/his observation on a checklist of students' behaviour. S/he also prepares sociogram during initial sessions on group discussions to provide feedback on learning in a group. Sociogram provides accurate information on behaviour of the individual student, number of interactions between two students, interaction pattern in the group, most preferred students during the process of interaction, acceptance of a student in a group and so on. In fact sociogram helps to understand the social interaction within the group. It helps the teacher to better design the group for learning in group. It helps the teacher to identify the student that is a central figure in the learning process and influence the behaviour of rest of the students in the learning process. It also helps to identify the students who have withdrawn from the learning process. They are neither initiating interaction nor responding to the interaction process. These types of students may have variety of problems so far learning in groups is concerned. The teachers can identify their problems and they can be counseled. Sociogram helps to identify the sub-learning groups in large learning groups. It helps to better understand the acceptance and rejection of a student in interaction process. It helps to identify the need of power, need for affiliation and need for achievement of different students. It helps to understand the technical soundness and level of previous learning of students. Sociogram is a very good tool to understand the social behaviour of students in learning process. Teacher can harness the potential of their learning behaviour for better learning designs in groups. A sociogram of group interactions is shown in Exhibit 3.33.

Exhibit No. 3.33: Use of sociogram

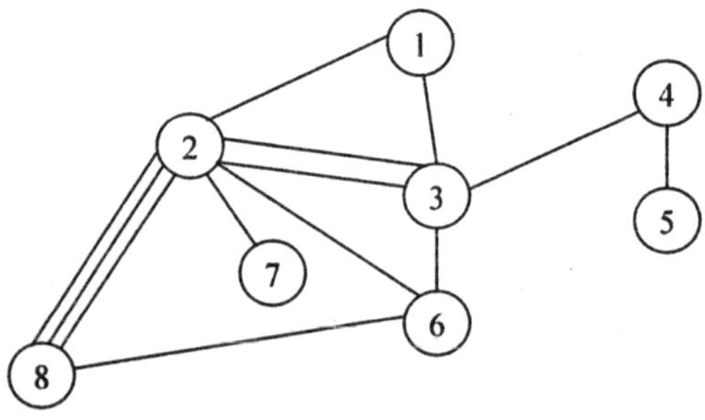

The focus of interaction is member 2. S/he has influence over the process of interaction. Student 8 has interacted with 2 and student 5 is isolated. The

3. Example of Force Field Analysis

An example of force field analysis is given in Exhibit 3.63. This example is related to introducing learner centered approaches in technical institution. The concep* of learner centered approaches is new to technical institutions so they have used various strategies to design and implement the major change.

Exhibit No. 3.63: Introducing learner centered approaches

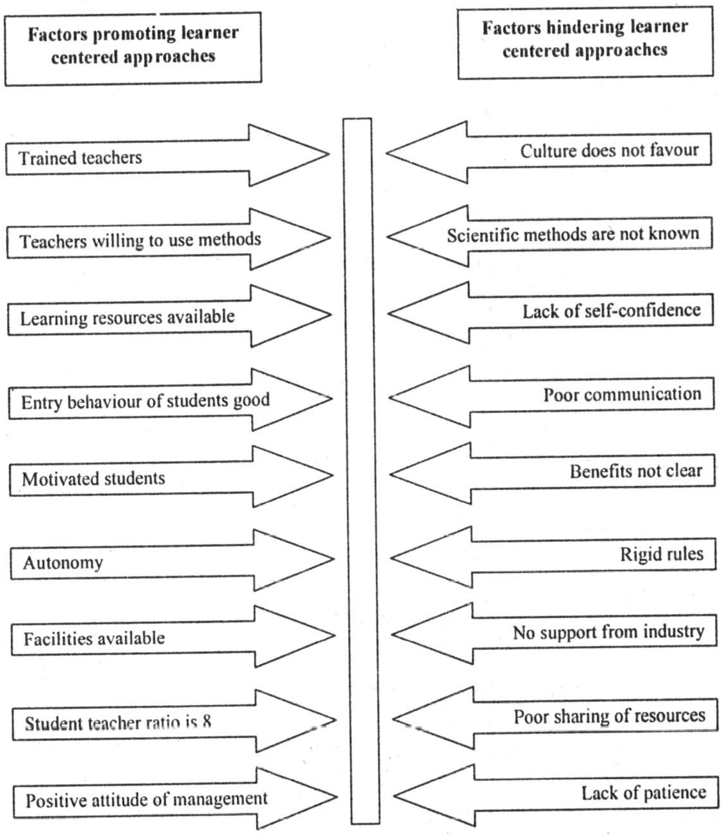

4. Summary

Force filed analysis is a method to involve students in learning process. This process helps to develop cognitive skills such as problem solving, decision-making, planning, communication, reasoning and creativity. It also develops the skills related to consensus seeking, influencing and agreeing. It develops the skills related to self-management, self-learning, self-control and self-initiation. It creates fun and enjoyment during the process of learning.

5. Activity

Carry out force field analysis for developing risk-taking attitude. Identify the factors responsible for risk taking attitudes and factors hindering risk-taking attitude. Priorities the factors and draw force field analysis diagram.

3.16 TUTORIAL

1. Introduction

All the students are not alike and equal so far learning is concerned. They come from different background, have different interest, are not proficient in communication, lack confidence, come from different academic background with individual learning style, and personal problems. During the course of study they are unable to make pace with the teacher and other students because they have specific problems related to learning. In a large class size teacher may not concentrate on individual learning problems that may leave behind a student because of a small learning problem. In engineering study most of the topics, subjects and learning exercises are interconnected. Having problem at any stage one cannot progress further with ease and joy. There may be anxiety, tension, and disinterest in the students for a particular subject or groups of subjects. They may ignore the learning in a particular subject.

2. Purpose of Tutorials

Tutorials are organized for solving learning problems of students. Learning problem may be related to learning of the concept, theory and process. It may be related to completing an assignment, project and research work. It may be related to interconnection between subjects and interdisciplinary issues as well. Tutorials are organized by a teacher to solve learning problems of students and make them flow in the learning process. Practice related learning problems are solved through arranging an expert from the industry.

3. Type of Learning from Tutorial Classes

Tutorial classes produce variety of learning. Some of the indicative learning is listed in Exhibit 3.64.

Exhibit No. 3.64: Learning produced through tutorials

➢ Self-learning habit ➢ Validation of learning ➢ Confidence for learning ➢ Identifying learning problems ➢ Attainment of higher level of skills	➢ Flexible learning approach ➢ Socio-emotional encouragement for learning ➢ Communication skills ➢ Receiving feedback

4. Guidelines for Organizing a Tutorial

To reap the benefits of tutorial method teachers are required to play altogether different role. S/he demonstrates listening skills and show empathy for the students. S/he acts as a counseller, guide, supporter, encourager, facilitator and friend for the student. S/he should follow guidelines listed in Exhibit 3.65.

Exhibit No. 3.65: Guidelines for organizing and conducting tutorials

- Every alternate day organize a pre-declared tutorial class at any convenient time before or after institutional hours or during the free time of students.
- At the beginning of the semester declare the guidelines for organizing tutorial classes. The guidelines can highlight the type of learning problems would be solved, manner in which solved, preparation to be done by students before coming to the class etc.
- Ask students to spell out the learning problem, difficulty in learning and efforts made by students to solve the learning problem. Encourage students to share the problem openly.
- Listen students carefully and try to understand the cause of the learning difficulty. The cause of learning difficulty of the student may be in the subject you are teaching or it may be in other prerequisite subject. Test the learning of the students related to the topic. If s/he satisfactorily responds to the test again try to diagnose the cause of learning difficulty and test the learning related to the cause. You will surprise that the problem is because of lack of conceptual clarity, or poor understanding of the theory, or because of abstract concept, or because of lack of

(Contd.)

(*Contd.*)

visualisation of part from whole or whole from parts. Provide psycho-emotional support to the students during the process of solving their learning problems.

- Solve the learning problems of students professionally. They should be encouraged to attend the tutorials.
- In tutorial classes you perform the role of a guide and learning problem solver. Student wants your support to solve the problem and build confidence in the subject. In tutorial classes you are not an instruction provider. Try to minimize the inputs related to learning problem.
- If more than one student are attending tutorial classes and any student react on the learning problem of the fellow student, provide her/him an opportunity to solve the learning problem.
- There is no need to teach the students during tutorial classes. You can provide cues or reference for removing the learning difficulty.
- Encourage positive attitude for learning in tutorial classes. Provide different point of view to make the student think.
- Tutorial should not be another classroom teaching in which all the students are present for listening a teacher. If it is the case review your classroom teaching learning process.
- Tutorial classes should be frequently organized for students doing major projects, assignments, and research study to boost their morale. Tutorials for major projects demonstrate teacher commitment for the learning process. It is a good way to provide recognition to their progress.

5. Summary

Tutorials are organized by teachers to solve learning and specific problems of the students. Tutorial sessions are necessary where self-learning is promoted by a teacher using various methods of learning. The teacher produces effective learning in students using tutorial classes. This method of learning is based on various modes of learning such as self-learning, learning through struggle, learning from self-feedback, learning from mistakes and problems. This method develops the habit of learning to learn. The teacher should follow some guidelines to produce effective learning through tutorial classes. These guidelines are organize tutorial classes every alternate day, solve specific learning problems of students, use bright students in solving the problems of slow learners, encourage students to think, encourage students to refer learning resources, promote positive attitude for self learning, provide constructive feedback for improvement in learning and so on.

6. Activity

Prepare a list of criteria and observe the learning problems of students. Note down these learning problems and organize some tutorials to solve the problems.

3.17 ASSIGNMENTS

1. Introduction

A student should be involved in the learning process to make the learning meaningful and joyful. The responsibility of learning should move from a teacher to students. Students should be more active in the process of learning than a teacher. A professional teacher can make the students active designing the complete process of learning student based. Students should be the prime mover of learning process. Assignments are designed by a teacher to develop variety of competencies in students. Output of learning assignment is a good measure of quality of learning. The progress of individuals and groups can be monitored assessing output of assignments. Assignments in areas of specialisation can create interest to pursue a particular discipline throughout the course of study.

2. Types of Assignments

There are varieties of assignments that can be designed by a teacher. The assignments can be classified on the basis of place of doing the assignments, nature of assignment, types of skills development and students task. There could be other classifications depending upon the subject and type of learning. Assignments can also be classified on the basis of size of the group such as individual, small group, medium group and large group. Assignments can be classified on the basis of routine assignment and special assignment. It can be classified as minor or major. Major assignments are given at the end of a term in vacations. The classification of assignments is shown in Exhibit 3.66.

The design of assignment depends on the training, creativity, ability, experience and attitude of the teacher. Every year the teacher can design different types of assignments to stop copying practice and bring variety in instructional process. An indicative list of assignments is shown in Exhibit 3.67.

Exhibit No. 3.66: Classification of assignments

Location	Nature	Skills development	Student task
Classroom	Case study	Problem solving	Literature Review
Laboratory	Project work	Decision-making	Study of a process
Field/industry	Role-play	Planning/design	Production
Library	Game	Evaluation	Observation

Exhibit No. 3.67: Learning assignment

➢ Self-study of the chapter ➢ Viewing a film ➢ Visiting an industry ➢ Conducting survey ➢ Solving theoretical problems ➢ Preparing a plan ➢ Designing a product ➢ Analyzing failure ➢ Comparative study ➢ Analysis of a case	➢ Research study ➢ Designing a software ➢ Preparing a report ➢ Writing a paper ➢ Evaluating the effectiveness and efficiency of a process ➢ Application of theory in practice ➢ Predicting the future technology ➢ Preparing observation report ➢ Investigating a case

3. Learning Produced through Assignments

Assignments are good means to inculcate the habit of self-learning in students. Students bear the responsibility for learning through doing assignment. Assignments inherently apply the concept of learning by doing, learning through struggle, learning by mistake, learning by self-evaluation. Assignments inculcate the habit of taking initiatives, visualizing the situation, learning to learn new things. It is a strong medium to involve students in learning process. Assignments create learning challenges for students so they consider learning as challenging process. They foster thinking with reference to an issue or a situation. Assignments provide enough flexibility for learning and they suit to individual learning styles. Assignments provide opportunities to incorporate for various modes of learning listed in Exhibit 3.68. Assignments are considered good tools of assessment of attainment of competency and proficiency level. The output of the assignment can be maintained to show as an evidence of efforts made by students to attain the competency. The output of assignments helps the certifying agency to look behind the stages of learning carried out in order to attain the competency.

Exhibit No. 3.68: Learning produced through assignments

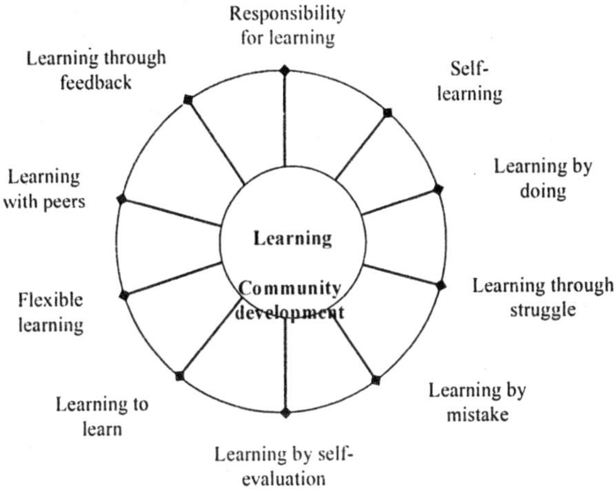

Properly designed learning assignments produce variety of learning in all the three domains of learning. The assignments produce learning listed in Exhibit 3.69.

Exhibit No. 3.69: Learning produced in different domains of learning by assignments

Cognitive Domain	*Psychomotor Domain*	*Affective Domain*
➢ Comparative skills ➢ Application skills ➢ Analysis skills ➢ Planning skills ➢ Evaluation skills ➢ Writing skills ➢ Organizing skills ➢ Communication skills ➢ Presentation skills	➢ Application skills ➢ Imitation skills ➢ Precision skills ➢ Manipulation skills ➢ Use of multi skills ➢ Maintenance skills ➢ Fault finding skills	➢ Attitude for safety ➢ Concern for environment ➢ Attitude for cleanliness ➢ Attitude for recording the progress ➢ Attitude for mutual cooperation

4. Guidelines for Designing Assignments

Assignments are designed by a teacher to produce desired level of learning in students. They are part of lesson plan and provide opportunity for applying the learning in a given situation. Assignments should be carefully designed to suit the learning needs of students. A teacher should follow guidelines listed in Exhibit 3.70 to design assignments.

Exhibit No. 3.70: Guidelines for designing assignments

- Prepare a possible list of assignments in a particular topic, or group of topics or a subject.
- Define the purpose of assignment and write the objectives to be achieved through assignment. Inform the students what is expected from them in the assignment.
- Decide whether it is an individual assignment or group assignment.
- Decide the type of assignment you are designing.
- Provide complete information on the assignment along with guidelines to be followed.
- Make explicit the minimum level of output of the assignment.
- If you are required to provide resources keep them ready for handing over to students.
- If it is library assignment ask librarian to extend help and cooperation.
- If it is field or industry based assignment prepare instruction to be followed by students in the field or industry.
- Get permission and confirmation from industry to complete the assignment.
- Inform the marking criteria and their weightage to students in advance.
- There should be close supervision of assignments being performed in workshop or industry. Teacher or supervisor should see that students don't violate safety rules.
- Always provide immediate feedback to trainees on their performance on assignment.
- Provide timely guidance to students to prevent delayed submission of work.

5. Experience of a Teacher Using Assignment as Predominant Method of Learning

There are teachers who deliberately designed the whole subject/cluster of competencies as an assignment for students to produce conscious and attentive learning in classroom. The teacher has prescribed a standard textbook to students. Every student brings this test book in the classroom. The assignment technique of the teacher follows a sequence listed below:

Teacher informs the students to read a particular topic at home and note down the difficulties. At the beginning of the class s/he emphasis the importance of the topic from learning point of view, examination point of view and application point of view. Then s/he asks any student randomly to read the topic for 5-10 minutes. Then s/he randomly selects a student and asks question on the portion of the topic read by previous student. The selected student answers the question. The teacher acknowledges right answer with reward. If student has replied partially correct answer in that case teacher and rest of the students help him to give complete correct answer. If student fails to give answer, teacher asks another randomly selected student to give summaries what has been read. If student summarizes the learning teacher provides him reward. If second student fails to do so s/he asks third student to re read the topic. Otherwise ask the third student to read the further part of the topic. Same learning sequence continues till the closure of the class. At the end of the class teacher summarizes the learning and consolidates the learning points. S/he also informs about next days topic and asks students to come prepared. At the completion of the topic teacher answers questions of students and summarizes learning points. S/he gives assignments to students to be submitted in writing. Students work on assignments given by the teacher and submit the assignment on due date. They seek guidance for completing the assignment. The process of reading and writing assignment continues till the completion of the subject and achievement of learning objectives. The learning outcomes are measured through a comprehensive test.

The teacher who predominantly uses the assignment method has shared his experiences and pointed out that

- Assignment method requires little planning
- It involves all the students in learning process
- All the students progress with same pace
- It improves reading, writing and presentation skills of students
- It create joy and fun in the classroom
- There is no anxiety during the time of examination
- There is no need to prepare visuals
- Learning becomes the habit of students

6. Use of Assignment with Other Methods of Teaching Learning

Assignment can be used with many methods of teaching learning. It is a good vehicle to involve students in learning process. The use of assignment depends on number of factors such as topic, learning objectives, competence of a teacher, availability of time, level of students, preparedness of a teacher etc. General combinations of teaching learning methods are listed in Exhibit 3.71 for ready reference.

Exhibit No. 3.71: Use of assignment with other methods of teaching learning

Lecture ⇒ Assignment ⇒ Lecture ⇒ Assignment

Demonstration ⇒ Assignment ⇒ Buzz group ⇒ Plenary

Self-study ⇒ Lecture ⇒ Assignment ⇒ Presentation

Case study ⇒ Assignment ⇒ Discussion ⇒ Summarization

7. Summary

Assignments are considered to be powerful tools to involve students in learning process. Professionally designed assignments produce intensive and deep learning. Assignments help to integrate the learning caused by other methods of teaching learning. They provide an opportunity to use principle of learning by doing, learning through struggle, learning through self-evaluation. Assignments involve the self of the students in learning process. Assignments produce learning in all the three domains of learning. The output on assignment is a direct measure of learning of students.

8. Activity

Design various types of assignments such classroom, laboratory, field, library, home, and internet. Divide the class in two groups and ask one group of students to complete these assignments. Use alternative strategy to achieve same learning objectives for other group and compare the results.

3.18 ACTION LEARNING

1. Introduction

With the advent of internet facility and accessibility to all kinds of information within no time the importance of classroom and a traditional teacher is decreasing at a very fast rate. The facility of digital library, e library, internet, learning resources center is substituting a teacher so far information part of learning is concerned. There is a significant change in the behaviour of the student. They are living in high technology driven era. They are empowered to gain information within no time at a cheaper rate. Teachers using traditional methods of teaching and learning would loose their credibility very soon. Student will not attend and participate in their classes unless they get and experience something unique and different. To bring the students in campus of the institution teachers have to come out from their traditional role and they should perform a role close to professional world. Action learning method is one of the many powerful methods that need to be used in classroom, laboratory, workshops, and during industrial training of students for their professional development. Action learning is a powerful method of learning for developing all kinds of professional skills. It brings the real world in the campus of the institution. Or the campus of the institution goes in the world of work and learns from the problems, challenges and opportunities of the world of work. As the name implies it is a process of learning by doing but certainly it is not a process of gaining experiences.

2. About Action Learning

Professor Reg Ravans promoted the powerful method of learning called action learning. Later on many scholars have worked on this method of learning in different areas of professional life and benefited from it. It is social process of learning in which people learn from each other's experiences. It has multiplying effect on learning and learning group. The learning group learns collectively and helps each other to learn in the situation where the solution is not available to any one in this way the action learning is different than learning from each other. Questions are posed to in conditions of ignorance, risk and confusion, when no body knows what to do next. The depth and breadth of questions to the group has significance in action learning. Reg Ravans has pointed out that asking fresh question on the situation is key to learning. Students learn to fulfil their learning needs asking deep and challenging questions about learning in a situation. The learning is manifested by challenges of learning situation. The learners encounter the situation challenging their experiences, previous learning and they explore new perspectives to the situation. In the process of learning learners are empowered to collaborate, cooperate, criticize and provide feedback. They are free to challenge existing policies, rules and practices. Whatever they learn in the learning situation they transfer it into real life situation. Mike Pedler has propagated the learning spiral. According to him there has to be a problem. There has to be ownership of the problem. There has to be building up of action and learning system. This learning has to be utilized for development. The learning is put to the situation so it may create conflict and tension challenging existing identity. Again the new learning situation for action learning is created.

Action learning is different from other methods of learning such as case method, role-play, simulation, project method, learning by doing in the sense that the students challenge existing knowledge, processes and practices and come out with different, new and unique solution to problem that saves time, money, efforts and resources. They implement the solution and reflect upon it. Learning is cautiously produced at every step. The new learning is validated. In the learning process the learning is tested, corrected and re-corrected for learning. In fact it inculcates the habit of learning to learn. Action learning is a flexible, adoptive, creative, active, reflective and continuous way to learn. It provides an opportunity for continuous learning and empowers students for learning process.

3. Real Life Situations for Action Learning

There are varieties of real life situations that can be brought in the campus of the institution or the students can be taken to the real life situation for learning. Some engineering situations are risky and require safety precautions that should be simulated in the classroom before students are exposed to the real life situation. Real life situations demanding actions are listed in Exhibit 3.72.

Exhibit No. 3.72: Real life situations for action learning

➤ Problem solving ➤ Designing strategies ➤ Decision-making ➤ Improving efficiency of the process ➤ Designing systems ➤ Designing change	➤ Evaluating the success of the programme ➤ Identifying risk ➤ Experimenting ➤ Involving people ➤ Obtaining commitment of people ➤ Team building

4. Learning Produced through Action Learning

Action learning is a process of developing profession related skills. It is a process that provides an opportunity to apply learning on real life situation at the same time learning from the actions through reflection. Action learning provides a scope for variety of learning and it facilitates the process of competency and proficiency development. Students develop the habit of learning to learn, continuous learning and questioning assumptions of others and their own. Teachers and students appreciate, experience and feel the level of excitement and magic of learning participating in process of action learning. The learning produced by action learning is listed in Exhibit 3.73.

Exhibit No. 3.73: Learning produced through action learning in engineering students

Skills

Planning skills	Visualizing skills	Application skills
Analytical skills	Synthesis skills	Integration skills
Investigative skills	Evaluation skills	Thinking skills
Forecasting skills	Design skills	Information collating
Report writing	Presentation skills	Questioning skills

Attitudes

Attitude of inquiry	Attitude for safety	Attitude of tolerance
Team spirit	Concern for others	Respecting diversity
Attitude of accuracy	Attitude of saving	Attitude of serving
Attitude of systematic working	Attitude for respecting others	Attitude of experimenting
Attitude of cleanliness	Attitude of cooperativeness	Attitude of collaboration

5. Role of the Teacher

The teacher is required to play altogether different role for using method of action learning in classroom/laboratory/workshop/industry. This role is different than traditional and conventional role. The role of a teacher for action learning is demanding and the teacher should be trained to conduct action learning for learning purpose. In organizing action learning teacher acts as a resource person or adviser or consultant. S/he does not impart any instruction to the action-learning group. The role of the teacher is listed in Exhibit 3.74.

Exhibit No. 3.74: Role of the teacher for conducting action learning

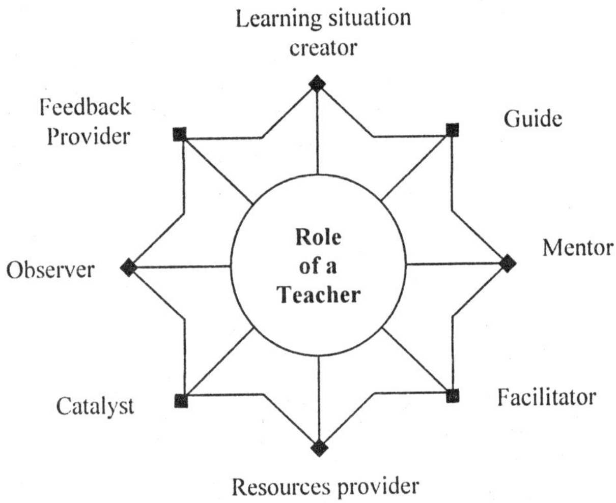

5.1 Learning Situation Creator

Teacher has to bring a problem from real life situation in the classroom with all details of the problem. The problem can be described in words or it could be video recorded. Students are assigned different roles related to character of the problem. Teacher creates learning facilities in the learning setting.

5.2 Guide

Teacher guides the students to solve the problem so far process part is concerned. Then students are put in a real life-learning situation. They work on a problem and explore, search and visualize the solution to the problem. They ask questions related to problem solving and generate altogether new, different and non-existent solution to the problem. They may see the problem from different perspectives. They collectively learn about the problem and its solution. Teacher guides each step of learning.

5.3 Mentor

Teacher acts as a mentor for students in the process of action learning. S/he takes the interest in the learning process and learners. S/he provides necessary energy to the learning process and encouragement to learners. S/he acts as a senior manger in the learning process and provides right guidance at right time during the process. In fact teacher delegates the control of learning process in the hands of the students. So it is a mentoring for learning.

5.4 Facilitator

Teacher helps in the process of learning, organizing the resources for learning and providing constructive feedback at every stage of problem solving. S/he reinforces the correct learning and asks to correct the wrong learning. S/he facilitates the process of action learning by providing psychological support such as modifying the communication, resolving conflict between group members, providing additional resources for learning and arranging interaction with industry people.

5.5 Resources Provider

Teacher is considered to be the expert in the subject and s/he is required to have latest information on theory and practice. S/he should be aware about the current practices in the industry or world of work. The students may consult her/him for guidance at a particular stage. S/he should be able to provide academic as well non-academic guidance to students. S/he acts as a learning resources provider.

5.6 Catalyst

Students are not mature to learn on their own at this stage so during the initial phases of action learning a teacher should encourage them to ask new and different questions on problems and solutions. S/he should encourage them providing cues for asking questions and reflecting on responses.

5.7 Observer

Teacher is required to observe the whole process of action learning and note down the points for providing the feedback. S/he should use all senses to observe the process of learning. S/he should provide equal emphasis on process of action learning and process of learning. S/he should provide the feedback on depth and breath of learning. The feedback should be provided to the group as a whole and group members on individual basis.

5.8 Feedback Provider

The teacher should act as a feedback provider on the learning process of the students on action learning project. Whatever s/he has noted during observation process on feedback point that should be properly organized and at the summarisation phase s/he should provide constructive feedback for improving learning through action learning. The feedback can be provided on process of learning, approach to solve problem, method of asking questions, depth and breadth of questions, assumptions, performance of the members during the process of action learning, behaviour to be promoted and practiced, transfer of learning, and evaluation of learning.

6. Abilities of a Teacher to Conduct Action Learning

Teachers should develop competencies to conduct action learning for producing learning. They can acquire the competencies through formal training programmes or working on action learning project as a participant. The competencies of teacher to perform their role effectively are listed in Exhibit 3.75.

The teacher is required to demonstrate different types of attitudes during the action learning process. Right attitude foster the learning process. The attitudes required to conduct the action learning are listed in Exhibit 3.76.

Exhibit No. 3.75: Abilities of a teacher to conduct action learning

➢ Ability to describe problem or opportunity ➢ Ability to organize learning resources ➢ Ability to create learning environment ➢ Ability to create openness, flexibility and diversity in learning process and approach to solve problem	➢ Ability to observe actions, learning and progress of the project ➢ Ability to promote participation ➢ Ability to encourage the students for deeper learning ➢ Ability to provide feedback on learning ➢ Ability to summarize and consolidate learning

Exhibit No. 3.76: Attitudes of a teacher to conduct action learning

➢ Patience ➢ Empathy ➢ Openness ➢ Cooperativeness ➢ Commitment	➢ Tolerance ➢ Appreciation ➢ Mutual respect ➢ Value diversity ➢ Sympathy

7. Action Learning Process

The students go through step by step learning process in action learning programmes. The flow chart of application of action learning is shown in Exhibit 3.77.

The problem for learning is the key to action learning. The teacher cautiously selects real life situation for learning. The situation may be related to the problem or opportunity. The problem is assigned to small group of students. The teacher selects more than one situation and ask students group to pick up a problem according to their ability and interest. The problem should be challenging and foster thinking of students. The students as well as teacher should not know the solution of the problem.

The group members define the problem from different perspectives and holistically. They probe question on each definition of the problem and try to test the validity of the definition of the problem at the same time they learn to define the problem in a better way. Once the problem is defined and validated by the group reflection on learning takes place. At this stage teacher provides constructive feedback to students on the application of theory and approach of defining the problem. S/he reinforces the learning took place during the definition of the problem and

Exhibit No. 3.77: Steps of action learning

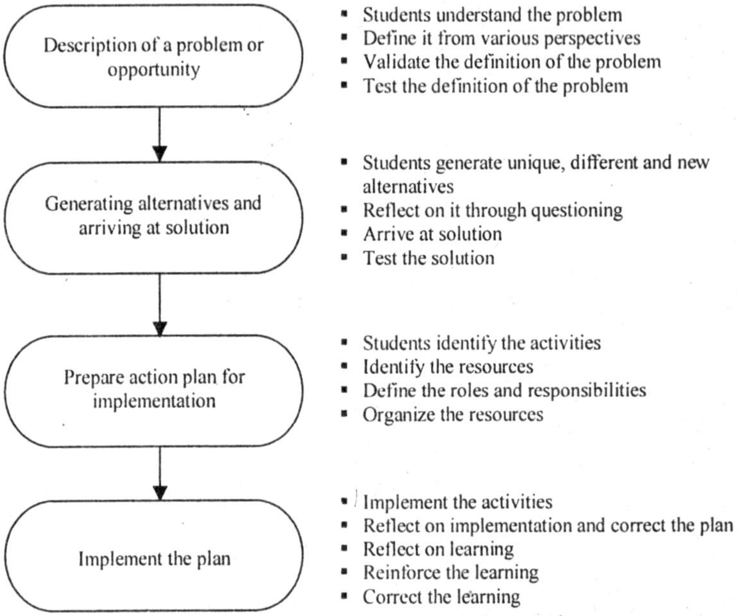

supplement the definition from her/his views. If necessary s/he asks the students to review the definition in the light of the feedback or new perspective. The students review the problem and reflect on learning and re conceptualize the problem definition.

Students generate the alternatives using collective talent and wisdom. They do not follow traditional methods of problem solving but look at the solutions from different perspectives. The process of generating the solutions is guided by the teacher so for learning process is concerned. Teacher can participate in generating the alternatives with postgraduate students but not with undergraduate students. S/he encourages the students to challenge each alternative they have generated and generate new and different alternative. During the process of generating alternatives concrete questions are asked to test the soundness of alternatives. After each step of asking questions and modifying the alternatives the learning points are reviewed. The learning is consolidated selecting appropriate examples from the alternatives and process of generating alternatives.

The alternatives are evaluated against the criteria set. The criteria can be tough and different than routine to foster the thinking and learning process in the same situation. The criteria can create stimulus and further challenge for generating more and different alternatives. Again the learning process should be reviewed before making final decision. The teacher reinforces the learning outcomes and summarizes the learning.

Then comes the preparation of action plan and organizing the resources to implement the solution in real life situation. Group members define their roles and responsibility and implement the solution. The teacher observes the process of implementation and provides guidance to perform in right way as per learning. The students monitor the progress on implementation and corrective actions are taken. On successful implementation of the solution the results are analyzed and reflection on problem solving and its process is carried. The learning points are noted and reinforced by teacher. Teacher encourages students to promote action learning in future in their employer's organisation.

8. Summary

Action learning is a powerful method of learning through problem solving and reflection. The previous learning is used for learning new and different things. It is practiced in groups in real life situations. The real life situation which is challenging, unique, different and unfamiliar to people is a good means to produce learning in students and teacher. The learning is consciously noted, tested, reflected and reinforced for application in a newer situation. Action learning provides a scope for continuous purposeful learning in real life situation. Students develop learning to learn skills and continuously use it for learning purpose. They learn to formulate hypothesis, test and implement. Higher level of skills and attitudes are developed in students using action learning. It promotes holistic and strategic thinking skills. It also develops right kind of attitudes in students. It provides an opportunity to transfer learning to real life situation. It prepares students to accept uncertain, risky, new and different situations in real life. The action learning process naturally satisfies the inner learning needs of the students.

Teacher plays a significant role in the process of action learning. S/he encourages students to think and challenge the assumptions and old practices and come out with a fresh view to situation and solution to a problem. S/he consolidates, reinforces, and encourages continuous thinking and testing of new ideas. S/he plays a role of a mentor, facilitator, encourager, resources provider, guide, and feedback provider to process of learning.

9. Activity

Identify a competency or groups of competencies that can be developed through action learning. Design the action learning situation based on real life situation and conduct the session. Note down your experience and share with your colleagues.

3.19 SELF LEARNING

1. Introduction

Every student has unique physical and psychological characteristics and learning styles. The desire or need for self-learning arises when students decide to achieve something challenging or pursue a career in a particular discipline. Now a-days students are self-conscious about their career. Self-learning starts from the point of consciousness that learning is important and worth to make the career bright. Self-learning is common in all the students. Self-learning is an essential element of learning process because all learning needs are not satisfied in the institution. Some students take special courses offered by educational and professional organisations. These courses add value to opt a particular profession or help in pursuing the hobby. Some students come from a business family and they want to pursue their business after completing the programme so they are more interested in practical and application aspects rather than theory. Some students have ambitions and want to establish their enterprise for particular products or services or both so they are interested to learn entrepreneurial skills.

There are bright students who are very fast in learning so they want to learn additional competencies in order to get higher job or job of their choice. Students take initiatives for self-learning to achieve learning objectives. The time of effectiveness and learning is different for individuals. Some students are effective in learning in the morning. They get up early and study the learning material. Some students are effective in learning in the night. They continue study till mid-night. Whatever may be the effectiveness of time of learning. Self-learning has important place in the process of learning. Students own this method of learning. They feel need of the learning and put honest efforts for learning. They use their own styles of learning.

The professional organisations want students with self-learning maturity so that they can spontaneously deal with any type of the situation for the benefit of the customer and organisation. Professional organisations want adoptive and adaptive students who can cope up with the change. They want students with learning attitude who can take up dynamic nature of roles who can shift from one division to another and one location to other. They want students who are technically as well as culturally adoptive and accommodative. Some multinational organisations have already added this dimension for selecting the students.

2. Concept of Self-Learning

Self-learning is defined as learning by own initiatives. The student feels a need to learn something that may be related to curriculum or may not be related to curriculum. S/he may get an idea for learning new skills from external source. The student explores the sources of information on her/his own and learns individually. The source of information may be teacher, book, internet, subject expert, magazine, journals, industry, private tuition, video film, online programme, distance learning programme etc. S/he may join a group of students who are also interested to learn same skills. If there is a group of students they explore the source jointly and learn individually and collectively. The source of learning may be the group members themselves. In such situation they assemble according to their convenience and put efforts for learning. They follow the group norms of learning and become a learning group rather learning team.

According to Carl Rogers human beings have a natural potential for learning. Self-initiated learning, which involves the whole person of the learner, feelings as well as intellect, is most lasting and pervasive. Independence, creativity and self-reliance are all facilitated when self-criticism and self-evaluation are basic. The most socially useful learning in the modern world is the learning of the process of learning, a continuing openness to experience and incorporation into oneself the process of change.

3. Cycle of Self-Learning

The learner goes through various stages of internal self-learning cycle. The successful experiences of learning of one cycle further motivate the learner to repeat the cycle. If the experiences are not positive the learner may quit the learning cycle at any stage and there are less chances of repeating the cycle. The various internal stages of learning cycle are stated in Exhibit 3.78.

Exhibit No. 3.78: Stages of learning cycle

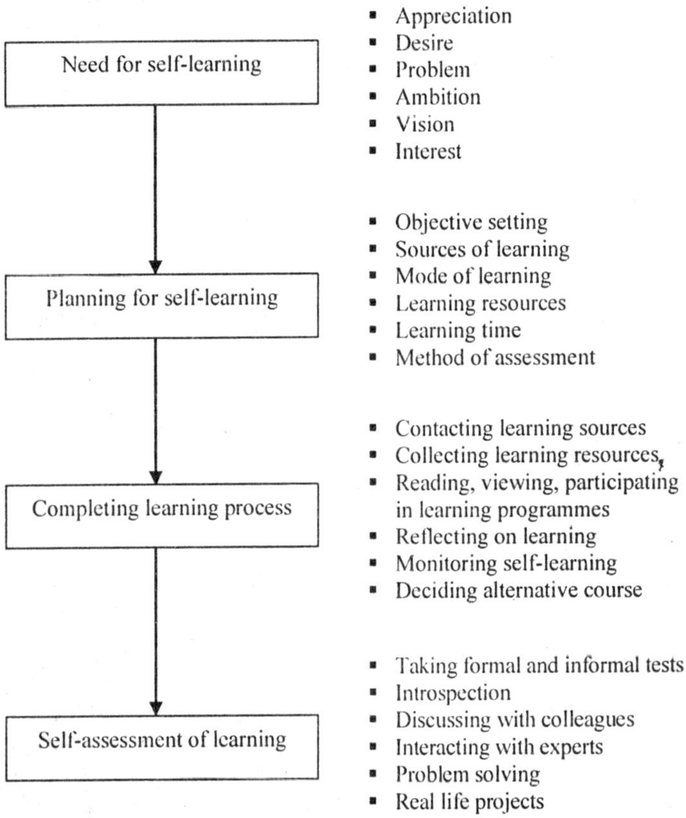

3.1 Need for Self-learning

The students appreciate that there is a need for self-learning. The appreciation comes from within. S/he feels the need and thinks that s/he can fulfill the need on her/his own. S/he realizes that s/he has a potential to satisfy the learning need. As per Maslow's theory of motivation this learning need is inherent and everyone wants to climb the ladder up to self-actualisation level. The students get variety of stimulus from the environment and they resemble their personality with a role model and they want to become like that. This desire creates an inner urge to achieve something on her/his own. In some learning situations students face problems and they want to solve the problem using their knowledge and skills. The wish to solve problem encourages them to learn. Right from childhood some students have ambitions to achieve something attractive. This ambition is inner and it continuously work and unconsciously encourages the students to learn to achieve it. Some students get motivated after joining the formal courses and they create a vision to achieve and put efforts for the same. Some students have hobby to do something and enjoy. They learn to pursue the hobby. So need for self-learning is surfaced from inside on the basis of some strong and attractive stimulus.

3.2 Planning for Self-Learning

Once identifying the needs in clearly understandable terms students set the learning objectives. These learning objectives are manageable and achievable. These may be achieved in sequence or simultaneously. Once the objectives are finalized the student explores the sources of fulfilling the objectives. In this endeavour s/he takes the help of many related people. S/he decides the mode of learning as well as time of learning. The students may select more than one mode for self-learning. In fact they use as many modes as possible because they are anxious to learn. It is in their benefit because they learn from various points of view with change in stimulus. Students search learning resources to achieve the objectives. The learning resources varies on a wide range such as books, journals, audio, video, television channel, learning packages, tuitions, coaching, friends, teacher, parents, professionals, seniors and so on. Apart from this they look for formal education programmes. They decide the time for various learning activities and dead lines for learning objectives. Students also decide the method of assessment of learning. This is also based on self-assessment.

3.3 Completing Learning Process

Students take decision to implement the plan or quit. If they quit it means they do not have strong determination to satisfy the need. If they take steps it means they are firmly determined to achieve learning objectives. At this point of time they should take steps to reschedule their time and discard trivial activities and find more time for self-learning. Students contact the sources and collect the learning resources. They fully get involved in learning process. They remove the hurdles and barriers from the path of learning and go though learning experiences with full enthusiasm. They reflect upon the amount and depth of learning and find alternative learning experiences and events in case of difficulty. They trace the progress of learning against the plan and decide further course of study. They learn to take self-feedback on the progress of learning. Self-feedback is rewarding and motivating for them to continue on the journey of self-learning.

3.4 Self-Assessment of Learning

Students test the progress on learning comparing it with learning objectives. They use variety of tests to assess the level of learning. They take formal test to gauge the quality of learning and measuring effectiveness and efficiency of self-learning method. Apart from formal tests they use non-formal tests such as applying the learning in real life situation to assess the competence level and learning gaps. They take views of colleagues, experts, teachers and other related persons on their learning method and achievement. They seek their guidance to improve the process of self-learning. On achievement of a competency they take projects and apply their learning to achieve project objectives. They get immense level of feedback during the process of completing the project.

The successful completion of one learning cycle boosts up the confidence of the students for self-learning. They come out of fear of failure and become better self-learner. The repetition of cycle increases maturity for learning and over a period of time students become fast learner. They develop the confidence of taking out wheat from the chaff at a faster and effective way. They learn learning to learn skills and thinking to think skills.

4. Some Patterns of Self-Learning

As stated earlier each student is unique entity and has unique learning style. The ways of learning of students are stated in Exhibit 3.79.

Exhibit No. 3.79: Ways of learning adopted by students

- Some students learn in the classroom and then revise the lesson as early as possible at home. They come with their difficulties and clarify it with the teacher.
- Some students study the learning material in advance, which the teacher is supposed to teach. They attend the class sincerely, take down the notes and come back attending the class. They revise the lessons taught in the classroom. If they have difficulty they clarify it with teacher or senior or classmate.

(Contd.)

(*Contd.*)

> - Some students attend the classes regularly and maintain the record of what has been taught in the class. They collect the learning material accordingly and learn just before the examination.
> - Some students learn from examination point of view during the examination period. They learn under pressure from their classmates.
> - Some students have no faith in the teacher and institution because of various reasons such as quality of instruction is not good, teacher is very slow in covering the curriculum, teacher is very fast in teaching the topic, shorter semester duration, difficult things are not covered in the classroom, irregular classes, and so on. So they take private tuition and learn on their own.
> - Some students want to learn higher-level skills or develop expertise in a particular area. So they join a group of interested students or go for coaching, or receive training in any organisation.
> - Some students have hobby to read and learn about other disciplines. Management is a very common discipline that is learnt by students on their own using various modes. The most commonly mode is reading books written by Gurus of management. Some students join personality development classes to improve their communication skills and confidence to face the interview.
> - With the advent of internet and information technology numbers of universities and professional bodies have started variety of programmes for students pursuing career in different areas of specialisation. Students learn on their own surfing internet and watching television. They have access to digital libraries from there they search material of their interest to learn.

5. Advantages of Self-Learning

There is a Chinese proverb that says teach a hungry man how to fish instead of feeding him a fish. Promoting and inculcating self-learning habits in students have numerous advantages. The list of indicative advantages is stated in Exhibit 3.80

Exhibit No. 3.80: Advantages of self-learning

> - Students explore the self and potential available in them for self-learning and self-development. They see personal change in way of responding to learning situation. That helps them to design strategies to pursue their hobby, interest and career on their own.
> - Self-learning develops skills of learning to learn that is necessary for continuous learning. Students survive and develop in changing

(*Contd.*)

(*Contd.*)

environment and develop coping, adoptive, and adaptive skills. Students feel that they are better in learning.

- Self-learning refines the thinking process. Students easily learn new concepts, principles, models and procedures.
- As they get success in self-learning they get more motivated to learn on their own. They get more deeply involved in the learning process. They keep on setting new learning objectives to achieve.
- Students empower themselves for learning process. They feel that learning is their own responsibility and they own the learning process. The teacher can gradually shift the responsibility of learning to students.
- Students become self-disciplined for learning process. They progress in desired manner. Self-learning provides full flexibility in learning to students.
- Self-learning is self-rewarding and rewards are immediate in terms of learning outcomes that is highly satisfying. The satisfaction leads to further motivation for learning. This cycle of feeling need for learning, planning self-learning, learning outcomes, self-satisfaction from learning outcomes, further motivation for learning continues.
- Self-learning is always purposeful because it is identified by the self for the self with a purpose.
- Self-learning builds confidence to accept learning challenges and trying new methods of learning.

6. Self-Learning Skills

Students learn self-learning skills cautiously. These skills are learnt during the process of learning. The self-learner may take the help of other experienced students to develop the self-learning skills. The engineering students should develop self-learning skills to remain stable in corporate world. The indicative list of self-learning skills is shown in Exhibit 3.81.

Exhibit No. 3.81: Self-learning skills

- Learning need assessment
- Drawing learning profile
- Listening
- Visualizing future
- Reading with concentration
- Remembering the significant learning points
- Associating learning with previously learnt concepts
- Notes taking or marking significant points on reading material
- Apply learning in a specific situation

(*Contd.*)

(*Contd.*)

- Observing the new environment
- Hypothesizing, testing, assessing and developing new solutions, methods and procedures
- Planning self-learning
- Selecting most effective learning mode
- Inbuilt the rewards in the learning process setting learning objectives
- Feeling sense of achievement
- Assessing learning
- Changing learning style
- Receiving feedback
- Thinking skills
- Prioritizing the learning requirements

7. Methods of Self-Learning

There are various methods of self-learning that can be used by students and can be promoted by teachers. These methods incorporate the provision of individual needs and individual differences between students. The individual differences may be in the form of using words, remembering, recalling, creativity, study habits, application of learning, interest, learning styles, learning maturity, interest for learning, learning needs, learning goals and so on. Technical students are required to read specifications, manuals, instruction sheets, procedures catalogues, signs and signals, operating instructions, maintenance procedure and so on. They are expected to read and follow the instructions effectively and efficiently. The self-learning methods provide an opportunity to choose feasible method of learning. Self-learning methods are many and provide a wide range of choice to students. Students should use self-learning methods as well as self-assessment techniques for positive and constructive feedback for improvement. These methods are writing conferences, discussions, reflection, periodical self-evaluation, interview and introspection. Students get immense feedback for self-improvement using self-assessment methods. It should be a part of the self-learning methods. The self-learning methods are briefly describes in subsequent paragraphs.

7.1 Reading

The most common and simplest form of self-learning method is reading. Students should develop reading skills for various purposes such as get familiar with technical terms, pronouncing the words properly, fast reading, locating the new information, interpret the data, improve upon technical terms, reading the graphs and interpreting, drawing conclusion, reading between the lines, reading intensions of writer, and ultimately learn new skills. The students should ensure that they have selected right learning material that would satisfy the learning needs. The learning material should match to their level of understanding and it is easy to learn. Students formulate the learning objectives or a teacher assigns objectives or they are given in the learning unit. The purpose of self-learning is to create interest for learning. The purpose of learning should be clear, specific and challenging. It should be based on the needs of the self. It should be related to ambitions of the learner. The student should feel that s/he can achieve the purpose through self-learning. Reading plays a very important role in self-learning. The students should follow systematic approach for effective and efficient learning. The self-reading can be done by students following self-learning cycle shown in Exhibit 3.82.

Exhibit No. 3.82: Self-learning cycle

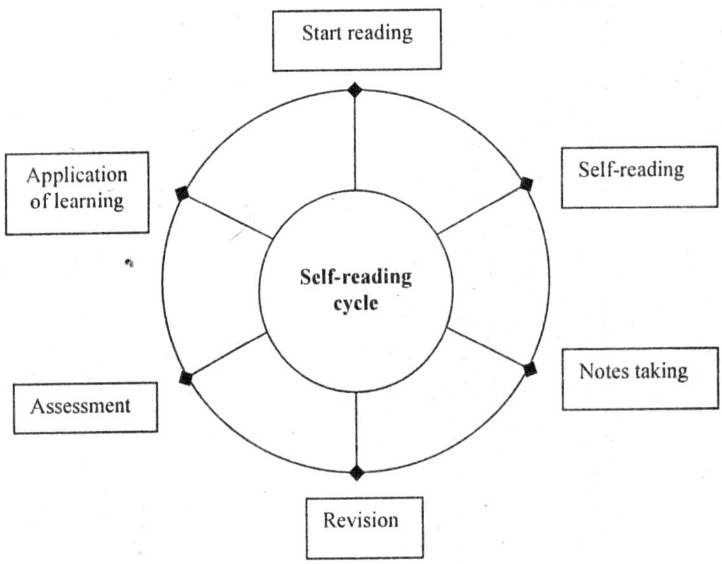

Start Reading: The student selects the learning material that satisfies learning needs and fulfill the learning purpose. Initiation of reading process is very important step in learning through self-reading. Students put lot of efforts and time in searching, selecting and bringing home the learning material. They always think to start reading but they do not initiate the reading process because of many reasons.

Self-reading: Develop the habit of different types of reading such as fast reading, scanning the material, reading and pausing, reading between lines, reading and remembering, reading and memorizing, reading and thinking, reading and recalling, reading and notes taking and so on. The habit of reading is difficult to develop because only one sense is involved in the process, that is sight. There are other reasons such as book is bulky, it requires continuous and frequent sittings, it is written for general readers, and not for specific readers, disturbances from the environment, it is heavy to read and it partially fulfils the learning needs.

Notes Taking: Notes taking are very important skills that make you learn important points and tell you about the source of information. Notes taking make you go with reading so you go along with text in the reading material. Notes taking are helpful in many ways such as revising the key points, linking the present learning with previous learning and *vice versa*. Apart from sight it involves other sense that is touch and breaks the monotony of reading process. It makes you alert for reading and learning. It reminds you for learning through reading. It energizes for further reading. It is a link between previous learning and further learning. While taking the notes write down the name of source of information, page number, access number, key words, their definition, main learning points, and their links with previous learning, its applicability in future and so on. Take the notes legibly, use appropriate words, follow a particular style, use symbols and signs, diagrams and figures, etc. Take the notes in logical manner to reach ultimate learning outcome. Notes can be taken in question form. The answer is taken from the reading material. The whole purpose of notes taking is to make the learning deep, easy and instantly retrievable. The notes should be taken in a way to substitute the original reading material. Notes are also taken during the process of learning methods such as lecture, demonstration, group discussion, presentation, seminars, conferences, symposium and so on.

The students should understand their learning curve and accordingly do the self-reading. They should develop the habit of concentrating on the learning material. They should develop skills to learn fast and remember things through self-reading. The speed of reading can be increased many fold using techniques such as concentration, skipping the familiar and known sentences, connecting the learning with previously learnt things, turning the pages that are familiar, reading the headings and moving forward, understanding the diagrams, making mental map of the learning.

Revision: On completion of one learning unit or lesson or learning event review the learning. Review is carried out hurriedly scanning the literature or reading the notes taken or recalling the learning points and so on. Students review the points where they have apprehension of forgetting. The process of revision is carried out just immediately after completion of one learning unit. The process of revising the learning is performed after each learning unit and previous learning is revised along with unit learning. The links to previous learning are established to bring continuity in learning process. Basically the purpose of revision is to prevent forgetting. The learning is structured orderly and logically in order to make it purposeful. The way to revise the learning is make a summary of learning in your language and words. The second way is to draw a diagram of what you have learnt that may be the process or diagrammatic model or association of concept with practice example. The third way is assigning symbol to each significant term and put it on paper, the fourth way is to draw a map of interrelated things, fifth way is challenge the learning through questions and so on.

Assessment: On completion of one unit the student take a test on review questions. If review questions are not given in the lesson s/he frames the question and answers them. If s/he is able to answer the questions confidently and satisfactorily s/he feels rewarded. The students get an opportunity to identify learning difficulties and learning gaps at this point of self-assessment. The student should fill up learning gaps and clarify doubts to make the further learning enjoyable.

Application of Learning: After taking a test and qualifying it to the satisfaction level s/he thinks about application of learning in real life situation or in next learning event. S/he establishes a proper link between theory and practice that helps to enrich next learning cycle. S/he also assimilates the learning with previous learning so that link between the previous learning and next learning is maintained. The application of learning refines the learning and stimulates thinking process. Then proceed further for next unit of learning material.

7.2 Multi-media Packages

Multi-media packages are designed and disseminated by professional institutions on various topics of interest. Get these multi-media packages and learn according to instructions. These packages provide opportunity for learning, reviewing, testing and remedial measures. As name indicates these packages are based on variety of media so create interest to learn.

Professionals design most of the multi-media packages considering principles of educational psychology and educational technology so they assure pre defined level of learning.

7.3 Distance Learning Programmes

There are number of universities and open universities offering wide range programmes right from certificate programmes to Ph.D. programmes. The students can register in these programmes and achieve learning objectives. These programmes are designed for self-learning mode only. The learning material is designed to suit the individual requirements and they provide variety of learning resources such as students guide, learning modules, assignments, case studies, audio cassette, video cassette, computer aided instructions and so on. These universities organize counselling sessions to solve learning difficulties and provide feedback on progress of learning.

7.4 Learning through Observation

Self-interest of achieving competencies and proficiency encourages observing the processes, methodology, behaviour, style, and performance. Students learn many complex concepts and principles observing the practices. During the process of observation students mainly use sight and they also take the help of other sensory elements. Students learn attitudes from observation. They learn to initiate the process of manual skills development from observation only. People learn to copy almost everything through observation. Students should learn to observe things objectively and minutely. They should learn to observe those things that are not visible for example they see a machine operating they should be able to analyze the cause, concept and principles responsible for operating a machine.

8. Self-Evaluation

Self-evaluation is a key to commitment to learning. Students should learn to evaluate progress on learning against their capabilities. Students profit more from self-evaluation than any other evaluation. Students should learn to consciously evaluate the progress on learning and provide self-recognition. Self-evaluation provides sense of satisfaction and colours the feelings. Self-evaluation largely depends on evaluation by teachers.

If the evaluation by a teacher is positive, students would rate herself/himself positive. The criteria for evaluating the self-learning should be related to self and it should not be compared with other students. Otherwise it may create dissatisfaction and inferiority complex. Self-evaluation should create positive interest for future learning. Students should be encouraged to maintain the record of self-learning that is a base for evaluating the progress on learning. There are other evidences of evaluating the self-learning such as enhancement in speed of reading, quick comprehension of situation, comparatively less mistakes, problem prevention, better planning, easy retrieval of information and application, establishing connections, systematic way of learning and so on.

9. Role of the Students in Self-Learning

The self-consciousness of the student plays a very important role in self-learning. Students analyze the needs, desires and ambitions and adopt to do learning and self-learning to fulfil the same. In fact self-learning helps her/him to fill up the specific gaps of formal learning. Today students and their parents are aware about their career and they have a vision of their life. They plan each and every activity and learning process as well. They take most effective ways of learning. The students should follow the guidelines stated in Exhibit 3.83 for self-learning.

Exhibit No. 3.83: Guidelines to be followed by students for self-learning

- Try to know the self-inside you, your self-esteem, and goal of the life. Try to craft vision in precise and clear terms. You can take the help of various tools and techniques such as Johari's window, strengths, weaknesses, opportunities and threat analysis, assessing your aptitude and so on for crafting vision. You can take the help of the professional and counsellors for deciding the path of career.
- Understand the profession in which you expect to achieve your vision or pursue career, or start your enterprise or develop further. The internet is a good way to understand and explore the profession. The senior students working in that profession may provide you relevant and latest information.
- Understand the provisions of the curriculum and skills imparted through formal instructional methods. Try to relate the competencies mentioned in the curriculum with the path you want to choose.
- Compare the required competencies with the curricular provisions and try to identify the gaps. Find out the strategies to fill up the learning gaps. There may be some competencies that you may develop on your

(Contd.)

(*Contd.*)

own. Identify the sources of information and learning resources that can fulfill your learning requirements. ➢ Identify the learning gaps that you can fill up on your own through self-initiatives and self-study. Collect the learning resources on such competencies from various sources. ➢ Search the learning resources that can fulfil the learning gaps. The learning material may be available in many forms such as reference books, text books, manuals, handouts, professional journals, websites, video programmes, telecasts on television channels, coaching classes, industries and organisations, annual reports, reports of government, research reports, experts, teachers, your colleagues, senior students of your institution, programmed learning material in print or non print form, computer aided instructions and so on. ➢ Plan the self-learning events using various resources and ways of learning suiting to your style of learning. In built small breaks of two to five minutes after every 30 minutes of study. ➢ Arrange and organize the resources for self-learning in sequential and logical order. ➢ Learn consciously, sincerely, and honestly keeping in view your vision and ambitions. Try to initiate self-learning and remove barriers from the process of learning. You can take the help of your colleagues, senior students, teachers and professionals for removing the barriers of learning.

10. Role of a Teacher in Promoting Self-Learning

Teacher plays a very important role in creating self-learning opportunity for students. Teacher can gradually inculcate the habit of self-learning in students. Self-learning is a very good method to develop skills of learning to learn. In fact it empowers the students for lifelong learning. Self-learning provides an opportunity for flexible learning. Learning opportunities satisfies students' desires, needs and ambitions. Teacher should promote self-learning in effective and efficient way. S/he should follow guidelines stated in Exhibit 3.84.

Exhibit No. 3.84: Guidelines to be followed by teacher to promote self-learning

The teacher should
➢ Always create interest in learning. S/he should link and relate it with the professional life. S/he should tell the importance of the learning for obtaining job of choice and career advancement opportunities. ➢ Diagnose the learning needs of the students, arouse it and motivate them

(*Contd.*)

(*Contd.*)

to satisfy the needs. Considering the needs of the students teachers can call an expert to guide the students on what to study, how to study, when to study, where to study, and how to develop self-learning skills and habits.

- Guide students to craft vision, or articulate the ambitions. Guide them to harness full potential to achieve the mission. Help them to pursue the hobby.
- Design learning resources in simple language that creates interest of the students to learn from it. Establish the learning resources center in the institute with self-learning facilities.
- Provide easy access to students for learning on their own in the learning center. Have variety of learning material in the learning resource center. Enrich learning resources center contributing the learning resources for it. Digitize the learning center for easy access and retrieval of information. Create facilities for self-learning in the institution.
- Identify the sources of self-learning resources in different disciplines and procure them or inform the students about them. The easiest task is selecting the learning resources available in the market and suggesting the students to go through it.
- Design simple, easy, legible, grammatically correct, organized logically and sequentially, and stimulating to read learning material for students. Create interest in learning linking the content with practice. Provide opportunity for recalling, reviewing, reflecting and assessing learning.
- Inbuilt feedback on progress of learning in the learning material. Provide cues and constructive feedback in the learning material.
- Use the concepts such as simple to complex concept, concrete to abstract concept, whole to part and part to whole, theory with illustrations and examples, particular to general in developing self-learning material.
- Define the key words, new terms and unfamiliar things. Explain abstract concepts with analogy, examples and non examples.
- Develop multi-media to enrich self-learning process. Design small and easy learning units for students. The learning material should encourage learning.
- Organize tutorials, guidance and counselling session for students who have taken self-learning path or you have provided self-learning assignment.
- Create self-learning environment in the institution. Ensure that there is a balance between self-learning and formal learning. Plan self-learning as a whole in your department and allocate time for the same. Students should not be over or under loaded for self-learning so for time is concerned.

(*Contd.*)

(*Contd.*)

- Use question answer method during lecture and demonstration to motivate students to think and reply.
- Exhibit supportive, positive, appreciative, stimulating and rewarding environment for self-learning in the institution.
- Plan formal learning to promote self-learning opportunities in it. Learning methods such as group discussions, creativity sessions, role-play, game, simulation, field visits, training in industry, projects, assignments, action learning and quality circles are formal methods to promote self-learning in the institution.
- Analyze the success of self-learning strategy and refine it based on the feedback.
- Promote self-learning in the institution for teachers and staff members. They should learn to enhance effectiveness and efficiency of transfer of learning.

11. Research on Self-Learning

Agrawal & Sakesna (1989) have reported that the students are above average on comprehension, average on concentration, high on task orientation, high value on interaction, high value on drilling, average on supports, high value on recording and difficulty in reading foreign author books. Analyzing the study habits they have noted suggestions such as students should improve on comprehension and concentration component of study habit. Books written by Indian author should be made available to them for better understanding and learning. Students should be encouraged to refer the other available literature. They should be trained to take notes. They should be encouraged to think and work independently, and to set goals according to their competence. They should be encouraged to know their strengths, weaknesses, opportunities and threats.

Ganjoo & Verma (1999) have noted that in polytechnic 66 per cent teachers have reported high degree of positive opinion towards self-learning. 66.6 per cent teachers have showed strongly negative and 33.3 per cent teachers have expressed positive attitude for self-learning. They have noted overall findings mentioning that every third teacher is having strong positive opinion and attitude towards self-learning, strongly positive opinion but negative attitude and negative opinion and negative attitudes towards self-learning. They have studied the opinion on five-point scale on parameters listed in Exhibit 3.85.

Exhibit No. 3.85: Parameters of study on opinion of teachers for self-learning

Sl. No.	*Parameters of Study*
1.	No welcome of different point of views on controversial issues
2.	Learning is a life long process
3.	Most important learning is specialisation in a subject
4.	Teaching is indeed a challenging job
5.	Nobody enjoys learning, it is always a compulsion
6.	It is knowledge from which power is derived
7.	Reading improves communication skills
8.	Knowledge is real wealth
9.	It is better to pursue power instead of knowledge
10.	I like to encourage discussions
11.	Given a choice, I would like to change my occupation
12.	I like to satisfy my curiosity by reading as much as I can
13.	Teaching is a monotonous job, because you have to repeat same content again and again
14.	Life is bondage, but knowledge is liberation
15.	One can learn up to a certain age, after which learning is not possible
16.	Successful people are generally well read people
17.	Communication skills will depend upon what you gained from the experience
18.	Knowledge is the essence of life therefore continued education makes life meaningful
19.	Most important learning is know how to learn
20.	Teachers enjoy good social status in our system
21.	Most learning needs are generally not best met through training. Therefore self-learning is essential for teachers
22.	More you know, more worried you are, that is why, ignorance is bliss
23.	Not to know is bad, not to wish to know is worse
24.	I like reading as most enjoyable hobby

(*Contd.*)

(*Contd.*)

Sl. No.	*Parameters of Study*
25.	Knowledge for the sake of knowledge is pursued by those who do not have other useful work
26.	I am proud of my decision to become a teacher
27.	More you read, more clearly is gain
28.	Learning can be a source of joy
29.	In today's world money is more important than knowledge
30.	Reading books is a most boring hobby
31.	Even teacher can learn something from their students
32.	To know our own self is most important from self-learning
33.	I am an experienced teacher, therefore self-learning is now irrelevant for me
34.	If I can earn money by learning than only I will learn new things
35.	More you read more you get confused
36.	Teachers are always put at low profile in the society
37.	Learning about outside world is more important than learning about self
38.	Bookish people are generally unacceptable in life
39.	Essence of life lies in accumulation of means of physical comfort
40.	It is hard for a teacher to admit his ignorance openly and frankly.

They have noted recommendations for improving self-learning in the institution. The recommendations are stated in Exhibit 3.86.

Exhibit No. 3.86: Recommendations for promoting self-learning

- ➤ There is a need to design and implement flexible approaches for promoting self-learning at institutional level.
- ➤ An information center should be opened at state level to provide information about distance learning programmes conducted by national and international institutions.
- ➤ The teachers should be encouraged to become member of various libraries. The membership fees should be reimbursed to them by the institution.
- ➤ The institutions should subscribe for national and international journals.

(*Contd.*)

(Contd.)

- Learning resources development and utilisation center should promote self-learning for teachers and students.
- The purchase procedure in the library should be simplified and library should be modernized. The library of different institutions should be networked.
- Teachers should be provided opportunities to share learning experiences in the institution, at state and national level.
- Staff development policy at institute level should make provisions for incentives to promote self-learning.
- Informal learning groups should be encouraged in the institution to enhance self-learning and creativity sessions should be organized in the institution to promote thinking.

12. Summary

Self-learning is one of the important and foremost methods of learning. It empowers the learners to learn and learn continuously to satisfy the learning needs. The student gets satisfaction because it satisfies the immediate learning needs of the students. Concept of self-learning is wide and varied. It does not mean that student learn each and every thing on her/his own. Student takes the help of teacher, professionals, experts, colleagues and any other person to identify and satisfy learning needs. The self-learning may be related to curriculum, co-curricular activity, and altogether different to pursue hobby. Self-learning is carried out knowing the self, crafting the vision, designing the strategies to achieve vision, initiating the self-development, self-reading, reviewing learning, testing learning and applying learning in real life situation and linking it with further learning. There are various methods of self-learning such as reading, going through multimedia package, joining interest group, registering in distance learning programme or on line learning programme. Observation plays an important role in learning motor skills. Students should develop the habit of self-learning and observing. Teachers play a significant role in promoting self-learning.

13. Activity

Assess Your Reading Skills

Recall the self-study you have done in this semester and mark your honest assessment in the assessment sheet given below:

Assessment Sheet for Reading Skills

Sl. No.	*Criteria*	*Extent of Effectiveness*		
		High	*Medium*	*Low*
A.	*Planning*			
1.	Assessment of learning			
2.	Self-learning objectives			
3.	Selection of self-learning resources			
4.	Selection of self-learning mode			
5.	Organisation of self-learning resources			
6.	Allocation of time to each learning event			
7.	Method of assessment of self-learning			
B.	*Self-Learning through Reading*			
8.	Reading skills			
9.	Initiation of reading			
10.	Determination for reading			
11.	Interest in reading			
12.	Fast reading			
13.	Slow reading			
14.	Reading between the lines			
15.	Reading behind the lines			
16.	Reading graphs			
17.	Reading figures			
18.	Reading charts			
19.	Reading signs			
20.	Familiarity with terms			
21.	Understanding reading instructions			
22.	Interpreting data			
23.	Drawing conclusion on the basis of data			
24.	Forming a complete picture on the basis of data			
25.	Linking present reading with previous learning			

(*Contd.*)

(*Contd.*)

Sl. No.	*Criteria*	*Extent of Effectiveness*		
		High	*Medium*	*Low*
26.	Linking present reading with future learning			
27.	Scanning the material and establishing linkages			
28.	Reading and note taking			
29.	Reading and underlining the important learning points			
30.	Reading loudly with clear pronunciation of each word			
31.	Reading silently			
32.	Reading and day dreaming			
33.	Getting bored during reading			
34.	Reading under disturbing conditions			
35.	Continuous reading for long hours			
36.	Short reading with long and short breaks and linking previous reading			
37.	Reading and taking pause and thinking			
38.	Reading and asking questions to self			
39.	Reading and rereading			
40.	Reading and linking it to practice			
41.	Reading and dealing with reading difficulties			
42.	Reading and improving reading on the basis of feedback from previous reading experiences			
43.	Reading and noting down the reading and learning difficulties			
44.	Reading and thinking creatively			
45.	Reading and memorizing			
46.	Reading and recalling			
47.	Reading and clarifying learning difficulties from teacher and colleagues			
48.	Reading and associating it with previously learnt concepts and principles			

(*Contd.*)

(*Contd.*)

Sl. No.	*Criteria*	*Extent of Effectiveness*		
		High	*Medium*	*Low*
49.	Listening the self while reading			
50.	Rewarding reading			
C.	*Revision of Learning*			
51.	Scanning the previous pages			
52.	Browsing the underlines			
53.	Reading the notes			
54.	Recalling and reciting the key learning points			
55.	Linking the forward and backward learning			
56.	Making summary of learning points without referring the reading material			
57.	Preparing mental map or spider diagram or process flow chart or logical tree diagram or flow diagram			
58.	Draw symbols indicating learning			
59.	Challenge the learning through questions			
D.	*Self learning through Multi-media Packages*			
60.	Reading			
61.	Watching			
62.	Relating to practice			
63.	Arranging resources			
64.	Attempting tests			
E.	*Observation of Work Place*			
65.	Understanding of practices			
66.	Understanding the underlying concepts and practices			
67.	Appreciating the attitudes required to perform the task			
68.	Appreciating the norms of working			
69.	Appreciating the professional ethics			

(*Contd.*)

(*Contd.*)

Sl. No.	*Criteria*	*Extent of Effectiveness*		
		High	*Medium*	*Low*
70.	Understanding the values of the organisation			
71.	Appreciating the amount of energy required to perform the task			
F.	*Assessment of Learning*			
72.	Take formal tests			
73.	Attempt the tests given in the learning material			
74.	Ask your friend to ask question on the learning			
75.	Apply the learning in real life situation and see the results			
G.	*Application of Learning in Real Life Situations*			
76.	Games			
77.	Simulation			
78.	Role-play			
79.	Demonstration			
80.	Practice exercise			
81.	Action learning			
82.	Library assignments			
83.	Internet assignment			
84.	Industrial assignments			
85.	Home assignments			
86.	Classroom assignments			
87.	Laboratory assignments			
88.	Design			
89.	Development			
90.	Visualisation			
H.	*Summative Assessment*			
91.	Demonstration of competency			

(*Contd.*)

(*Contd.*)

Sl. No.	*Criteria*	*Extent of Effectiveness*		
		High	*Medium*	*Low*
92.	Criteria for assessing competency			
93.	Validity and reliability of assessment			
94.	Certification of competency			
95.	Feedback for refining competency			
96.	Assessment of impact of learning			

3.20 DRILL AND PRACTICE

1. Introduction

Drill and practice has been a traditional method for making students to learn new information and skills. Drill and practice helps the students to remember the important facts, rules, precautions, data, and skills. Drill and practice is necessary to impart significant skills necessary to perform key functions. So that students can use the knowledge and skills to perform significant important tasks without much of pressure and help. In drill and practice students develop the skills without thinking the reasons behind it. Drill and practice consolidates the skills in the behaviour of the students. Drill fixes the skills and practice refines it. This method is based on saying practice makes a man perfect. Drill and practice is a method to develop and refine cognitive, affective and motor skills. In China defense skills are developed using this method only. The warriors are trained to a stage that even in sleep their senses work and they deal with the actual attack of the enemy. There is a need to develop certain skills in engineering students to an extent that even in unconscious working they practice the right skills.

2. Learning from Drill and Practice

As described earlier drill and practice develops higher level of skills in all the three domains of learning. During the process of drill and practice students learn by mistakes, self-feedback and correction, experiencing the anxiety of real life situation, receiving the feedback from the teachers and peers. Students use all the senses of learning to perform the task during the process of drill and practice. They learn dedication, sincerity and integrity. In developing competencies drill and practice is essential and prerequisite condition. This method initiates the process of proficiency development. Students get an opportunity to do experimentations after attaining certain level of proficiency. They get an opportunity to transfer skills in different situations. They develop observational skills during the practice. The teacher can design variety of drill and practice experiences for the students assigning different responsibilities to different students to develop leadership, followership, communication, problem solving and conflict resolving skills in students. Students like drill and practice because they see meaning in it for learning and performance. They get an opportunity to learn skills step by step under the observation of a teacher. The good point in drill and practice is that they are not required to attend long lectures. They have a good change in the process of learning, as they are the driver of the learning process. They develop skills and then deduce and learn about the theory behind competency. The list of skills and competencies that can be developed by this method is given Exhibit 3.87.

Exhibit No. 3.87: Skills developed through drill and practice

Cognitive Skills	*Affective Skills*	*Psychomotor Skills*
➢ Planning ➢ Problem solving ➢ Information gathering with a purpose ➢ Observing a method ➢ Preparing reports ➢ Trouble shooting ➢ Presentation ➢ Influencing	➢ Taking preventive measures ➢ Healthy relationship ➢ Observing rules ➢ Team spirit ➢ Maintaining hygienic condition ➢ House keeping	➢ Drawings ➢ Handling the equipment and machine ➢ Selecting right tools ➢ Maintenance of machines ➢ Integration of movements of body parts to perform the complex task ➢ Calibration ➢ Performing task in a team

3. Method of Use of Drill and Practice

The drill and practice method when used with other methods of learning creates effective learning in all the students. In producing common competencies in engineering students it is combined with lecture, demonstration, and practice. But the combination of methods of learning depends on the competency to be developed, entry behaviour of the students and competence of the teacher. The alternative combinations of various methods of learning are shown in Exhibit 3.88.

Exhibit No. 3.88: Combination of learning methods with drill and practice

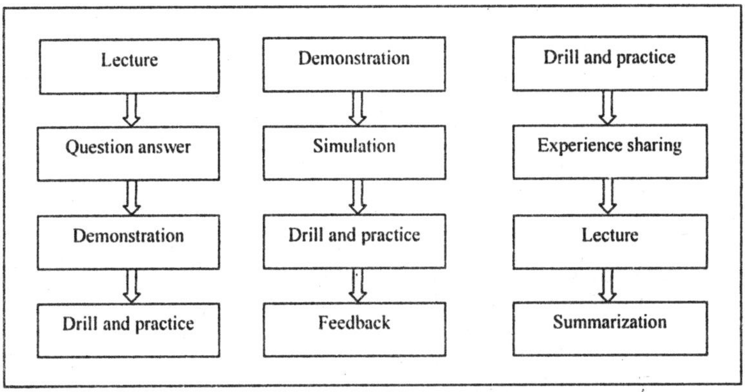

4. Method of Drill and Practice

The trained teacher should analyze the competency to be developed in the students using drill and practice along with other methods of learning. The principles of learning are kept in mind to design drill and practice sequences. The drill and practice should be designed in series of learning stages. It is designed in way that students realize that the competency or skills can only be developed by drill and practice method. It means it should create natural environment for learning a particular competency. It is not necessary that students learn theory behind the competency but they should appreciate and practice right method. The teacher observes the drill and practice and if s/he finds wrong learning of the skills s/he should provide remedial actions. In fact this is the limitation of the drill and practice that the wrong learning is very difficult to correct. A driver is not required to learn about the centrifugal and centripetal forces, friction and lateral friction, contact area of tire with the road and so on. But s/he is certainly needed to drill and practice correctly to drive on various types of road curves. S/he should have complete sense of control of speed, applying breaks, operating clutch and steering, and following safety rules. The drill and practice is conducted using steps stated in Exhibit 3.89.

Exhibit No. 3.89: Steps of drill and practice

- Analyze the competency and see whether it can be developed combining drill and practice with other methods of learning.
- Designing drill and practice sequences and exercises.
- Prepare detailed instruction schedule along with attention points for the students. If necessary prepare manual, worksheet, work book, instruction book and practice book.
- Decide what to do and how to perform the task.
- Decide what to observe and how to observe. Prepare an observation sheet to objectively assess the skills of the students. What to observe is divided in two parts that is outcome of the performance and method of performance.
- Arouse the interest of the students for learning the competency and its relevance with the professional life.
- Inform the students about what and how part of performing the task.
- Explain each step of skill development and provide enough opportunities to drill and practice. The steps in skills development should be short and interesting.
- Emphasize the core skills of the competencies during the practice.
- Provide opportunity to practice skills as per instruction in different situation. If necessary guide and assist them with part demonstrations.
- Ask them to analyze their performance, outcome of performance and compare it to the standard. If there is no deviation provide recognition to learning.
- Ask them to identify the deviation in the performance and method of performance.
- If they fail to identify the gap in performance and method of performance offer feedback and ask them to take corrective action.
- Provide opportunities to take corrective actions through self feedback or feedback from others.
- Develop skills to take the feedback from the progress of the work.
- Decide other methods of learning that are necessary to develop the competency.
- Check the attainment of competency to pre-defined level.
- Provide independent assignments for refining the competency and attaining higher level of proficiency.

5. Summary

Drill and practice method of learning has been in use from the time unknown to develop psychomotor skills. The beauty of this method is that students are not required to learn theory and they are directly put to the task. This method of learning provides opportunity to participate in completing the task. Students appreciate that the task is important and it needs to be performed. They also appreciate that accuracy and proficiency is required in performing the task. They see meaning in the learning. They experience the anxiety and stress of performing the task. The teacher analyses the competency to be developed and selects methods of learning in combination with drill and practice. S/he prepares the detailed plan for carrying out the drill and practice. If required s/he prepares the manual, work instruction and practice exercises for the students. The teacher provides step by step instructions and the students perform the task. The students are trained to receive feedback from the progress of the work and from their peers. The teacher also observers the performance of the students and provides them feedback for corrective action. S/he also provides remedial instruction using part demonstrations, practice exercises and minute observations.

The immediate knowledge of result plays a very important role in developing the competency and proficiency level. After attainment of certain level of competency and core skills the teacher provides variety of assignments to students. These assignments require the use of same competency by students in altogether different situations. After developing the competency students are exposed to theory. So that they can plan for completing the task, use the competency to perform the task, find the fault and take corrective actions. They learn to work independently in variety of situations.

6. Activity

Design drill and practice learning method to develop complex competency in students and implement it.

4

Management of Learning in Laboratory

> ***Objectives:*** The readers will be able to:
>
> 1. List the need and importance of learning in the laboratory
> 2. State the types of learning takes place in the laboratory
> 3. List principles of learning used in laboratory
> 4. Describe the modes of learning used by students in laboratory
> 5. State learning methods used in laboratory
> 6. Describe various combinations of learning methods used in laboratory
> 7. Explain steps followed in producing learning in laboratory
> 8. Describe the procedure for developing attitudes in laboratory
> 9. Explain the process of assessment of learning in laboratory
> 10. Design plan for producing stated competencies in laboratory

1. Introduction

Laboratory has significant place in process of learning. Laboratories provide an opportunity to apply the knowledge, skills and attitudes learnt in the classroom. The students learn concepts, principles and theory in order to develop competency. Classroom provides necessary information to them through various modes of learning and instructions. Students verify the information, relationship, cause and effect etc. They perform experiments to verify the principles and arrive at conclusion. They get an opportunity to develop, design and innovate new concepts and principles.

2. Learning in Laboratory

Students get an opportunity to lean in all the three domains of learning.

Teacher designs the experiments keeping in mind the requirements of learning objectives and competency. Students learn variety of concepts, principles, motor skills and attitudes in the laboratory. The first and foremost learning is that they see the machines, tools, implements, equipment, material, layout of the machines, various connections, charts, graphs, models, line diagrams, notices containing precautions and so on. They really see the world very close to real life situation. In fact the students use observation skills to learn in the laboratory. The students learn variety of and a wide range of knowledge, skills, and attitudes listed in Exhibit 4.1.

Exhibit No. 4.1: Type of learning takes place in the laboratory

Cognitive Domain ➢ Application of theory to perform a given task ➢ Planning and designing ➢ Interpretation of results and drawing conclusions ➢ Systematically recording the information ➢ Evaluate the effectiveness and efficiency of process, methods, and operations ➢ Diagnose the problem	➢ Analyze the problem and generate solution ➢ Synthesize the information collected and form principles or patterns or correlation ➢ Compare the methods, procedures and results obtained and find out the reasons of differences ➢ Selection of appropriate tools and techniques ➢ Report writing ➢ Presentation skills
Psychomotor Skills ➢ Apply the concept, principles and attitudes to perform the task ➢ Use hands, leg and eyes in integrated way to perform a task ➢ Make electric connections ➢ Conduct experiment	➢ Manipulate the variables to see the effect ➢ Assemble the parts produced separately ➢ Find fault in operation of a process ➢ Disintegrate the parts ➢ Modify the design
Affective Domain ➢ Attitude of inquiry ➢ Attitude of safety ➢ Following the instructions and norms ➢ Attitude of precision ➢ Concern for quality ➢ Concern for productivity ➢ Concern for energy saving ➢ Attitude of time management ➢ Respect for others	➢ Concern for protecting environment ➢ Concern for cleanliness ➢ Good house-keeping ➢ Attitude of exploring ➢ Attitude of discovery ➢ Systematic observation ➢ Attitude for care ➢ Attitude of respect ➢ Attitude of saving ➢ Attitude of learning

3. Principles of Learning

The learning in laboratory is very close to real life learning. The learning in laboratory is based on numbers of principles of learning. These principles are listed in Exhibit 4.2.

Exhibit No. 4.2: Principles of learning used in laboratory

➤ Meaningful learning ➤ Learning with a purpose ➤ Learning from part to make whole ➤ Learning from whole to learn about parts ➤ Learning from known to unknown ➤ Learning from analysis to synthesis ➤ Learning from concrete things to abstract	➤ Learning general things to learn particular things ➤ Learning from facts to rationalize ➤ Learning from psychological to logical ➤ Learning is integrated ➤ Learning is a natural process ➤ Use of more than one sense

4. Modes of Learning in Laboratory

The students get an opportunity to use various modes of learning in laboratory. They take the responsibility of learning and get involved in the process of learning. They become enthusiastic to apply the theory in practice. They learn individually and in teams. They use more than one sense for learning and use numbers of modes of learning. The significant modes of learning in laboratory are stated in Exhibit 4.3.

Exhibit No. 4.3: Modes of learning in laboratory

➤ Learning through observation ➤ Learning through experimentation ➤ Learning by doing ➤ Learning by committing mistakes ➤ Purposeful learning ➤ Learning through experiences	➤ Learning through imitation ➤ Learning through mistakes ➤ Learning through struggle ➤ Learning through creativity ➤ Learning through simulation and games

5. Methods of Learning in Laboratory

The teacher decides the method of learning in the laboratory considering the learning objectives, resources available, entry level of students, and sequence of learning in order to achieve competency. The teacher uses various methods in sequence in order to develop desired competency and proficiency level. An indicative combination of methods is shown in Exhibit 4.4.

Exhibit No. 4.4: Combination of methods used in laboratory

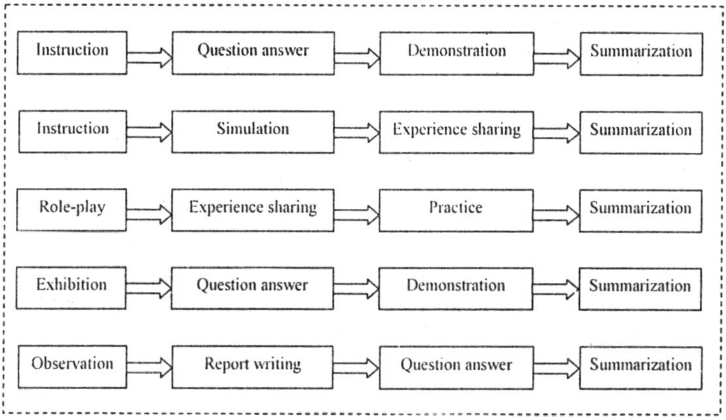

There are various methods used in laboratory such as demonstration, simulation, action learning, game, practice, role-play, multiple role-play, exhibition, assignment and so on. The involvement of students in the learning method varies from simply observer to independently performing. The students get an opportunity to practice whatever they have learnt in theory. They get first hand experience and feel of performance.

6. Guidelines for Teachers to Produce Effective and Efficient Learning in the Laboratory

The guidelines to produce effective and efficient learning in laboratory are stated in Exhibit 4.5.

Exhibit No. 4.5: Guidelines for teachers to produce effective and efficient learning in laboratory

Planning of Learning in Laboratory

- Inform the guideline and instructions to be followed in the laboratory.
- Inform about acceptable and non-acceptable behaviour, dangerous and non-dangerous things, must do and must not do activities.
- Analyze the job to be performed in real life situation.
- Identify the competencies required to perform the job.

(*Contd.*)

(*Contd.*)

- List instructional objectives for all the three domains in order to achieve the competency.
- Analyze the objectives and identify the learning requirements in all the three domains of learning.
- Plan and design the laboratory experiences, assignments, problems and projects. Demonstrations, games, action learning and so on. Design experiments for learning motor skills step by step one set of motor skills at a time.
- Develop laboratory manual to facilitate learning and save time on unnecessary activities.
- Distribute the manual to all the students.
- Ensure that the students have learnt prerequisite theory.
- Provide adequate information on complete performance of the task
- Analyze the job/task/activity to be performed by students in the laboratory. Find the list of motor skills, their sequence, relationship, concept or principle involved.
- Establish relationship between different sets of motor skills.
- Inform the students about all the learning events to be performed in the laboratory. The teacher should prepare diagrammatic representation of these sequences on transparency, flip chrat or power point slide. These events can be shown in the manual.
- Never design the rigid timetable for theory and practice. The laboratory work should be conducted according to learning plan and as per pre-decided timetable. The learning should go in proper order.

Execution of Learning plan in the Laboratory

- Arrange the resources in proper order before start of the practical.
- Demonstrate the performance of one type first and then ask the students to perform.
- Provide opportunity to practice one set of skills, observe performance, reward desired performance and provide constructive feedback on undesired performance. Demonstrate correct way of performing the task.
- Train students to take feedback on performance from the progress and quality of product, results, outcomes and so on.
- Observe the behaviour of the students on pre-defined parameters. These parameters are decided on the basis of learning attitude and learning approach.
- Provide immediate knowledge of results.
- Insist the students to prepare the report just after completing the practical and check it.

Summarisation of Learning

- Consolidate the learning.
- Link the learning with theory, practice and next learning.

7. Development of Attitudes

Attitudes shape the behaviour of the students. Students develop professional attitudes in the institutions during the process of learning. If students do not learn the attitudes or learn wrongly it is very difficult to shape the attitudes on the job. In fact there is no time to unlearn and relearn the attitudes on the job. Attitudes are demonstrated in the behaviour of the students. Attitudes are the feelings and beliefs of the students about equipment, procedures, rules, norms, ethics etc. There is a saying about learning attitudes that attitudes are caught it cannot be taught. The professional world requires lots of attitudes ranging from safety to customer relationship. The teacher should create professional environment in the institution so that students learn right attitudes and practice them in their professional life.

- The desired and undesired behaviour related to attitudes should be spelled out clearly to all the students
- The desired behaviour of the students should be reinforced immediately when they demonstrate the behaviour
- The undesired behaviour should be pointed out along with actions to be taken
- All the students and teachers should demonstrate the desired behaviour
- The teachers should act as a role model for students
- Provide opportunities to practice the attitudes under observation
- Observe the attitudes of the students and provide constructive feedback to them for practice and internalize
- Use attitude development methods such as demonstration, role play, simulation, game, practice, feedback and so on in the laboratory.

8. Assessment of Learning in Laboratory

The assessment of learning in laboratory is carried out based on the performance of the students against set objectives. The learning is assessed to identify the learning deficiencies and difficulties of students, planning remedial instructions, reinforcement of behaviour at right time with right rewards, providing immediate knowledge of results, developing intrinsic motivation for perfection and accuracy, developing positive attitudes for learning, providing emphasis on higher levels of learning, developing attitudes for learning to learn. The assessment of learning in laboratory is carried out on process and product. Process assessment is carried out to reinforce the desired actions, to take corrective action and to plan for higher levels of skills. Product assessment is carried out to assess the overall performance of the students on the product/learning outcome. It helps in assessing the planning work, organizing work, quality of work, efficiency of work, precision, accuracy, and utilisation of time. The communication skills and interrelationship of competencies are also assessed through viva-voce. The teacher should prepare the instruments to assess the learning using indicators of learning for process, product and integration of learning. An example of method of assessment of learning of civil engineering drawing is given at the end of this chapter.

9. Research Studies

Nayak & Kudesia (1995) have classified the competencies of laboratory technicians on three areas. They are personality, job proficiency and interpersonal relations. They have rank ordered the competencies related to personality, growth and stated in following order; maintaining punctuality and regularity, becoming mentally alert, becoming hard and sincere worker, attending and facing the problems sincerely and boldly, having positive/creative/innovative/cooperative/learning/managerial attitude, having stamina and energy, having neither too strict nor too lenient behaviour, using reasoning, becoming emotionally balanced, and thought provoking. They have rank ordered the competencies related to job and stated in following order:

- Receiving materials, samples, equipment, tools etc. for conduction of practical and arranging in laboratory
- Maintaining laboratory equipment, instruments and tools in good condition and keeping work area clean
- Following safety rules and regulation
- Fulfilling the role and responsibilities sincerely and resolving the encountered difficulties
- Following the norms and rules
- Updating the laboratory according to the requirements of project
- Organizing laboratory work effectively and assisting teachers in creative and innovative laboratory work
- Planning and conducting the activity systematically and arrange demonstration

- Preparing samples/specimen/circuit and check electrical connections properly before operating by students
- Guiding and assisting the students in completing their practical/ project
- Developing expertise on the job to work independently without guidance of faculty members
- Maintaining files, documents, and students record properly
- Involving new laboratory technicians in laboratory work for developing their skills
- Setting personal goals matching the organisational goals for improvement
- Attending managerial problems related to laboratory and making decisions for organizing laboratory activities.

They have rank ordered the competencies related to inter personal relation and stated in following order:

- Adjusting with teachers/students/environment/management and its policies
- Providing prompt services to clients/users
- Cooperating by working in team and groups without any conflict
- Understanding the problem of others and sharing their responsibilities
- Sharing resources with others available in polytechnics
- Fulfilling roles and responsibilities and respecting the feelings, ideas and thoughts of others
- Working without any prejudice and biased feelings
- Communicating effectively in dealing with others
- Taking decisions in the interest of others
- Giving more weightage to the needs and requirements of others.

10. Summary

Students have a feel of real life atmosphere in the laboratory. Whatever they have learnt in theory that they apply in practice. They develop right kind of attitudes to perform a particular job. They perform the task with coordination of muscles and activities. They do experiments and draw conclusions. Learning in laboratory is based upon principles of learning and students use variety of modes of learning in the laboratory. Teacher plans the laboratory work as per requirements of the curriculum. Teacher observes the process of performance against set of parameters. Teacher provides feedback to students for accuracy and precision. S/he reinforces the desired behaviour of the students. The assessment of learning is carried out systematically to provide constructive feedback for improvement and create interest for further learning.

11. Activity

Design the laboratory sheets to facilitate the learning in laboratory and assess the learning outcomes particularly attitudes.

Check List
Assessment of Civil Engineering Drawing (Process)

Name .... Roll No. ....

Direction: Circle "Yes" or "No" to indicate whether skill has been demonstrated.

Yes	*No*	*S. No.*	*Item*
Yes	No	1.	Student is able to plan various elements of structure conceptually.
Yes	No	2.	Student is able to draw rough sketch of plan.
Yes	No	3.	Student is able to select suitable scale.
Yes	No	4.	Student feels difficulty and discuss with peers/teachers.
Yes	No	5.	Student properly sets drawing sheet on drawing board.
Yes	No	6.	Student plans drawing sheet as per rules.
Yes	No	7.	Student brings instrument box.
Yes	No	8.	Student selects and uses appropriate instrument for different work.
Yes	No	9.	Student carefully handles instrument.
Yes	No	10.	Student uses curves for drawing curves.
Yes	No	11.	Student follows drawing rules/IS code.
Yes	No	12.	Student draws systematically.
Yes	No	13.	Student erases frequently.
Yes	No	14.	Student follows instructions.
Yes	No	15.	Student takes interest in work.

Rating Scale
Assessment of Civil Engineering Drawing (Product)

Name .... Roll No. ....

Direction: Indicate the degree to which the drawing fulfils the criteria.

S. No.	*Criteria*	*Poor*	*Good*	*Very Good*
1.	Lay out of drawing sheet	1	2	3
2.	Quality of pencil work	1	2	3
3.	Accuracy in dimension	1	2	3
4.	Frequency of use of symbols	1	2	3
5.	Details of different elements	1	2	3
6.	Labeling and dimensioning of drawing	1	2	3
7.	Quality of lettering	1	2	3
8.	Organisation of elements	1	2	3
9.	Suitability of scale	1	2	3
10.	Overall outlook	1	2	3

Structured Questionnaire
Assessment of Student in Civil Engineering (Viva-Voce)

Name .... Roll No. ....

Direction: Tick for correct answer.

S. No.	*Questions*	*Correct*	*Incorrect*
1.	How did you select instruments for drawing?		
2.	Which method did you follow for layout of drawing sheet?		
3.	How shall you explain the drawing to your assistant engineer?		
4.	How shall you explain the drawing to a mason?		
5.	Which method will you follow for layout of the structure?		
6.	How shall you take sanitary details?		
7.	How shall you take water supply details?		
8.	How shall you take electricity and air conditioning details?		
9.	Is the plan feasible for framed structure?		
10.	Whether details are sufficient for estimating the cost?		
11.	If required how shall you make necessary changes in the drawing during construction?		

5

Management of Learning Through Projects

***Objectives*: The readers will be able to:**

1. Define the concept of project
2. Describe the purpose of the project
3. List the role of the teacher in managing projects
4. State the types of projects
5. List the characteristics of project
6. Explain the type of learning takes place through projects
7. Describe the learning situations in which project should be selected
8. State the advantages of group projects
9. List the projects that can be assigned to students
10. Explain the criteria to assess the learning of the students in project method

1. Introduction

There are various higher-level of competencies, which the students are required to learn. These competencies may be related to integration of concepts, skills and attitudes learnt in various competencies. The project method of learning provides an opportunity to students to apply whatever they have learnt in the course of study. It invites the students to think and plan the strategy to complete the project work. During the process of completion of project they learn in all domains of learning i.e. cognitive, psychomotor and affective.

2. Definition of a Project

A project is a planned time-bound learning event designed by the teacher with specific learning purpose at the completion of learning process for the students to produce higher level of competencies in all the three domains of learning. Generally the project creates an opportunity to integrate the learning to perform the role or to solve the problem, or to create something new proficiently and prepare a report thereof. Teacher designs the learning project for students with detailed instructions to complete it. During the design of the project teacher plays an active role to create learning challenges for students. During completion of the project students play an active role to complete the project. They assume the learning responsibility for learning under the guidance of their teacher and resource person. This method provides scope for greater involvement of students in learning process. Projects are designed for providing real life exposure and experiences to students. They learn by doing the things and satisfy their needs of learning. Working on projects they are not away from real life so they enjoy the process of learning. They feel the excitement of real professional life. Project provides fairly good opportunity for learning by mistake, learning through experimentation, learning by doing and learning by reflection. Projects bring real life in the campus of the institution. Selecting and undertaking real life projects is a good means to bring potential employers in the campus. It is also a good means to enter in employers' organisation and building relationship for collaborative work.

3. Classification of Projects

Projects can be classified on various criteria such as number of students, time, size, theoretical or practice oriented. It depends on factors such as subject, curriculum provisions, time available to teacher, competence of the teachers, resources available, linkage with industry, size of the class, purpose of project, entry level of students etc. Learning projects can be classified on following criteria:

Number of Students: Projects can be designed for individuals and groups of students. The size of the group may be small 5 to 10 students or large 10 to 20 students. If it is designed for individual students and for a competency various aspects of the competency are designed and allotted to individuals. If the focus of the project is solving real life problem and it requires integration of knowledge, skills and attitudes of various kinds then the projects are designed for small or large groups. To produce higher level of learning in undergraduate programmes projects are designed for small groups. Group projects are assigned to have advantages listed in Exhibit 5.1.

Exhibit No. 5.1: Advantages of group projects

For Teacher	*For Students*
➢ Saves time ➢ Saves efforts ➢ Monitoring and review becomes easy ➢ Easy communication ➢ Learning and other problems are solved at students level	➢ Better clarity of project ➢ Opportunity for creativity ➢ Opportunity to bring out the talent ➢ Sharing of work ➢ Collective learning ➢ Use of different talents and interests ➢ Team work

Availability of Time: Time is a precious resource for teachers as well as students. Projects designed to be completed during vacation or at the end of the year are generally have longer duration say one month. There could be one small duration project in each year and one large duration project.

Theoretical or Practice Oriented: Projects should always relate to practice. Now-a-day there is a great pressure on institutions to contribute for the community development, work for privileged groups of society and economy. The institution can select projects with a purpose and assign it to students as a project work. Institution can take consultancy projects on which students and teachers can work together and earn for the institution and self. At the same time learn real life challenges. In some situations it is necessary to develop higher level of skills specially cognitive skills such as planning, analysis, synthesis, evaluation, design, innovations, design new products or services, problem solving, decision-making etc. In such circumstances real life situation description is given to the students and they are asked to work on the situation and prepare a report thereof.

4. Purpose of Project Method

The projects are designed and assigned to students to fulfil various purposes. These purposes are listed in Exhibit 5.2.

Exhibit No. 5.2: Purposes of projects

For Teacher	*For Students*
➢ To integrate learning in a meaningful way ➢ To introduce variety in teaching learning process ➢ To shift responsibility of learning to students ➢ To involve students in teaching learning process ➢ To gradually make students mature to take real life job ➢ To do some urgent work when students are working on a project	➢ To experience a real life job ➢ To solve real life problem ➢ To do experimentation ➢ To appreciate the linkage and importance of competencies they are developing ➢ To practice the theory they have learned ➢ To develop proficiency and expertise in a particular competency ➢ To innovate something that does not exist ➢ To appreciate human values

5. Learning Produced through Projects

Projects are powerful means to produce higher level of learning in all the three domains of learning. They produce learning in students as well as teachers. Projects provide an opportunity to the teacher and students to apply and transfer learning to new and different situations. Projects are carefully designed by teachers to produce higher level of learning listed in Exhibit 5.3.

Exhibit No. 5.3: Learning produced through projects

Skills	*Attitudes*
➢ Planning skills ➢ Visualizing skills ➢ Application skills ➢ Analytical skills ➢ Integration skills ➢ Investigative skills ➢ Synthesis skills ➢ Evaluation skills ➢ Problem solving skills ➢ Decision-making skills ➢ Thinking skills ➢ Forecasting skills ➢ Design skills ➢ Use of tools and equipments ➢ Information collating ➢ Report writing ➢ Presentation skills	➢ Attitude of inquiry ➢ Attitude of systematic working ➢ Attitude of safety ➢ Attitude of respecting others ➢ Attitude of tolerance ➢ Team spirit ➢ Attitude for environment ➢ Concern for others ➢ Respecting diversity ➢ Attitude of accuracy ➢ Attitude of experimenting ➢ Attitude of saving ➢ Attitude of serving ➢ Attitude of cleanliness ➢ Attitude of cooperativeness and collaboration

6. Projects for Learning

Teacher designs the projects for students learning. Projects are designed to be completed by students in the campus of the institute or in the industry or in the employer's organisation. Projects may be related to internet based. Whatever it may be it should have characteristics listed in Exhibit 5.4.

Exhibit No. 5.4: Characteristics of projects

It should:	
➢ be related to real life situation ➢ create challenge for students ➢ invite students to complete it ➢ cross the boundaries of the topics, competencies and subjects ➢ be interdisciplinary ➢ not be repetitive ➢ be completed in a well-defined time frame ➢ be feasible ➢ be related to higher level of learning	➢ create scope for further exploration ➢ be meaningful ➢ create scope for joyful learning ➢ be properly designed ➢ be clear to the students ➢ match with the entry behaviour of the students ➢ require systematic and scientific approach ➢ the product should be visible ➢ the learning should be evaluated

Design of the Project: The teacher should analyze the curriculum and define the learning outcomes of the project. S/he should prepare a plan to assign, instruct, provide resources, guide, support, and evaluate the quality of project. This plan can be made known to students. S/he should clearly explain the plan of the project to the students along with her/his expectations from the students. The quality of output of the project should also be explained to students at the time of assigning the project. If the project is being done outside the institution s/he should make all arrangements with the organisation in which students would complete project. At postgraduate level the students are matured enough to select the project under the guidance of the teacher. They are provided full autonomy to select the topic of their choice provided it should fulfill the learning requirement. The indicative list of subject of projects is given in Exhibit 5.5.

Assign the Project: The project is assigned to individuals or groups it all depends on learning competencies/objectives and design of the project. The teacher should specifically spell out the broad expectations, method of completing the project, resources support, process of obtaining

Exhibit No. 5.5: Students project

➤ Preparing a plan ➤ Designing a product ➤ Modifying a product ➤ Value addition in the process ➤ Reducing wastage ➤ Improving efficiency ➤ Studying a complex process ➤ Designing marketing strategy ➤ Designing additional features to a product or services ➤ Reducing drudgery ➤ Saving energy ➤ Protecting environment ➤ Designing networks ➤ Conducting various research studies ➤ Conducting failure analysis	➤ Diagnosing a problem ➤ Developing management information system for effective decision-making and reporting ➤ Solving a problem ➤ Developing alternatives ➤ Predicting crisis ➤ Undertaking risk analysis ➤ Creating awareness about new methods or technology ➤ Preparing presentations ➤ Designing a website ➤ Doing quality, energy, financial, cultural audit ➤ Survey ➤ Comparative study

guidance, evaluation criteria and marks allotted to each criterion. For first year and second year students teacher can help at each and every stage of the project to boost up the morale. But later on in third and fourth year s/he should inculcate the practice of independent handling of the project by students.

Supervise the Project: The first activity after assigning the project to students is to ask them to submit a plan of activities to complete the project. This plan is related to roles and responsibilities of the team members, approach of completing the project, resources and guidance required to complete the project, problems they are likely face, etc. This plan would provide good idea regarding the understanding of students about the project. At this stage teacher can provide constructive feedback to improve the quality of the plan to complete the project. S/he can brief the students on expectations, guidance, resources, and criteria for evaluating the outcomes of the learning. The next step of supervising the project is to monitor the progress of the project and provide adequate time to students for solving their learning problems. The teacher should ensure that every member of the team participate and contribute to complete the project. S/he should ask various members of the team questions related to progress of the project work, difficulties they are facing and their role in the project. S/he should convene meetings with agendas such as, experiences of doing the project, learning taking place, reflection on learning, motivation level of the students, etc. with team as per monitoring schedule. S/he should diagnose the learning problems and reinforce the learning with additional inputs and learning resources.

Preparation of Project Report: The project report is prepared on salient points of the situation. It is a structured report on approaches to situation. During this phase of the project students compile, classify, tabulate, test the results, interpret data and draw conclusions on the situation. They also list the learning occurred during the process of completion of the project. The project report is the reflection of learning of students on topic of the project. It should be noted by the teacher that learning takes in various shapes and forms and everything cannot be noted in the report.

Presentation of Project: The students groups are asked to make presentations on their project before the whole class for learning, sharing experiences, and reflecting. They should get an opportunity to make presentation on learning of associated competencies. During the presentation the teacher should relate the outcomes of the project with theory and practice. S/he should positively reinforce the learning. S/he should remove the doubts of students. S/he should remove the misconception formed during the process of completing the project. At the end of all the presentation s/he should summarize and consolidate the learning and encourage the students to work on projects in future with greater enthusiasm and energy.

Assessment of the Projects: The major part of the assessment is carried out during the completion of the project and presentation of the project. The purpose of assessment is to ensure higher and purposeful learning. The students should be awarded marks or grades on the basis of their contribution to complete the project against the declared criteria. The assessment criteria should emphasize on planning, execution, approach, novelty, creativity, effectiveness, learning efforts made by students, quality of data, level of interpretation, quality of conclusions, team spirit, quality of report, presentation of outcomes and learning and quality of report.

7. Guidelines for Effective and Efficient Project Work

Every method of learning has got strengths and limitations. The teacher should harness the strengths of the project method of learning. S/he should follow the indicative guidelines listed in Exhibit 5.6.

Exhibit No. 5.6: Guidelines for effective and efficient project work

- The projects should be selected from real life situation. It may be selected from society or industry or employers organisation.
- Projects should be allotted/selected to the students at the completion of the curriculum of most of the subjects/cluster of competencies in a semester to apply the learning in real life situation.
- The time for project work should be allotted in the semester timetable. It should not be considered extra learning activity. Every year new and different projects should be allotted to students. However they can review the previous years project reports.
- Each project should create enough challenge for the students to learn and apply interdisciplinary knowledge, skills and attitudes.
- The students should be provided adequate freedom to plan, implement and monitor the progress of the project.
- It should initiate professional maturity in the students. They should learn professional values along with technical knowledge and skills.
- It should be ensured that students use systematic approach to complete the project. They should apply the theory in true sense to real life situation.
- Projects should not be too ambitious to be completed. But they should be difficult and complex requiring variety of knowledge and skills.
- Projects should create enough scope for creativity, imagination, positive thinking, analytical thinking to achieve the objectives/competencies.
- There should not be redundant members in a project team. It should be ensured that every member of a project team take her/his share for completing the task and learning.
- Projects should be properly planned to minimize the wastage of time, resources and money.
- Teacher acts as a director, guide, supporter, facilitator, problem solver, mentor, encourager, sympathizer, information provider and feedback provider. S/he should be experienced, trained, sincere, devotee and good learner.
- Teachers should do more home work to produce learning through projects. They should have close link with the real life world.
- The learning gaps should be fulfilled and learning should be consolidated by the teacher.
- The institution should maintain the record of projects of students. It should be shared with other institutions in the network. The students and teachers should have accessibility to such projects.

8. Summary

Project method of students learning provides an opportunity to the students and teachers to work on real life situation. It crosses the boundaries of topics, subjects and disciplines and creates scope for applying the knowledge, skills and attitudes to resolve the real life situation. During the design of the project teachers learn and appreciate the challenges of real life situation. The students work on the project and learn by doing, committing mistakes and reflection. They have an opportunity to use creativity and talent to complete the project. They have a feel of professional life and prepare themselves for the professional life. Projects are assigned to students individually, in small groups, and large groups. It all depends on factors such as curriculum provisions, availability of time, learning objectives, level of students and linkage of the institution with industries, employers and society. Project method is beneficial for teachers and students as well because it produces concrete learning. It provides a scope for developing technical skills as well as human skills.

Teachers play a significant role in producing learning through projects. They should select right project for the students. The project should be challenging, creative, non-repetitive, demanding, flexible from real life situation, foster thinking and reflection, develop right kind of attitude and shift responsibility of learning towards students. The projects should be properly designed, assigned, carried out, reported, presented and evaluated. The teacher should ensure the right kind of learning of students from the projects. S/he should fill up the learning gaps, relate theory with practice and consolidate the learning.

9. Activity

Identify the competencies from curriculum that can be achieved through project method. Prepare a plan for carrying out project method of learning. Note down the experiences related to producing learning through project method and share these experiences with your colleagues. Identify the ways of value addition in project method of learning.

6

Management of Learning at Work Place

Objectives: The readers will be able to:

1. Define the concept of learning at work place
2. Describe the purpose of learning at work place
3. List the objectives of learning at work place
4. State the types of learning take place at work place
5. Explain the type of learning takes place at work place
6. Describe the steps to be followed by a teacher to produce learning at work place
7. Explain the method of assessment of learning at work place
8. State the role of the teacher to manage learning at work place
9. State the role of the resource person to manage learning at work place
10. Describe the importance of teachers learning at work place

1. Introduction

The retraining cost of engineering graduates to take up a job is very high. Cost of retraining is wastage of time, money and efforts. Students having no exposure to learning in industry take longer time to understand their role and perform professionally. They are not confident to willingly come forward to accept new responsibilities. They do not understand the work situation holistically. They do not appreciate the importance of quality, effectiveness and efficiency. They do not understand the complete role to be performed by them. They perform what is told to them. They depend on other persons for trivial decisions and activities.

Management of learning at work place plays a significant role in refining the competencies of the students. Students get an opportunity to come out from the campus and see the world of the work. They see the application and integration of the theory in real life situation. They have a feel of real life experiences. They get an opportunity to see the development trends in the industry. They see the complexities involved in the industrial organisational processes. Students appreciate the need of working in a professional way. They appreciate the need of positive approach and high value for quality of products and services. They appreciate the importance of effectiveness and efficiency that they read in books. They have a feel of risk involved and uncertainties in work situation.

Another aspect of organizing learning at work place is that the institutions and industries supplement and complements the business of each other. They are not separate entity. The industries must share the responsibility to develop professionals and share the cost of learning through extending their resources for work place learning of students. The institutions have their own limitations of resources, hands on experiences and expertise. This limitation can only be overcome through managing learning at work place. The work place training of students establishes a strong link between industry and institution to take up collaborative assignments for mutual benefit.

2. Objectives of Work Place Learning

Learning at work place should be a major part of the learning process. Learning at work place serves many purposes. Some of the indicative objectives of learning at work place are listed in Exhibit 6.1.

Exhibit No. 6.1: Objectives of learning at work place

- To expose the students to have a feel of world of work.
- To observe the organisation structure, process, way of working, technology, work culture, work life of people in the industry/at the work place.
- To create strong feel of quality, effectiveness, efficiency, customer relation, cooperation, collaboration, working in a team, conflict, safety, environment protection, energy conservation, wastage reduction, and so on.
- To identify the gap between theory and practice and fulfil it.
- To relate theory with practice.

(*Contd.*)

(Contd.)

- To collect learning material from the industry such as manual, works instruction, technical specification, process description, roles and responsibilities, safety precautions etc.
- To develop an ability to critically observe the processes, phenomenon, events, and practices.
- To learn trouble shooting and decision-making skills.
- To develop ability of planning, organizing, influencing and controlling.
- To understand the technical, social, environment, economic, political, managerial aspects of job.
- To understand the modern trends in functions of industries/organisations
- To appreciate the importance of right kind of attitudes and values for performing the role/job.
- To know the laws, rules, regulations followed in industry/organisation.
- To suggest solutions to problems.
- To suggest innovations in order to increase productivity and quality.
- To practice and refine the competencies learnt in the institution.
- To prepare professionally competent engineers to accept the challenges of world of work and stay in competition.
- To develop the professionals to cope up with all types of changes such as technological, functional, procedural, cultural and perform professionally without affecting the quality, effectiveness and efficiency.
- To learn fast and develop new competencies as per needs of the business of the organisation.
- To willingly accept and perform multiple tasks at high proficiency level without any resistance and stress.

3. Type of Learning at Work Place

The learning in industry/organisation is based on real life situation. So it provides variety of learning opportunities. Students learn to take instructions from the manager and plan the job accordingly. They directly use the competence to perform the job. They feel the anxiety of working in real life situation. They learn from trial and error that means making mistakes. They learn to receive feedback from the progress of the work. They observe the safety rules and norms of functioning on shop floor. They learn to establish relationship and seek help from unknown people. They learn the methods of solving problems spontaneously. They practice and refine their technical, social and managerial skills. They learn to transfer the skills on new jobs. If they are on long-term placement they do experimentation as well as research work.

Students use all the senses in coordinated manner for completing the task and learning. The work place learning incorporates various modes of learning such as learning by doing, learning by observation, learning to receive feedback, learning by mistakes, learning by experimentation, learning by thinking, learning by problem solving and so on. In fact the initiation of competency development takes place in the campus and proficiency is developed at work place. There is a lot of scope for deciding the type of the job and career after completion of the study. The students have an opportunity to closely look the job requirements. They can remove their doubts and perception about a particular job and take better decisions.

4. Management of Learning at Work Place

Management of learning at work place is difficult than management of learning in the institution because at work place students develop competency and proficiency in real life situation. They are expected to perform the task. Management of learning at work place is a teamwork. The teacher or resource person alone cannot manage the training effectively and efficiently. They require the cooperation of all related members in the institution and industry. The success of management of learning depends on many factors. These factors can be appropriately addressed through systematic planning, implementation and evaluation of learning. A generic model of management of learning at work place is shown in Exhibit 6.2.

Planning of learning of students at work place is very important function of a teacher. The whole process of learning at work place depends on planning of learning events. Subject teachers in consultation with industry persons carry out planning of learning at work place. They plan academic as well administrative aspects of learning. The planning assures the quality of learning at work place. It helps to minimize and prevent many likely problems. The teacher and students get confidence to successfully learn at work place through proper planning. Generally the questions such as what to learn, where to learn, how to learn, who has to learn, when to learn, who has to report, what learning material to collect, what is the format of the report, what to record in report, how to present the report etc. are addressed through planning.

4.1 Analyze the Curriculum and Identify Learning Needs at Work Place

The subject teachers analyse the curriculum of all the subjects and find out the competencies that need to be developed at work place. They produce prerequisite learning in the campus using experience of learning

Exhibit No. 6.2: Planning of learning at work place

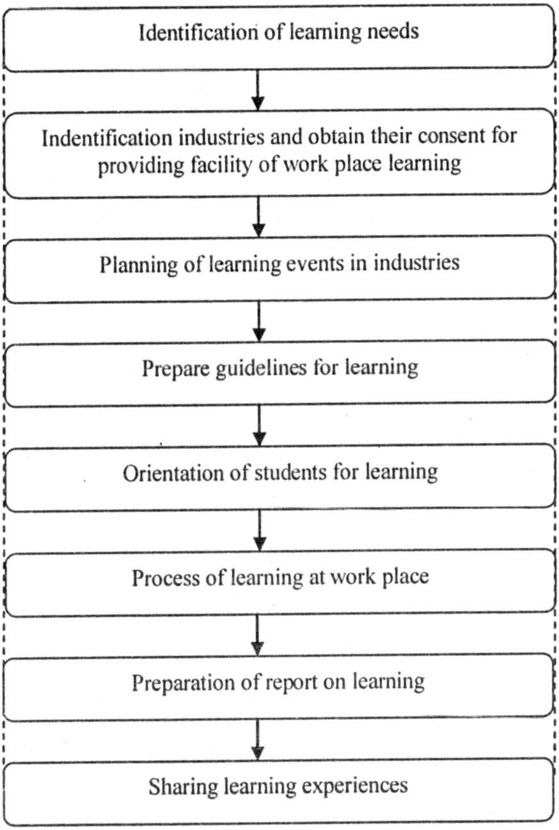

method in classroom, laboratory and library. They plan for all inputs, learning modes, learning methods and learning assignments and so on to transfer learning at work place. Teachers look at work place learning from integrating the learning point of view, developing the desired competency and proficiency. Generally learning at work place is organized after completion of the semester that is not a good practice because students do not consider it as a part of learning. It is not well planned also. The training at work place should be planned at the later part of the semester when students have completed learning in the campus and they need to refine the competency and get exposure to world of work. The learning at work place should be mentioned in the curriculum document and in competency plan. The subject teacher should prepare a list of competencies and indentify learning needs in each competency that can be fulfilled by learning at work place.

4.2 Identify the Industry/Organisation and Seek Their Consent

The subject teachers have a list of industries that fulfills the learning needs of the students. They should keep on updating the list along with brief profile of the industry. They should identify the industries where the students can be placed for learning with the specific objectives. The industry is selected on the basis of fulfilling the learning needs, modernisation level, professionalism, capacity to produce learning, capacity to absorb the students of the institute, networking with the institution, level of interaction with the institution and so on. The teachers should also consider the choice of the students within the framework of the curriculum. A group of students may have interest in research and development, the second group may be interested in production, and the third group may be interested in planning and design. The fourth group may be interested in marketing and logistics and so on. Their interest should be considered to place them for work place learning. At the beginning of the learning at work place the students may be given full exposure and later on they can be placed for learning in their area of interest.

Teachers should contact the industry personnel or human resources development department and discuss with them the learning needs of the students. Teachers should try to take the consent of industry for organizing workplace learning of students. They should visit the industry and plan the learning events for the students. Teachers should put sincere efforts in planning the learning events in the industry. The learning events are planned as per learning needs of the students and learning objectives. While planning the teacher should see the requirements of the competency. The teacher should take the consent of the industry on the learning plan and s/he should ask the industry to provide a resource person to ensure effective learning.

4.3 Plan the Learning events in Industry

Teachers plan the broad learning events at work place in different sections of the industry. They plan the manageable learning events and assignments for the students. If the learning at a work place is planned for a longer duration say one-month students should be assigned specific assignment and a coach should be appointed. These learning events and learning assignments are planned in consultation with different sections of the industry. They plan and communicate the learning parameters for the students as well.

4.4 Prepare Guidelines for Learning at Work Place

Teacher should prepare the guidelines for the students for learning at work place. The guidelines should be prepared on headings such as objectives of learning at work place, learning events, learning parameter, learning activities of students, rules to be followed during the process at work place, format of learning report, documents to be collected from the industry, boarding and lodging arrangement, contact person, resource person from the institution, and so on. Teacher should educate the students about the methods of learning at work place.

4.5 Orient the Students for Learning at Work Place

The teacher should orient the students for learning at work place. The orientation should cover academic, administrative, financial and managerial aspect of learning. A comprehensive written guideline is an effective tool for orientation of the students. Apart from the guidelines the teacher should address the students on importance of learning, objective of learning, learning plan, problem solving mechanism, support, help and guidance available during the process of learning at work place, learning outcomes and format of reporting and presentation of learning. The teacher and industry person should be clear on their roles and responsibilities. Teacher should also explain the monitoring and review mechanism to prevent confusion during training. The teacher should also explain about evaluation of learning and criteria for evaluation before they go for work place learning. The teacher should make it clear to students that they are being placed for learning and not for performing. So the students should devote more time on learning rather than performing.

4.6 Process of Learning at Work Place

Students get significant opportunities to learn at work place. They should learn to exploit these learning opportunities. Students should learn about the functioning of the industry in totality but they should deeply learn about the competencies stipulated in their plan. They should exhibit behaviour listed in Exhibit 6.3 for effective and efficient learning at work place.

Exhibit No. 6.3: Behaviour to be exhibited by students to learn at work place

- Study the guidelines for learning at work place sincerely and design the strategy for learning at work place.
- Prepare a list of questions to be asked in the industry. These questions may be related to technology, techniques, culture, stress level of the employees, challenges at work place, stories of work place, crisis faced by employees, future development, preparation required to take up the job, hazards of the profession and so on.
- Contact the resource person and pay full respect to her/him. Establish congenial relationship with her/him. Show full commitment for learning. Inform her/him that you are willing, ready and open to learning.
- Develop the skills to see the things in totality and differently. Try to relate the work of different sections with the core business of the organisation. Understand the relationship and nature of coordination required between different sections.
- Learn to translate your anxiety in questions. Learn to ask questions to resource persons and self about anxiety, doubts and problems.
- Share the learning and validate it with incharge of shop floor or the resource person. Learn to reflect on learning at work place.
- Initiate the action even in difficult, complex and risky situation with full confidence. Be careful during the action in dangerous situation. Learn to confront and solve problem.
- Learn to establish relationship between cause and effect, means and end, process and product, quantity and quality, efforts and time, core and peripheral processes and so on.
- Learn to receive feedback in positive way and use it for further learning
- Learn to seek clarification.
- Learn to seek and record information systematically. Learn to interact and interview significant persons. Learn to document experiences in the form of notes, anecdotes, incidences, case studies and diary.
- Observe the process of instruction providing to subordinates, meetings, performance assessment sessions, audit, briefing and so on.
- Observe the norms at work place.
- Develop observation and imitation skills.
- Organize learning in logical way.
- Assess the progress of learning after each learning event.
- Scan the material such as vision document, quality policy, operation manual, norms, values, code of conduct, rules, specifications, drawings, manuals, note sheets and so on.
- Participate in seminars, training programmes, functioning of quality circle and informal meetings.
- Discuss the learning points and issues in groups and with other resource person.

4.7 Report on Learning

The students are asked by teacher and resource person to submit a report on learning. The students learn report writing and presentation skills during the process of preparation of report. The companies coming to recruit students for job often refer the report. It is useful to industry from the point of view of improving management of learning at work. It is useful to the institution to assess the effectiveness of learning at work place and for better planning in future. It helps to assess the learning of students at work place to recognize their efforts and provide constructive feedback. Report is useful to teachers for providing latest information on industries to next batches of students. Teachers use it for designing assignments and case studies, picking examples, preparing handouts and learning resources. Teachers update their information about industry and latest trends. They update learning resources, curriculum and facilities in laboratory. They develop positive attitude towards continuous learning and updating their learning to create learning environment and learning conditions for the students. They learn to plan for supporting resources for better work place training. The quality of report works as benchmark for the next batch. The report provides a feel of learning at work place and efforts required to learn at work place to next batch.

4.8 Presentation of Report

The students are asked to make a brief presentation of learning and learning experiences at work place. Departmental teachers and all the interested students attend this presentation to know about the latest trends and experiences of students. They get an opportunity to interact on issues, share the experiences, note significant learning points and provide constructive feedback for continuously improving academic climate in the institution. The presentation session helps to encourage rest of the students to take up the learning at work place in a positive and challenging way.

4.9 Assessment of Learning

The assessment of the learning plays a very important role for the students. They get the recognition of learning efforts and rewards for learning. At the same time they get the constructive feedback for improvement in demonstration of competency. If necessary, teacher provides them additional inputs and opportunity to learn at work place. The assessment of learning is carried out against the learning needs of the students and curricular requirements. The learning of students is assessed against pre-defined parameters against learning objectives or competency. The technical performance is measured on parameters such as knowledge brought at work place, planning for performance, organisation of machine, tools, equipment, material, accuracy in performance, efficiency in performance, quality of product, wastage of time, material and energy, and so on. The human skills are measured on parameters such as establishing relationship with people at shop floor, leadership or follower-ship, effectiveness in communication, asking questions, clarifying doubts, helping fellow member, trusting people and so on. The attitudes are measured on parameters such as concern for safety, concern for saving, house keeping, respect for others, cleanliness, note taking, tolerance of undesired behaviour of others, positive approach to learning and so on. Apart from this the general abilities such as creativity, problem-solving, decision-making, thinking holistically, establishing connections among situations and learning, risk taking, working in uncertainty, working with confidence, working without stress and anxiety are assessed. The resource person and students observe their learning process against defined parameters and note down the level of performance. The learning is also assessed on the basis of quality of report, presentation and dealing with the questions. The students are required to demonstrate the competency. If they get success to demonstrate the competency they get further course of action otherwise they go for remedial treatment.

5. Role of the Teacher for Managing Learning at Work Place

The teacher plays a significant role in planning, organizing, monitoring and evaluating work place training of students. The performance of teacher can enhance the effectiveness and efficiency of training at any level. The teachers should be trained to manage work place training of students. They should be trained to perform activities listed in Exhibit 6.4.

Exhibit No. 6.4: Activities to be performed by teachers to manage learning at work place

- Assessing the curricular needs and identifying needs that can be produced at work place.
- Assessing learning needs of the students in the form of competencies to be developed/refined at work place.

(*Contd.*)

(*Contd.*)

- Establishing relationship with industry for organizing work place learning and assuring placement in advance.
- Planning of work place learning at industry in consultation industry persons.
- Orienting the students on ways of learning at work place, norms to be followed, learning parameters, format of the report, report writing, assessment criteria, material to be collected and so on.
- Assuring the quality of learning at work place through continuously monitoring the progress of learning and solving learning problems.
- Maintain record of work place training.
- Assessment of leaning of students through reports, presentation and viva voce.
- Using the learning experiences of the students for various purposes such as preparing anecdotes, incidences, case studies, assignments, power points, simulations, games, and so on.
- Updating the resources in laboratory, library, learning resource center and self-learning center.
- Revising the curriculum.
- Improving the quality of work place learning.
- Undertaking collaborative assignments.

6. Role of Resource Person for Managing Learning at Work Place

The resource person from industry plays significant role in transferring learning and developing right competency in the students during work place training. In fact they transfer whole life learning to students in a limited time. They transfer the cream of the cream to students. They are the person who creates interest in students to enter in professional life with full energy, enthusiasm and creativity. They develop confidence in students to deal with challenge, uncertainty, competition and crisis. They should perform activities listed in Exhibit 6.5.

Exhibit No. 6.5: Activities to be performed by resource persons to manage learning at work place

- Receive a copy of guideline and understand the learning needs and interest of students.
- Study the plan prepared for work place learning and design strategy to implement it.
- Organize an orientation session and explain the work place learning plan to students and receive their comments, suggestions and expectation.

(*Contd.*)

(*Contd.*)

- Clearly tell the students your expectations and norms to be followed by them during work place learning. Ensure that they have understood your expectations and norms to be followed. Seek their commitment for observing the rules and regulation.
- Orient them about complete process of learning. So use whole to part and part to whole methods.
- Define the specific terms used in your industry/organisation. If possible provide a written copy of the same to students.
- Plan and organize learning events professionally. After each learning event provide immediate knowledge of results that works as reward and source of taking corrective action.
- Demonstrate what of and how of competency. During the process of demonstration use the actual machine site and exhibit your competency on it. You can take the help of graphs, process diagrams and other figures. The resource person should explain all types of body movements and senses working to perform the task. After demonstration of set of skills the resource person should provide an opportunity to students to ask questions. Then s/he should invite students to perform the task under guidance. Once you are satisfied you should provide opportunity for practice to students. The resource person should assess the learning on the basis of the product and provide the information to students.
- Provide an opportunity to master one set of skills and then move to next difficult set of skills and so on. Simultaneously integrate the previous learning with present learning. Try to use your inside teacher. Have high expectations about learning from students. They must feel that learning is demanding and challenging.
- Observe the behaviour of each student and record it on the sheet provided by institution.
- Create learning challenges for students and provide them opportunity to think creatively and apply knowledge, skills and attitudes to perform the task or solve the problem or to do small innovations.
- Always create suspense in the learning process to enhance the interest and curiosity of the students.
- Promote self-learning through stimulating assignment, problems and projects.
- Demonstrate, guidez, support, help and coach the students when it is necessary for learning.
- Inculcate positive attitudes for confronting the problem, accepting the challenge, managing the crisis, planning and implementing innovations etc.
- Provide constructive feedback for improving the competency and behaviour.
- Share the experiences related to professional life and learning from these experiences.

(*Contd.*)

(*Contd.*)

> - Provide important and significant information to students related to profession and relationship.
> - Provide opportunity of experience sharing to students. Show interest in information provided by them.
> - Review the learning every day and ensure that students are maintaining diary of learning and learning events.

7. Research Studies

Agrawal & Jain (1987) have identified 27 areas of collaboration between institution and industry and classified them under primary, essential and desirable. The areas and their classification is stated in Exhibit 6.6.

Exhibit No. 6.6: Areas of collaboration between industry and institution

Primary Areas of Collaboration

1. Organizing field/industrial visits for students.
2. Organizing industrial training during vacation for students and teachers.
3. In plant training of students.
4. Campus recruitment/placement of students in industries.
5. Summer or part-time employment of students.
6. Participation in curriculum development or curriculum updating process.
7. Extension lectures by field engineers.
8. Use of institutional resources/facilities by industry personnel.
9. Appointment of field engineers as part time lecturer and examiners.

Essential Areas of Collaboration

10. Involvement of students on live projects of industries.
11. Organizing seminars, conferences, and workshops in collaboration with industries.
12. Organizing continuing education programmes.
13. Undertaking joint projects for solving industrial problems.
14. Undertaking joint publication and media development.
15. Establishment of production center in the institution.
16. Establishment of vocational training center.
17. Involvement of industries in rural development programmes.
18. Involvement of industries in entrepreneurship development programmes.

Desirable Areas of Collaboration

19. Undertaking industrial consultancy work by the faculty members.
20. Conducting researches relevant to industries.
21. Exchange of staff.

(*Contd.*)

(*Contd.*)

22.	Recruitment of technical personnel for the industries.
23.	Establishment of alumni association.
24.	Association of institution with professional bodies.
25.	Exchange of invitations for different types of functions.
26.	Donation of equipments, industrial products etc. to the institution by the industry.
27.	Awarding scholarship, stipends etc to meritorious and poor students.

The collaboration between industry and institution is reported very low except organizing industrial and field visits. They have reported that industries and institutions have realized the importance and implication of having deeper collaboration. They have suggested that proper steps should be taken to improve the collaboration. They have suggested that work culture has to be imbibed in the faculty and students, concrete steps should be taken by principal and senior faculty members to tackle the attitudinal problems of faculty members, teacher training and staff development activities should be organized to enhance the competence of the teachers, trained and competent teachers should take up problems of industries, institutions should be granted autonomy to revise the curriculum according the needs of the industry, legal binding for collaboration should be imposed and suitable body should take the whole work at state level in coordination with institutions. They have suggested a model to connect the missing links involving all the stakeholders. They have suggested the role of all the functionaries to enhance the collaboration.

Gupta & Jain (1992) have reported that teachers of all the disciplines have perceived high utility of industrial training in instructional process. Instructional processes includes parameters such as correlating the engineering principles with practical examples, reinforcing the engineering theory/law with respect to current industrial practice, selecting relevant and interesting examples for classroom teaching, solving practical problems during the classroom teaching, collecting relevant drawings, photographs, specifications, samples, etc. to enhance the effectiveness of teaching learning processes, understanding and subsequently using the industry oriented handouts, examples cases etc. designed by experts, conducting laboratory instructions more effectively and selecting live projects from industry.

They have reported that teachers of all the disciplines have perceived high utility of industrial training in developmental processes. Developmental processes include creating industrial environment in the work culture of the institute, solving practical problems systematically and scientifically, appreciating job function, duties and responsibilities of the technician, preparing technical reports and project proposals, collecting sample, data, information which could be converted into useful, relevant and industry based instructional material print and non-print (including handouts, work books, text books, cutouts, slides, films, models etc.), and designing variety of new and purposeful laboratory experiences. They have reported that teachers of all the disciplines have perceived average utility of industrial training in promoting interaction with industry. Promoting interaction with industry includes parameters such as developing consultancy services, conducting continuing education programmes, testing of material, solving industrial problems, arranging and managing training for students, finding out employment opportunities for passouts, involving industry in different activities of the institution, sharing resources, and generation resources.

They have noted that there were shortcomings in industrial training of teachers. These short comings are training was not relevant to subject they are teaching, duration of training was insufficient, curriculum is not relevant to industrial practices, industries do not extend full cooperation, monitoring of training was poor, lack of environment and resources in the institution to utilize experiences gained in the industry. Industries have also expressed that teachers do not have specific objectives and there is a big gap between curriculum and industrial practices. They have noted suggestions to improve the existing training system. Their suggestions are stated in Exhibit 6.7.

Exhibit No. 6.7: Suggestions for improving effectiveness and efficiency of industrial training programme

- ➢ Industrial training of teachers must be compulsory and continuous according to individual needs and requirement.
- ➢ Fresh graduates joining the institution as teaching faculty should be trained in industry for 3 to 6 months.
- ➢ Objectives of the training should be clearly formulated and circulated to industry well in advance. Training should be planned systematically.
- ➢ Placement of teachers for training should be in choice of industry.
- ➢ Guide should be provided during the training to provide new and relevant information and to relate the theory with practice.
- ➢ Effective and continuous monitoring should be carried out to solve academic and non-academic problems.
- ➢ Duration of the training should be flexible according to needs.
- ➢ Assessment of learning should be jointly done by industry and institution.

(*Contd.*)

(*Contd.*)

➢ Positive environment should be developed in the institution for industrial training and its utilisation.
➢ Teachers should take interest to utilize the experiences gained in industry.
➢ Adequate facilities should be provided to teachers during training and utilize the experiences of the training in the institution.

Gupta & Jain (1992) have suggested a model for industrial training of teachers. This model is shown in Exhibit 6.8.

Exhibit No. 6.8: Model for industrial training of teachers

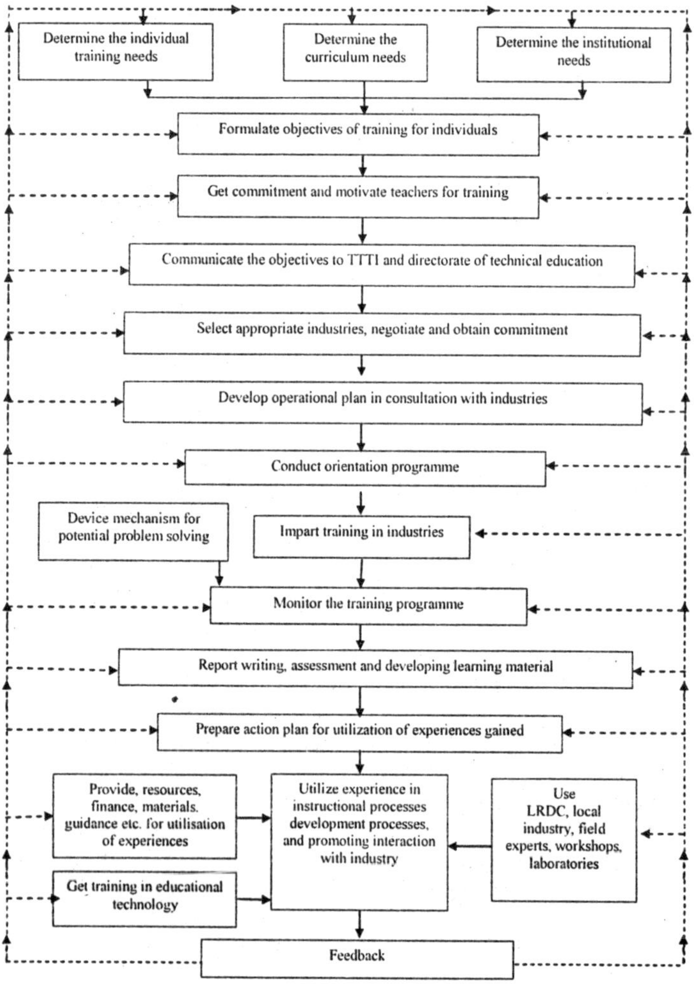

Sahu & Lalla (1996) have reported on training process that there is no formal system for the preparation of the training programme, orientation of students for industrial training, formal system of guidance and counselling. They have further reported on training monitoring that there is a practice of maintaining daily/weekly diary by students during their industrial training, the present monitoring system requires joint efforts by industry persons and faculty members of polytechnics to monitor training programmes. They have concluded on training evaluation that there is a necessity of pre-determined norms to evaluate outcomes of training. They have suggested that joint evaluation of industrial training by industry persons and faculty members of polytechnics is necessary, there is a need of planned follow up procedure for training programmes and on the job assignments motivate the trainees. They have reported on the feedback of the training that there is need of developing feedback mechanism and this can be obtained through well-designed proforma.

They have reported on content that training programme content helps the students to co-relate theoretical knowledge with industrial experiences. They have recommended that the contents of the training programmes should be decided and training should be scheduled to make it convenient to concerned parties. They have recommended objectives of industrial training after completion of first year, second year and third year. After completion of first year students should gain experience in various fields through collecting information about tools and terminologies. After completion of second year students should understand mining procedures and in third year students receive training on managerial and behavioural functions along with technical competence. They have noted recommendations for improving industrial training of students of mining discipline. These recommendations are stated in Exhibit 6.9.

Exhibit No. 6.9: Suggestions for improving industrial training of mining students

Broad Suggestions: The industrial training needs should be identified systematically. A detailed curriculum of the industrial training should be formulated and provided to students stating objectives of training, contents of training, schedule of training, learning assignments, evaluation scheme etc. The students should be given sufficient input before they go for industrial training through orientation programme. There should be formal system of guidance, training and monitoring in the industry. Students should be given on the job assignments. A transparent evaluation scheme of learning of students should be jointly evolved by institution and industry. An effective feedback mechanism should be developed to monitor the progress of learning.

(*Contd.*)

(*Contd.*)

A Model: The polytechnic teachers should identify a person in industry and finalize the training programme on the basis of curricular needs. Then the orientation of students, implementation, monitoring, report writing and evaluation formats are prepared. The industry is informed about the training schedule and training curriculum. The students are oriented on industrial training in totality. Then students are placed in industry for training where they collect information, learn skills, do assignments and practice skills. Teachers and industry against monitoring schedule jointly monitor training. Students prepare a detailed report on various parameters of learning such as information collected, practices adopted in industry, new technology, assignments completed, participated in discussions etc. The learning is evaluated on parameters such as training report 30 per cent weightage, seminar presentation 15 per cent weightage, on job assignments 15 per cent, daily diary maintenance 10 per cent and report of monitoring team 10 per cent weightage. The feedback of students is collected on effectiveness and efficiency of training along with administrative help.

Structure of Industrial Training: A detailed structure is described for industrial training of mining students. This structure suggests imparting broad based training in first year, advanced training in second year and competency integration and refinement training in third year.

Kechkar & Saxena (1998) have reported that teachers have perceived high utility of industrial training in instructional processes, developmental processes and promoting industry institution interaction. Teachers of autonomous institutions are using experiences of industrial training in a better way. Teachers are using experiences of industrial training in areas listed in Exhibit 6.10.

Exhibit No. 6.10: Use of experiences of industrial training

- ➢ Organised industrial visits of students.
- ➢ Developed print instructional material.
- ➢ Arranged expert lectures of eminent industry person.
- ➢ Encouraged students to participate in technical exhibitions.
- ➢ Developed non-print learning material.
- ➢ Guided industry based live projects.
- ➢ Contributed in industrial training.
- ➢ Conducted entrepreneurship development programme for students.
- ➢ Contributed for internal revenue generation.
- ➢ Modernised laboratory.
- ➢ Maintained equipments and machine.

They have reported that favourable factors and constraining factors for utilizing the experiences of industrial training. These factors are listed in Exhibit 6.11.

Exhibit No. 6.11: Facilitating and constraining factors affecting utilisation of experiences of industrial training

Favourable Factors	*Constraining Factors*
➢ Self-interest of trained teachers ➢ Students interest ➢ Encouragement from higher authorities ➢ Availability of sufficient number of industries in required area ➢ Information and other material supplied by industry ➢ Cooperation of other staff	➢ Shortage of teaching staff ➢ Vast syllabus and shortage of time ➢ Lack of funds ➢ Not teaching the subjects learnt in industry ➢ Lack of incentives ➢ Lack of good laboratory facilities ➢ Poor library facility ➢ Lack of planning and coordination

Soni & Kudesia (1996) have reported that teachers trained in industry have expressed that their horizon of knowledge has widened and interaction with industries has increased. Their views are stated in Exhibit 6.12.

Exhibit No. 6.12: Opinion of teachers on utilisation of industrial experiences

- ➢ They can develop certain qualities and competence in the polytechnic students as per need of the industries.
- ➢ They can develop confidence in planning and evaluation of a project and can guide students in conducting experiments and developing skills to work on machine and equipments.
- ➢ They can develop instructional material, learning packages and models related to the working of industries.
- ➢ They can contribute in bringing positive change in technician education system and help in identifying the areas where modifications may be done in the current curriculum with special reference to the working of industries.
- ➢ They can use competencies and capabilities in modifying and implementing curriculum as per the need of industries.
- ➢ They can impart industrial training to students according to the latest technology and practices adopted by the industries.
- ➢ They have become practical person and they can improve teaching learning process related to industry.

(*Contd.*)

(*Contd.*)

- They can demonstrate the machines/equipments which are normally not available in the workshops/laboratories.
- They can design any programmes related to the industrial training to be imparted to the students and can monitor training programmes organized for students in a better way.
- They have become better in interpersonal communication.
- They can provide guidance for maintaining the machines and equipments in workshop and laboratories.
- They can guide students to solve industrial problems.
- They can conduct research work related to industrial operation/safety/ procedures etc. They can write articles related to the industrial working and production to be published in journals and periodicals.
- They can organize industrial visits and industrial tours as per requirements of curricula.
- They can conduct practical accurately as per requirements of industries and other organisations.
- They can design and implement continuing education programmes according to the need of the industries.
- They can provide guidance to entrepreneurs for establishing their units.
- They can provide consultancy about office management and automation for small scale industries.
- They can prepare specifications for purchasing machines.
- They can quote more examples and illustrations from industrial background during teaching learning process.
- They can develop deeper understanding in some of the different techniques related to the product/construction process/quality control/ maintenance system/safety system/pollution control/designing the processes/material testing/instruments etc.
- They can use the knowledge and competencies gained during industrial training in modernisation of laboratories and workshops.
- They feel competent to perform changing roles effectively.
- They can act as a consultant and professional for industries.
- They can exchange their views, thoughts, and experiences freely and frankly with industry people.
- They can explain about quality control in industry.
- They can create industrial environment and work culture in polytechnic.
- They can make polytechnic students aware of duties and responsibilities required for a successful technician to work in industries.
- They can motivate their subordinates/students for participating in different activities related to industry/institute interaction.
- They can pursue the industries for arranging campus interviews and for sharing resources and expertise.

Soni & Kudesia (1996) have noted number of suggestions to improve the effectiveness of industrial training of teachers. Some of the significant suggestions are stated in Exhibit 6.13.

Exhibit No. 6.13: Suggestions for improving the effectiveness of industrial training of teachers

- A list of qualities and competencies required from the polytechnic passouts by the industries may be prepared. This list should be kept in mind for formulating and conducting industrial training of teachers.
- The list of industries using most modern technology should be prepared and teachers should be placed in selected industries
- Each teacher should solve at least one industrial problem during the training period to have a feel of industrial problems.
- Each teacher should design at least one continuing education programme for industry persons
- Apart from technical and managerial training teachers should learn entrepreneurial skills during the training. They should prepare case study of one successful entrepreneur
- Teachers should learn the industrial work culture and adopt it in their polytechnic situation
- Teachers should be encouraged to undertake research work during industrial training and publish it in the journals
- Teachers should learn automated store purchase procedure, documentation and inventory management procedure
- Teachers should develop competencies related to functioning of industry in different sections such as production, project planning, manufacturing process, quality control, maintenance, safety system, pollution control, design and process, material testing, stores management, marketing and research, quality control and so on
- Teachers should acquire competencies to become consultant to industries.

Jha & Khambayat (1997) have concluded that level of performance in different areas of industry institute interaction is below satisfactory. They have noted that the relevance of diploma programmes and quality of passouts depends largely to the extent of interaction between polytechnics and industry. They have recommended that the polytechnics should be given full support, autonomy and basic infrastructure to bring out positive changes. It requires regular monitoring with feedback mechanism. They have listed facilitating and constraining factors responsible for industry/institute interaction. These are stated in Exhibit 6.14.

Exhibit No. 6.14: Factors facilitating and constraining industry/ institute interaction

Facilitating Factors	*Constraining Factors*
➢ Location of the polytechnic in the proximity of industry ➢ Cooperation from industry ➢ Availability of conveyance facility ➢ Inclusion of industrial training in the curriculum ➢ Excellent passout performance ➢ Reputation of polytechnics ➢ Staff initiatives ➢ Expertise and experiences of faculty ➢ Efforts of training and placement officer ➢ Committed staff ➢ Well equipped laboratories	➢ Polytechnic is located in under developed area ➢ Lack of conveyance facility ➢ Reluctance of staff ➢ Inadequate support to training and placement officer ➢ No separate provision of funds ➢ Low corporate image of the polytechnic ➢ Poor response from university ➢ Shortage of staff ➢ Lack of publicity about potential of polytechnic ➢ Rigid norms for testing and consultancy ➢ Poor academic and administrative leadership ➢ Tight academic schedule ➢ Lack of interest among students

Kulkarni & Khambayat (2000) reported that polytechnic students are placed in industry for 8 weeks to get exposure of industrial working. Teachers also receive training in industry. Every year 2 to 5 teachers are placed for industrial training. They have reported that industrial work culture on parameters such as commitment to work, concern for quality, team work, creativity and innovation, adaptability to change, systematic planning, interpersonal relationship, time consciousness, participative decision-making and optimum utilisation of resources is practiced in institutions. They have suggested strategies to promote these parameters in institution.

Kapse, Saxena & Khambayat (2001) have identified 14 competencies for mechanical engineering students. They have stated that industrial training is not compulsory for students but students are going for training on their own, training is finalized in consultation with industry; institute has not prescribed any training manual, students attend training regularly and maintain daily diary, evaluation methods are known to students and feedback is taken after completion of training. They have reported problems as well these are faculty members of respective institute and industry person do not monitor and evaluate training jointly, design of training is inadequate to develop competencies, students do not get prerequisite input before they go for training, formal orientation programme is not organized for training, training is not planned in advance, training is mandatory and evaluation system is missing in the training. They have proposed to organize industrial training for students after every year and total duration should be three months. They have proposed the competencies, activities and duration. They have suggested that a comprehensive manual for industrial training of the students should be prepared addressing the detailed curriculum of training, performance criteria, and assignments. The institute should implement the training seriously in consultation with industry in a planned and systematic way.

Saxena & Jain (2003) have recommended that teachers and supporting staff should be trained in industry. This can be done through variety of modes like formal training, taking up suitable positions in industry, exposure to new technology, projects and industry problems. This training should be well planned, monitored and evaluated by polytechnics and industry. Similarly well-planned industry/field visits, training, and interactions should be organized for the students. They should be encouraged to take up industrial problems and projects as project work. Institute should sign memorandum of association with industries in this matter. Industry/field experts should be involved in teaching learning process. They can be involved through seminars, conferences, symposium, workshops, lectures, projects, problems solving exercises and assessment of students learning. Faculty members should get involved in in-house human resources development programmes for industry personnel and their clients. Such events should be jointly sponsored and organized in a collaborative manner.

8. Summary

The work place learning of students is essential. It covers the learning gaps and provides an opportunity to see the world of work in totality. It creates interest and attraction for a specific job in the students. The employers should also share the cost of the training of the students and provide opportunity for work place training in their organisation. The work place training reduces the learning time of a particular competency and it integrates the learning of various competencies. Students get an opportunity to have a feel of professional life. They appreciate the importance of quality, effectiveness, efficiency and professionally working. They learn to accept the challenges and face the competition.

They learn to work in uncertainty, new, different, and unfamiliar situations. They learn to work with different professionals to perform the task. They appreciate the need and importance of right approach, positive attitude, accuracy, safety, norms and ethics, forward looking, continuous learning and culture of the organisation.

The teacher should plan the work place learning of students in consultation with industry resource persons. The teachers should maintain the information of all employing and potential employing organisations. They should establish good relationship with them and plan collaborative activities including work place learning of students. They should prepare guidelines for managing work place learning. They should orient the students before they go for work place learning. The students should establish good relations with resource persons in the industry and show their willingness to learn sincerely. The resource person should orient the students and provide them well-designed opportunities for learning. They should create challenges for learning using various modes such as demonstration, practice, assignments, problems, projects and questions. They should share the experiences and inculcate positive attitudes for professional life. They should assess the learning after every learning event and provide recognition for desired learning and constructive feedback for improvement. They should observe the behaviour of the students on predetermined parameters. They should help, guide and encourage students to learn right skills and attitudes in right way.

The students prepare a report on work place learning. They submit the report and make presentation on pre-defined date, time and place. Interested teachers, and students of other classes attend the presentation. Students are given an opportunity to answer the questions of audience and share their experiences. After presentation they attend *viva-voce* conducted by teacher. The work place learning is assessed asking students to demonstrate competency. The teacher consolidates the learning and provides constructive feedback for improvement. The work place learning enhances the relationship and collaborative work between industry and institution. It creates win-win situation for one and all.

9. Activity

Design guidelines to organize learning at work place for students.

7

Teacher as a Manager of Learning Process

Objectives: The readers will be able to:

1. State the importance of the competency and proficiency of teachers
2. State the cluster of competencies required in a teacher
3. List the importance of shifting from training to learning organisation
4. Establish the relation between people and learning organisation
5. Design strategies to enhance motivation level of teachers
6. Design strategies to enhance commitment level of teachers
7. Design strategies for time management
8. List factors responsible for satisfaction of teachers
9. Design strategies to minimize role conflict
10. Design strategies to transform the institution in learning organisation

1. Introduction

The fast changes in the external environment have compelled institutions to introduce the changes to satisfy the needs of the employers and other stakeholders. The advancement in the field of technology, educational technology, educational psychology, training technology, curriculum development, methods of assessment of learning, information technology, accessibility to information has provided an opportunity to technical institutions to enhance its effectiveness and efficiency and make its services and products more satisfactory in continuously changing environment. Earlier educationist, technologists and policy makers used to talk about continuous updating of knowledge and skills of teachers. Now the tone has changed and people are talking about proactive approach of change, holistic development of teachers to make them competent and proficient in the changing world. They are demanding for professionalism and same level of services as offered by any international organisation.

The competency based technical education can only be seen in reality when teachers possess the competencies that need to be developed in the passouts. The institutions have corporate culture and function as an enterprise. The institution have capability to face the competition, take risk, manage crisis, fulfil sudden demand of the employers, satisfy the requirements of law of the land, bench mark its services and products with the best provided by any organisation, continuously change and excel for the development of the economy and society. The institute creates the environment comparable to the corporate world. Provide package comparable to any international organisation. This is possible only through competent and proficient teachers as a manager of learning of students.

2. Competencies of Teachers

The competency and proficiency development of students is possible when the teachers are competent and proficient in developing competencies in students. Apart from it they should be competent in producing the learning. Some researches have been conducted in the past on competencies of teachers. But due to fast change in the whole environment many competencies are becoming outdated and redundant. Now the institutions are enjoying a wide variety of autonomy and flexibility at the same time they are facing competition, crisis and problems. They also have immense opportunities for the development and growth. They are crafting their own vision, transforming strategies and processes to achieve the vision. In such varied situations it is difficult to prescribe the competencies and proficiency level for teachers and other significant functionaries. The competencies should emanate from the vision, missions, strategic plans, programmes and projects of the institution. The common competencies for all the teachers in one institution may not serve the purpose and it is difficult to develop also. There is a need to have wide spectrum of competent and proficient teachers to carry out key functions of the institution. The competencies are broadly classified in categories stated in Exhibit 7.1.

Exhibit No. 7.1: Categories of competencies of technical teachers

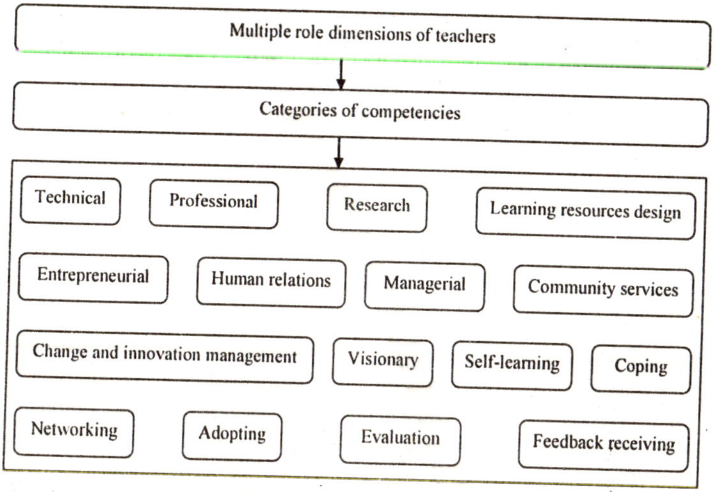

3. Shift from Training of Teachers to Learning Organisation

The concept of training is becoming obsolete and now professionals are promoting the concept of learning organisation. It is an organisation in which people develop capacity and capability to strive for achieving organisational goals, missions, and vision using processes of continuous learning. It is an organisation in which learning, thinking, and analysis of learning is encouraged to create innovative, forward looking and moving ahead organisation. It is an organisation in which people learn collectively about the business of the organisation, its problems and future. They also learn individually and collectively to devise the ways and means to develop continuous learning environment in the organisation. People working in the organisation know that future of the organisation is dependent on their ability, capacity and creativity. They appreciate that the future of the organisation is dependent on their continuous learning about the changing business of the organisation. They learn and contribute to meet the changing requirements of the organisation.

The organisation provides opportunities to its employees for learning and development. The organisation appreciates that ways of learning for different people are different. The learning organisation motivates employees to learn about the changing business of the organisation and provides ample opportunities for continuous learning. Employees use their competencies for excellent contribution. The meaning of learning is continuous analysis of the core business and experiences taking place in the organisation. Sharing work related experiences with individuals and teams. Experience sharing in the organisation creates mutual learning and brings positive changes in the work related behaviour of people. Positive change in work related behaviour produces positive change in the performance of continuously changing organisation. In learning organisation human resources are the focus for all developmental activities. A relationship between learning organisation and people is shown in Exhibit 7.2.

Exhibit No. 7.2: Learning organisation and people

In learning organisation people:	
➢ are considered as resources and not as a burden on the organisation ➢ learn from their mistakes and they take measures not to repeat the mistakes ➢ do experimentation to produce better results ➢ are empowered to perform the duties ➢ are granted autonomy to perform the task ➢ are considered a source of creative and innovative ideas ➢ are encouraged to participate in all important decisions related to development of the organisation	➢ are encouraged to question the rationale of important decisions and policies of the organisation ➢ are motivated to question on ineffective strategy or policies ➢ are encouraged to carry out formative appraisal of the performance and take steps to bring continuous improvement ➢ are trusted on their performance and capability ➢ perform the tasks on the basis of mutual trust ➢ are always ready to break work boundaries to perform new task ➢ are encouraged to take risk

4. Dimensions of Learning Organisation

Learning organisation has varied dimensions in doing business. The significant dimensions of learning organisation are stated in Exhibit 7.3.

Exhibit No. 7.3: Dimensions of learning organisation

➢ Shared vision, missions and goals ➢ Shared values, beliefs and ethics ➢ Strong values for learning ➢ Ample learning opportunity ➢ Learning culture ➢ Use of variety of learning approaches ➢ Flexible learning methods	➢ Effective communication ➢ Collective understanding of changing business ➢ Learning is a part of the business ➢ Rewards are associated to learning ➢ Adequate learning facilities ➢ Feedback on performance

5. Paradigm Shift—Traditional Organisation to Learning Organisation

It is little bit difficult to convert traditional organisation in learning organisation during the initial stage of efforts but there is no alternative to it. Government or private organisation can be converted to learning organisation in a planned way. People working at different leadership, managerial and supervisory positions should initiate the direction setting process. They should take the exercise of shared visioning or revisiting the vision statement to set the direction. This exercise should be carried out participatively. They should derive the missions, goals and objectives and prepare strategic, perspective and annual plans involving employees and stakeholders. The strategies should be evaluated and analyzed participatively to assure their effectiveness and efficiency. The organisation should create learning opportunities for its employees so that they can learn using their own learning style and time to ensure continuous improvement in the performance and bring innovations in work situation. The organisation should provide learning opportunity within and outside the organisation for collective learning. People working at significant positions in the organisation should push and increase momentum for collective learning. They should do so playing a role of trainer, guide, motivator, role model, supporter, coach, evaluator, recognizer, leader, problem solver, conflict manager, learning resources provider, learning opportunities provider, counseller, mentor, etc.

A well-equipped learning center in the organisation should be created to promote collective and self-learning. Good learning resources and a team of facilitators should support this learning resource center. The organisation should fix suggestion/complaint box to encourage people to drop spontaneous suggestions and complaints. The organisation should start a newsletter or magazine to share the information and experiences with internal and external stakeholders. Important information should be shared with affected and involved teams using booklets to avoid confusion and miscommunication. There should be electronic circulation for the information and experiences if facility is available in the organisation. The full potential of human resources and thereby other resources can be harnessed by organisation developing multidisciplinary knowledge, skills and attitudes creating learning organisation. It can overcome the problem of shortage of manpower, obsolescence and redundancy. In learning organisation people are naturally trained to assume changing role. They are deployed and redeployed. The organisation should consider learning as one of the processes of the business and allocate budget and resources for it.

6. Motivation of Teachers

Pathade & Shivagunde (2002) have reported that graduate engineers have joined the teaching profession because of following reasons listed in rank order; preference for peaceful life, enough opportunity to enhance knowledge and skills, natural liking for teaching, availability of job in the hometown or at a place of one's own choice, enough opportunity to enhance knowledge and skills, preference for human values, availability of free time to pursue social work, extra curricular activities, hobbies etc., liking for interaction with young people, social status, especially in rural society, contractual obligation with government, had no other options.

They have reported following barriers to job satisfaction listed in rank order; less opportunity to change jobs, loss of touch with professional practice, students with no motivation for learning, lack of professional ethics in peers, undesirable outside influence in the working of institution, low socio-economic status of teachers, absence of perks as provided in industry, rigid rules and regulation, students misguided by self styled leaders, and no challenge in job. Teachers are continuing in the teaching profession because of following reasons listed in rank order; peaceful life, liking for the job, enough time to attend to other engagements, good salary, high job security, cannot join industry now, well settled at one place.

They have made recommendations to make the technical teaching career an attractive option. These recommendations are; make the career financially attractive offering comparable pay scale and perks, service conditions, rewards and family welfare schemes with industry. To enhance the job satisfaction in technical teaching as career ensure selection of the teachers on the basis of aptitude, create more challenges in the job, train teachers in methods of teaching and technology, encourage and permit teachers to do consultancy and research work, provide adequate support to teachers for teaching, practice participative decision-making processes, modernize laboratory and other facilities, provide avenues for career growth. To improve career growth potential ensure faster career advancement for deserving teachers, provide advance education and training, encourage professional practice through consultancies, secondment to industry etc.

Dale & Kudesia (1998) have reported opinions of teachers about factors affecting job satisfaction. The factors are stated in Exhibit 7.4 in rank order.

Exhibit No. 7.4: Factors affecting the job satisfaction of teachers

Sl. No.	*Factors affecting job satisfaction*	*Rank*	*Satisfied*	*Dissatis-fied*
Social				
1.	Most of the person dislike teaching profession due to less respect in society	12		*
2.	A person becomes lazy and feels inferiority complex after joining teaching profession	10	*	
3.	The long-term summer vacation affects me much	6		*
4.	Indiscipline and unrest amongst students have created disliking towards teaching profession	21	*	
5.	I like teaching and interaction with students which enhances healthy relationship	5	*	
6.	In teaching profession, I not only feel sometime boredom but also feel tiredness in life	16	*	
Personal				
7.	Teaching is not only a respectable profession but also challenging one	7	*	
8.	I like teaching but the process of examination provides lot of dissatisfaction	23		*
9.	I do not only solve the academic problems of students but also guide in their studies which gives me satisfaction	3	*	
10.	In teaching profession a teacher not only develops his expression power professional qualities and capabilities	6		*
11.	In teaching profession one has sufficient opportunities to develop himself as an effective teacher and guide	7		*
12.	Disliking of discussion and delivering lectures	9	*	

(*Contd.*)

(*Contd.*)

Sl. No.	*Factors affecting job satisfaction*	*Rank*	*Satisfied*	*Dissatisfied*
Morale				
13.	I do not only enjoy teaching but also try to develop personality of students	2	*	
14.	I do not like to work under the pressure of principal and senior faculty	22	*	
15.	I dislike teaching profession because for partiality and favouritism adopted by principal and senior colleagues	18		*
16.	I become happy seeing my students attaining high positions in society and working efficiently in other areas	1	*	
17.	I like teaching because the chances of adopting corrupt practices and unfair means are too less	8		*
18.	The personality of learned and experienced teacher have motivated me to great extent to join teaching profession	13		*
Professional				
19.	In teaching profession one not only shows his abilities, intelligence and efficiency but enhances knowledge of one's subject	4		*
20.	In teaching profession neither problems are solved nor academic guidance is provided	17		*
21.	I get motivation and encouragement by principal and senior colleagues for performing my duties as an efficient teacher	14	*	
22.	My reading and writing habits inspired me to join the teaching profession	11	*	
23.	Education has become so much formal that it makes the educational environment monotonous	22	*	
24.	The lack of readiness to learn new teaching techniques and methodology makes a teacher inefficient	26	*	

(*Contd.*)

(*Contd.*)

Sl. No.	*Factors affecting job satisfaction*	*Rank*	*Satisfied*	*Dissatis-fied*
Financial				
25.	Wages paid in teaching profession are less for livelihood of my family	12		*
26.	In teaching profession lot of opportunities are provided for developing one's own abilities and also for getting promotions	19		*
27.	Teaching profession looks comfortable and easy to me	15		*
28.	Teaching profession does not attract bright scholars to join	24	*	
29.	I joined teaching profession because I could not get another suitable job	16	*	
30.	High officials do not care of teachers problem and difficulties which creates frustration among teachers	18	*	

7. Commitment of Teachers

Pandey & Gupta (1998) have reported that the polytechnic teachers have indicated a high level of commitment in activities related to student counselling, teaching, co-curricular and extra-curricular activities and innovation in instructions. They have reported medium level of commitment in student assessment and evaluation, curriculum development, laboratory instruction, departmental administration, revenue generation, and developing physical facilities. They have reported low level of commitment in developing learning resource material, continuing education, research and development, and community services.

They have studied the factors responsible for high/low commitment. They have reported factors responsible from high to low order. These factors are willingness, role status, information sharing, freedom, values and beliefs, participation, training and development, problem solving, job satisfaction, innovativeness, leadership, rewards, employee relations, involvement in profession, supervision, excellence, organisational pride, work practices, performance and team work. These factors are contributing positively to the organisational commitment.

They have suggested strategies to enhance commitment level of teachers at three levels. These strategies are suggested at Government, institute level and individual level on the basis of their authority and way of implementation. These strategies are summarised in Exhibit 7.5.

Exhibit No. 7.5: Strategies to enhance commitment level of teachers

Strategies at Government Level

- Reward system should be introduced by providing better future prospects, performance based promotion system and making provision of bonus/incentive for the teachers.
- Willingness of teachers should be enhanced by appreciating their contributions and providing resources timely.
- Role status of teachers should be improved by making role clear, self-explanatory and specific.
- Participation of teachers should be appreciably enhanced by communicating institutional goals clearly.
- Performance of teachers should be improved by introducing effective performance appraisal system.
- Creative thinking should be promoted among teachers by organising exhibitions, seminars and workshops.
- Opportunities should be increased for training and development by designing suitable policy on career development.
- Autonomy should be imparted to teachers by providing free and flexible environment in the organisational work settings.
- Job satisfaction of teachers should be enhanced by offering attractive pay scales and providing facilities.
- Competitions among institutions and within institution should be promoted for the excellence.
- Supportive policies relating to promotions, rewards, bonus etc. should be formulated.

Strategies at Institute Level

- Reward culture like patting on the back, providing assignments of choice and appreciating the accomplishments of teachers must be maintained.
- Teachers should be made familiar with the institute and its accomplishments to enhance their willingness.
- Role status of teachers should be improved by making it clear interesting, challenging and providing flexibility to perform roles.
- Personal and psychological problems of teachers should be solved by working together and creating open and supportive atmosphere in the institution.
- Valid information should be provided timely to teachers to avoid the reaching of distorted information.

(*Contd.*)

(*Contd.*)

- Participation of teachers should be enhanced by involving them in decision-making process.
- Organisational and personal pride of teachers should be enhanced by promoting social welfare activities, publicising institutional goals and recognising the talents, efforts, achievements of teachers.
- Performance of teachers should be improved by encouraging competitions in the institution.
- Team work should be promoted by forming team of interdepartmental members.
- Shared leadership should be promoted in the institution.
- Relationships among employees should be improved by encouraging team spirit and expressing concern to their problems.
- Creativity among teachers should be promoted by organising creativity sessions.
- Opportunities should be provided to develop skill and competencies.
- Autonomy should be imparted by avoiding unnecessary interference in work.
- Job satisfaction should be enhanced by guiding and counselling them for career development and fulfilling their personal needs.
- Values and beliefs should be shaped by inspiring and motivating.
- Excellence should be promoted by developing skills and competencies and maintaining effective communication.
- Effective feedback system should be introduced to keep informed for improvement in performance.

Strategies at Individusl Level

- Teachers should appreciate each other for their contributions and celebrate the success of fellow teachers.
- Teachers should discuss freely their problems and use their talent to solve them and assist fellow teacher to enhance the willingness.
- Teachers should help each others in making roles clear and performing it effectively and efficiently.
- Teachers should develop a sense of family feeling and solve each others problems.
- Teachers should discuss institutional issues freely and openly to promote information sharing.
- Teachers should utilise the available resources to perform their roles in best possible manner to enhance organisational and personal pride.
- Teachers should co-operate in each others work and learn from each other to improve their performance.
- Teachers should maintain face to face communication to avoid the formation of wrong perceptions and thus improve the relationships.
- Teachers should actively participate in seminars, workshops and solve the problems in new and better way to enhance creative thinking.

(*Contd.*)

(*Contd.*)

- Teachers should complete the assigned tasks timely to enhance their job satisfaction.
- Teachers should change their negative attitude and direct it towards the excellence of the institution.
- Teachers should guide and assist each other to accomplish institutional goals effectively and efficiently.
- Teachers should take active part and interest in departmental/institutional meeting to keep them informed.
- Teachers should extend co-operation and full support to the fellow teacher in performing their roles and completing assigned task timely.

8. Role Conflict

Jamuar & Gupta (1997) have reported that polytechnic teachers have experienced very high conflict on role inadequacy, role overload, personal inadequacy, role isolation, and role erosion. Teachers have experienced on role stagnation, role expectation conflict, inter role distance, role ambiguity and self-role distance. The role conflict is adversely affecting the physical condition and behaviour of individuals. The adverse effects of role conflicts reported to be very high on individual's physical health and behaviour. The adverse effects are increase in organisation dissatisfaction, decline in creativity, increase in disinterest, increase in tension, decline in performance, enhancement in anxiety, decrease in self-confidence, reduction in effectiveness, increase in demotivation, and decline in morale. The adverse effects of role conflicts reported to be high on individual's physical health and behaviour. The adverse effects are increase in problem of adjustment, increase in exhaustion, decline in inter personal relation, reduction in job involvement, increase in frustration, decline in commitment and job dissatisfaction. They have reported that role conflict is adversely affecting the organisation in various areas of behaviour. They have reported very high adverse effect such as increase in deterioration in climate, decrease in innovation, reduction in effectiveness, decline in morale, increase in indiscipline and increase in unfavourable culture. They have reported high adverse effect such as increase in complaint, increase in communication gap, reduction in inter personal relation, decline in commitment, increase in organisation dissatisfaction, increase in unrest, increase in absenteeism and increase in low job performance. Jamuar & Gupta (1997) suggested a strategy to prevent and minimize the role conflict based on the interview of experts, administrators, principals and teachers. They have suggested various elements of role conflict prevention/minimisation strategy. These elements are stated in Exhibit 7.6.

Exhibit No. 7.6: Elements of role conflict prevention/minimisation strategy

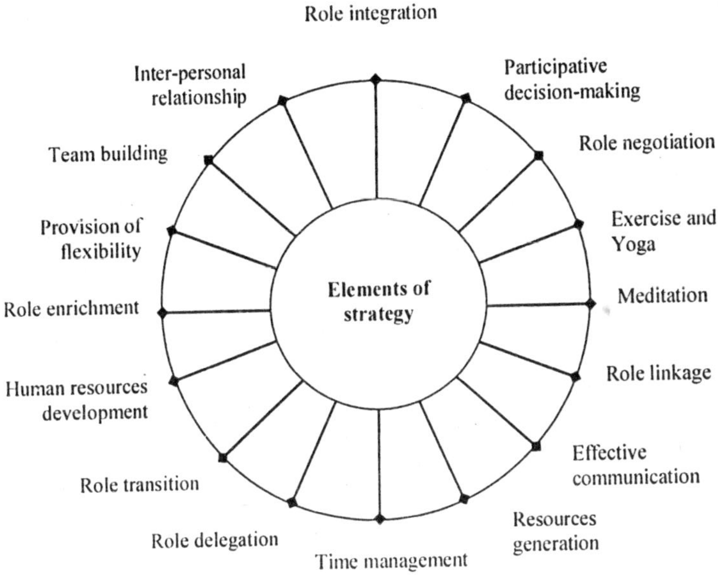

They have suggested a model to resolve role conflict of teachers in polytechnic. The model describes that role conflict resolution strategies should be designed considering the elements stated in Exhibit 7.6. The implementation of strategy will prevent, minimize, and resolve conflict in the institution that will result in effectiveness and efficiency at individual and institution level. The increased effectiveness and efficiency at individual and institution level leads to enhanced effectiveness and efficiency, healthy organisation and healthy person. The model is shown in Exhibit 7.7.

9. Utilisation of Time by Teachers

Nafade & Mathew (1999) have studied time utilisation pattern by teachers of autonomous and non-autonomous institutions on regular activities, intermittent activities and individual responsibilities on ten parameters. They have detailed out each activity on various parameters. The parameters are academic contact hours, preparation and assessment, research and development, guidance and counselling, administration, staff

Exhibit No. 7.7: Model of role conflict resolution

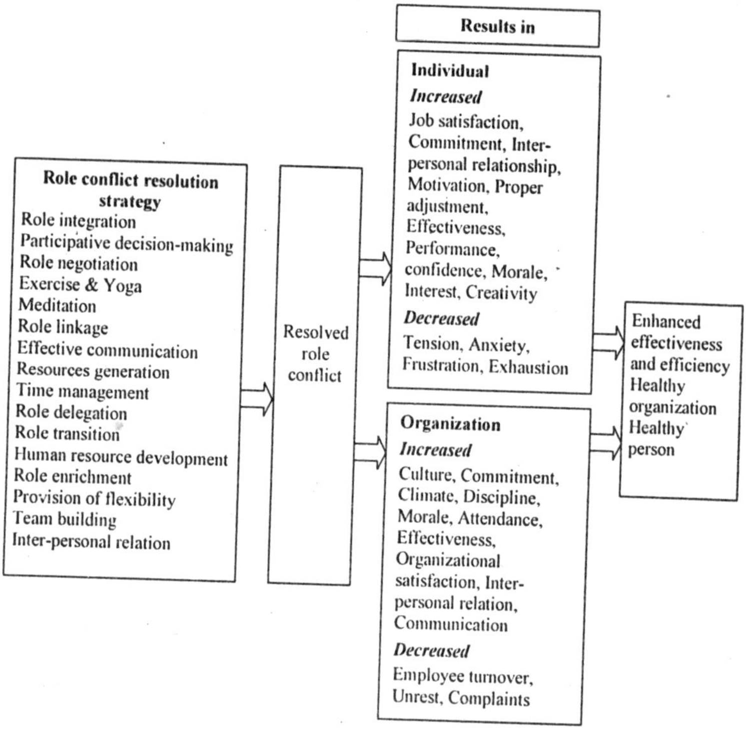

development, industry institute interaction, internal revenue generation, co-curricular and extra-curricular activities and other roles and responsibilities. They have reported that teachers have devoted about 46 per cent time on academic activities, 14 per cent time on administrative activities, 6 per cent time on preparation and assessment, 1 per cent time on guidance and counselling, and 6 per cent time on research and development. They have reported that teachers have intermittently devoted 34 per cent time on examination and assessment, 8 per cent time on administrative activities, 1 per cent time on guidance and counselling, 5 per cent time on industry institute interaction and 2 per cent time on research and development activities. They have reported that individuals are heavily loaded with administrative responsibilities and they are devoting 46 per cent time on it on weekly basis. The workload of teachers of autonomous polytechnics is 10 per cent higher than the non-autonomous polytechnics. They have noted that the time devoted on administrative activities surely affects the academic activities and teachers are unable to concentrate on it.

They have reported factors responsible for effective time utilisation. These are; time commitment, time analysis, role clarity, communication, priority selection of activities, planning of activities, delegation of work, personality traits and resource utilisation. They have suggested strategies for effective time utilisation at three levels as per levels of authority. These strategies are suggested at government level, institute level and individual level.

Strategies at Government Level: Strategies at government level are classified under three headings that are providing infrastructural facilities, formulating support policies and improving role status. Under infrastructure facilities they have suggested to provide separate cabin, departmental library, learning resource center, and staff quarter. Under support policies they have suggested to fill up the vacant positions; performance based monetary rewards, and facilities for physical and learning resources. Under improving role status they have suggested to improve role clarity through involving individuals in role development, flexibility to perform the role with accountability, regular performance appraisal.

Strategies at Institute Level: Strategies for effective utilisation of time at institute level are classified under four headings that are proper allotment of work, proper planning, improving administration, and enhancing willingness. Under proper allotment of work they have suggested that there should be uniform and equal distribution of work and the work should be allocated on the basis of experience, abilities and interest of the teachers. Under planning they have reported that the institute should prepare yearly and monthly plans and the implementation of the plans should be regularly monitored. The teachers should be informed about significant activities of directorate, board of technical examination and institution. Under administration they have reported that principal should reduce the involvement of teachers from prolonged administrative activities such as admissions. The administrative work should be allocated to suitable non-teaching staff. Proper record keeping method should be developed to keep a track on progress of activities of teachers. Under willingness they have reported that superiors should enhance the willingness of teachers using strategies such as provide necessary resources, allotment of work as per experience, ability and interest, guide teachers to do work, appreciate the achievements, participative decision-making, provide timely and constructive feedback, minimize interference in the work of teachers, promote information sharing and give freedom for innovation and creativity.

Strategies at Individual Level: Strategies for effective utilisation of time at individual level are classified under seven headings that are planning and priority selection of activities, time analysis and time commitment, delegation of work, proper communication, proper utilisation of resources, making role clear and personality traits. Under planning and priority selection they have suggested that teachers should prepare action plan month and year-wise along with academic calendar, maintain daily diary and time planner, use systematic approach to perform the task. Under time analysis and time management they have suggested that teachers should analyze the time and find out the ways to effectively utilize it, estimate the time required for a task, find out new and effective methods to perform the task, be aware about time commitment and punctuality. Under delegation they have suggested that teachers should delegate the clerical work to supporting staff. Under communication they have suggested that teachers should maintain the notes and record of meetings for quick retrieval, exchange information of interest, and share information. Under poor utilisation of resources they have reported that the procedure for utilizing the resources should be made simple, teachers should use resources for routine activities, and should use learning resources. Teachers should make the role clear with effective communication, realize the importance of their role and perform it effectively and efficiently. Teachers should use their talent in completing the task. They should develop the habit of problem-solving and decision-making in routine works. They must be clear about their strengths and weaknesses. They should work in a team to help each other. They should develop reading habit to keep abreast with the latest developments.

10. Performance Appraisal

Umale & Gupta (2002) have reported that the concept of performance appraisal is to identify the areas of strengths and weaknesses of a teachers, it is used as a control instrument and meeting the needs for certain purpose, it is used to differentiate the performance of teachers and accordingly grades are given, and it is a tool used for fear. The purpose of performance appraisal system is to decide rewards and punishment for teachers. It is used for giving promotions, clearing probation and awarding time scale. They have reported drawbacks of the existing performance appraisal system. These are weightage given to different areas arc not proper, specialized activities are given weightage but these are limited in nature. It is confidential therefore there is no chance for improvement, decisions for reward or punishments are taken at secretary level therefore it is more time consuming. There is no scope for immediate feedback on performance. It is used as a tool for creating fear for performance. There is a provision to convey excellent and poor grades only. It has more subjectivity. There is more than 10 per cent variation found in performance appraisal of same person by different appraisers. In existing performance appraisal system weightage given to academic areas is very less. Same format is used for appraisal of lecturers and workshop superintendent. Superiors appraise the performance only therefore it is not much contributing towards enhancement of performance of individuals and the institution. They have reported factors responsible for performances of individuals in rank order. These are teacher competence, knowledge, attitude towards work, confidence in work, commitment in the work, abilities, creativity and imaginativeness, proper planning and coordination, communication skills, expertise, job satisfaction, good health, and support from family. They have reported factors responsible for performance at institutional level in rank order. These are team spirit, feedback from stakeholders, institutional climate, students quality, staff development planning and implementation, effective leadership, comparable salary with other organisations, physical facilities and resources available, selection and promotion policy and criteria, environmental opportunities, opportunities to demonstrate competencies, grievance handling system, fulfilment of personal goals, transfers, recognition by peers and others, and financial incentives. They have evolved a performance appraisal system, which is participative, data based, open, task oriented, development oriented, constructive and less emotional. They have recommended that one academic year should be considered for performance appraisal. At the beginning of every year teachers should be asked to prepare a plan. The head of department and principal should approve this plan. The performance of a teacher should be assessed against approved plan at the end of every six-month. The performance of a teacher should be appraised twice in a year. Immediate feedback should be provided to a teacher on performance improvement. The decisions about rewards and punishment should be taken at regional level. The performance of the teacher should be appraised by self with 50 per cent weightage, head of department with 20 per cent weightage, principal with 10 per cent weightage, and students with 20 per cent weightage. They have proposed that 50 per cent weightage should be given to academic activities, 20 per cent to research activities,

10 per cent development and extension activities and 10 per cent to administrative activities. Performance grades should be assigned and communicated within one month after appraisal. Action on performance should be taken in two months and there should be a provision for making appeal in case of disagreement. They have suggested the formats and a model of performance appraisal. The model is shown in Exhibit 7.8.

Exhibit No. 7.8: Performance appraisal implementation model for polytechnics

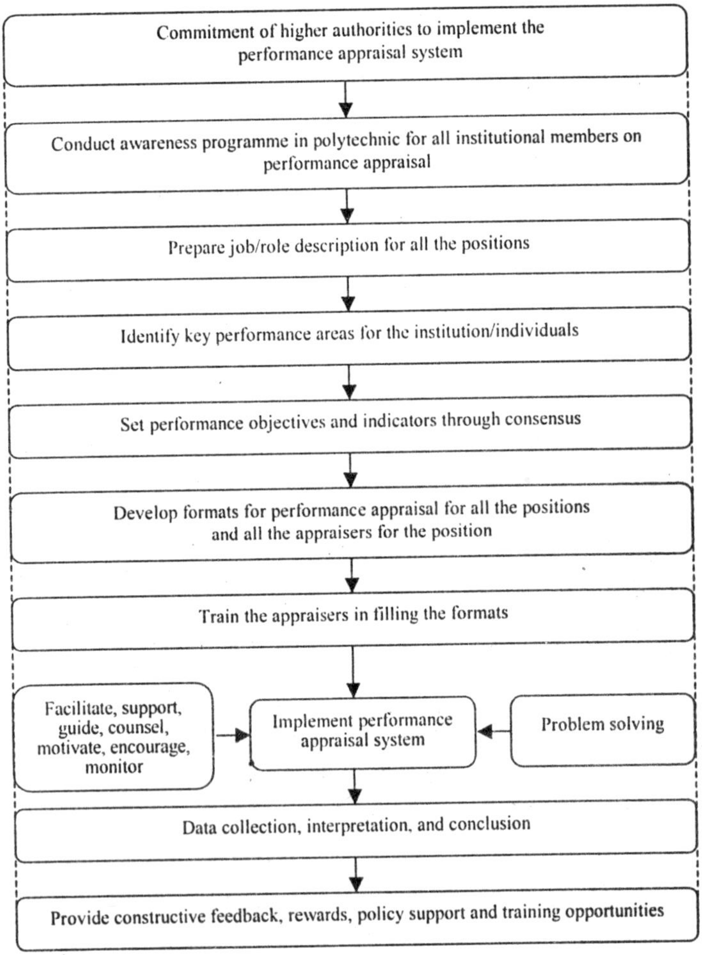

11. Competencies of a Teacher

Suraweera, Tiwari and Ganorkar (2001) have conducted a study on competencies required by technical teachers of Sri Lanka and suggesting alternative strategies of teacher training. They have prepared a list of competencies of technical teachers on the basis of literature review and experiences of the teachers and classified them under nine functional areas. These areas are plan, instruct, evaluate, manage, guide/counsel, public and human relation, professional role, industry institute interaction, serving special/exceptional students, teaching adults and use of computers. Technical teachers, their immediate supervisors, and teacher trainers validated the list of competencies. They have prioritized and classified the competencies as essential, desirable and optional. The list of competencies reported by researchers is shown in Exhibit 7.9.

Exhibit No. 7.9: Competencies of technical teachers

Sl. No.	*Competencies*
Essential	
1.	Teach (introduce, develop and summarize) a lesson
2.	Use class time effectively
3.	Manage available learning resources effectively
4.	Select teaching methods/strategies and supplies for a lesson
5.	Use positive reinforcement
6.	Manage students conflicts
7.	Construct a lesson plan
8.	Manage discipline in classroom, laboratory or workshop
9.	Evaluate students for skills
10.	Use correct oral, written, and non-verbal means of communication
11.	Select and develop instructional content for a lesson
12.	Evaluate students for attitudes
13.	Handle hostile acts of students decisively
14.	Evaluate students for knowledge
15.	Determine/select appropriate instructional media and teaching learning aids
16.	Present a lesson with the aid of chalk board
17.	Choose and use appropriate leadership styles to suite the context
18.	Sequence learning activities and experiences logically and psychologically
19.	Develop good working relationships (interpersonal) with other teachers and administrators

(Contd.)

(Contd.)

Sl. No.	*Competencies*
20.	Determine institutional (classroom, laboratory, workshop) and out of institutional learning experiences
21.	Monitor students progress and provide constructive feedback
22.	Demonstrate, respect, love, sympathy for students as growing, developing and feeling humans
23.	Provide progressive assessment to students in the form of classroom, home, Library, laboratory assignments
24.	Develop/instruct laboratory/workshop performance tests for skills
25.	Establish and demonstrate regular procedure for the proper use, storage and maintenance of tools and equipment
26.	Employ the techniques of oral questioning
27.	Assist students in schoolastics problems and motivate them to learn
28.	Develop good working relationship with other supportive staff (office, canteen, driver etc.)
29.	Direct students laboratory experience
30.	Work effectively in educational team
31.	Prepare overhead projector transparencies
32.	Be alert to and respond to latest technological developments and get oneself updated
33.	Formulate behavioural objectives
34.	Present concept or principle through demonstration
35.	Interpret cumulative students records and counsel the students according to data
36.	Plan for conducting demonstrations
37.	Present information using models, exhibits or displays
38.	Formulate essay, structured, essay and short answer type questions
39.	Monitor classroom/laboratory instructions and modify plans of instruction on the basis of the feedback
40.	Prepare handouts
41.	Evaluate ones own techniques and methods of teaching
42.	Present a lesson with use of overhead projector
43.	Direct students self-evaluation
44.	Formulate objective type questions
45.	Use drill and practice during a lesson
46.	Provide information and motivate students for self-employment
47.	Develop instructional units
48.	Use instructional techniques to meet the needs of exceptional students
49.	Identify and diagnose exceptional students
50.	Provide vocational guidance to students
Desirable	
51.	Analyze knowledge into facts, concepts, principles and procedures

(Contd.)

(*Contd.*)

Sl. No.	*Competencies*
52.	Present information by the use of project method for acquiring skills, attitudes and concepts
53.	Determine students needs, interests and goals
54.	Provide information on further education and career opportunities to students
55.	Present information through team teaching
56.	Recognize over signs of severe emotional distress in students and demonstrate awareness of appropriate intervention and referral techniques
57.	Evaluate techniques employed with teaching delivery, systems and strategies used
58.	Demonstrate information technology related skills which are essential for living in the internet era
59.	Conduct students parents teacher conferences
60.	Identify from the job description the skills and information to be taught for and appropriate job
61.	Use assignments as teaching method
62.	Construct laboratory sheets
63.	Analyze a duty, task or activity
64.	Recognize alcohol and drug abuse in students and demonstrate awareness of appropriate interventions and referred procedures
65.	Establish criteria for evaluation of lessons, units and course
66.	Evaluate industrial learning of students
67.	Develop a test for given specification
68.	Plan instructions for adults
69.	Employ a variety of instructional methods for example games, buzz session, brain storming session in institution
70.	Manage adult instructional process
71.	Formulate or identify course aims and select and develop instructional content for a course
72.	Develop case study problems
73.	Develop means for assessing individual contributions or learning which results from small group work
74.	Use internet for gaining knowledge
75.	Involve the industries in curricular activities for example curriculum development, expert lectures, industrial visits
76.	Develop case studies
77.	Use computer assisted teaching material in instruction
78.	Direct students in instructing other students
79.	Use computers to keep students record
80.	Use computers for presentations
81.	Involve industry experts in instructional planning, delivery and evaluation

(*Contd.*)

(*Contd.*)

Sl. No.	*Competencies*
82.	Give presentations to promote institutional programmes in the industry for example skill upgradation, continuing education programmes etc.
83.	Use e mail for messaging
84.	Use computer for preparation of print and non-print learning resources
85.	Direct a role playing
86.	Evaluate text books and reference materials using predetermined criteria to meet course objectives
87.	Use computers for word processing
88.	Develop instructional materials for computer assisted learning
89.	Organize exhibition to promote institution
90.	Teach through television using video cassettes
91.	Develop brochures to market institutional activities
92.	Provide consultancy to industries
Optional	
93.	Participate in e mail chat sessions

They have suggested alternative strategies to develop these competencies in teachers. They have suggested developing essential competencies in all the teachers using different long-term and short-term modes. They have suggested developing competency development modules to be used for distance learning programmes. The teachers for learning purpose use these modules and their progress is monitored at the institution level. A resource person is also allocated to the trainee teachers. The assessment of competency is carried out in the institution itself by a panel of experts.

Chaudhary & Gupta (1994) have reported the profile of polytechnic in which objectives of the polytechnic are prioritized. They have reported the profile of faculty on dimensions such as designation, qualification, teaching, industrial and research experience, training received, membership of professional body, priority for acquiring higher qualification, seminars attended, awards received, books written laboratory manuals prepared, papers published, and interest in training to other faculty members. They have prepared instruments to know the training needs of principal, head of department, lecturer selection grade, lectures, workshop superintendent, and project officer. They prepared three instruments for each category to know the training needs. These instruments are related to their level of involvement in various areas/

activities of the institution, training received in past in each area and training need. On the basis of analysis of training needs they prepared a plan for training for three years. They have shown alternative strategies for training in the plan such as in house or outstation, on the job or in industry. They have suggested significant generic skills for all the teachers. These are problem analysis, judgment, organisational ability, decisiveness, sensitivity, coping with stress, oral communication, written communication, range of interest, educational values and ethics.

They have suggested a systematic approach for staff development at institutional level. The significant steps of the approach are identifying training needs as per involvement of teacher in institutional activities, prior training and desired training. On the basis of training needs prepare training plans such as institutional level training operation plan, outstation training operation plan, plan showing alternative sources/strategies of training, plan for induction course, plan for acquiring higher qualification and plan for developing generic skills. Finalize the total plan of training at institution level. Motivate faculty and obtain their commitment for training. Prepare tentative expenditure schedule. Obtain approval from higher authorities. Devise procedure for administrative matters. Prepare monitoring plan at institution level. Identify the faculty to monitor. Implement the plan and monitor the progress. Solve the implementation problems and seek support of superiors. Reward the teachers for successful training and obtain feedback to improve the training plan for next cycle.

12. Summary

The teacher as a manager of learning process should be competent and proficient in carrying out the academic and non-academic business in a way to satisfy the learning needs of the students and ultimately satisfying the needs of the employers and other significant stakeholders. To design, implement and evaluate competency based curriculum teachers should develop capacity and capability at par with corporate world. The technical institutions should function on the lines of the corporate world. The teachers are the heart of the learning process and students are the blood. The heart and blood should function perfectly for good assured health of the institution. The competency and proficiency of teachers in management of learning process is key to good assured health of the institution. The institution should transform itself in the learning organisation to become center of excellence. The competency and proficiency of teachers is an essential and prerequisite condition to assure development of competency and proficiency in students. The institution should develop the whole spectrum of competencies and proficiency in teachers and significant functionaries. It should create opportunities, rewards and incentives for the teachers to perform professionally. It should attract professionals instead of incompetent and non-committed persons.

13. Activity

Activity 1

In this chapter you have appreciated the concept of learning organisation. Prepare a plan of your organisation to transform it in learning organisation. You can prepare the plan in following format.

Sl. No.	*Learning Events*	*Purpose*	*Participants*	*Duration*		*Resource Persons*	*Responsi-bility*
				From	To		
1.	Creativity sessions						
2.	Participative planning						
3.	Experience sharing sessions						
4.	Experimentations						
5.	Complaints analysis sessions						
6.	Opportunity analysis sessions						
7.	Use of technology for learning						
8.	Competition analysis sessions						
9.	Exploration exercises						
10.	Learning challenges						
11.	Learning projects						
12.	Self-learning opportunities						

(Contd.)

(*Contd.*)

Sl. No.	*Learning Events*	*Purpose*	*Participants*	*Duration*		*Resource Persons*	*Responsi-bility*
				From	To		
13.	Team learning exercises						
14.	Guided learning						
15.	Learning simulations						
16.	Meditation						
17.	Performance appraisal						
18.	Action learning exercises						
19.	Case study						
20.	Researches						
21.	Review of policies, rules and regulations						
22.	Collective planning						
23.	Seminars						
24.	Conferences						
25.	Meeting with customers						
26.	Formal training programmes						
27.	Workshops						
28.	Diagnostics						
29.	Interaction with stakeholders and experts						
30.	Learning games						
31.	Problem-solving sessions						
32.	Observation opportunities						
33.	Discussions—panel, group, focus group						

(*Contd.*)

(Contd.)

Sl. No.	*Learning Events*	*Purpose*	*Participants*	*Duration*		*Resource Persons*	*Responsi-bility*
				From	To		
34.	In basket						
35.	Quiz						
36.	Industrial training						
37.	e-learning opportunities						
38.	Study leave						
39.	Sabbatical leave						
40.	Advance educational programmes						
41.	Excursion/educatio-nal tours						
42.	Secondment of faculty members						

Activity 2: Assignment on Perception of People About the Institution

A list of statements related to learning organisation is given. Read statements serially and decide the extent to which it applies to your institution. Mark your response in appropriate column. 4 indicates full weightage and 0 indicates no weightage. If you do not respond to the statement it would be assumed that this is not applicable to your institution.

Sl. No.	*Statement*	*Extent*				
		4	3	2	1	0
1.	Training needs are analyzed every year and training plans are prepared on the basis of training needs					
2.	Competency based training programmes are designed					
3.	Most of the training programmes are organized in-house					
4.	People are conscious about learning					
5.	Academic interactions are frequently organized					

(Contd.)

(*Contd.*)

Sl. No.	*Statement*	*Extent*				
		4	3	2	1	0
6.	Self-learning is promoted by institution					
7.	People learn from all learning opportunities					
8.	Learning to learn concept is promoted					
9.	Faculty and staff members are encouraged to organize learning events such as creativity sessions, seminars, conferences, workshops, training programmes					
10.	Meetings are organized to learn about the academics and discuss academic problems					
11.	Variety of training learning methods are used in training programmes					
12.	Learner centered methods are used in training programmes					
13.	Latest learning resources are procured immediately					
14.	Teachers develop learning resources such as text books, work books, assignments, case studies, video films, computer aided instructions, modules, monographs, concept papers, guide for learning specific topics, etc.					
15.	Teachers do experiments for bringing improvements in academic processes					
16.	Teachers prepare academic plans					
17.	Teachers undertake consultancy projects					
18.	Effective team work prevails					
19.	Open and constructive feedback is accepted by employees					
20.	Use of learning media is very common in institution					
21.	Complaints and academic problems are welcomed by the institution					
22.	Concrete suggestions are implemented					
23.	Performance appraisal and development system is effectively used					
24.	Participatory approaches are used for long-term and short-term planning					

(*Contd.*)

(*Contd.*)

Sl. No.	*Statement*	*Extent*				
		4	3	2	1	0
25.	Management and educational tools and techniques are used for planning, implementation and evaluation of educational programmes					
26.	Employees follow values, norms and ethics					
27.	Changes are implemented collectively or in teams					
28.	People are developed to design and implement change					
29.	Learning opportunities such as attending out station courses, in-house courses, secondments, sabbatical leave, study leave, fellowship, exchange, industrial training are easily available					
30.	On the job coaching, guidance, counselling, mentoring is common					
31.	All types of learning is aligned to vision, mission and goals					
32.	Competencies and proficiencies level for all the positions is well defined and known to people					
33.	Full talent and potential of people is used					
34.	Seniors devote time to develop juniors using variety of methods					
35.	Training and learning activities are monitored					
36.	Impact of training and learning is assessed					
37.	People are developed to accept future challenges					
38.	Risk taking for learning is common					
39.	Self-learning center, learning utilisation center and digital library is fully functional and used					
40.	Training need analysis, training implementation, learning resources development, achievement measurement processes are in place					
41.	Team building exercises are carried out					
42.	Action learning is common in teams					
43.	People think strategically					
44.	Learning from failures and mistake is common					
45.	Communication is effective and efficient					

(*Contd.*)

(*Contd.*)

Sl. No.	*Statement*	*Extent*				
		4	3	2	1	0
46.	Interdisciplinary learning is practiced					
47.	People are often deployed and redeployed					
48.	Joint learning events are organized with industry and sister institutions					
49.	Systems and processes are designed, implemented and refined jointly					
50.	Documentation of experiences					
51.	Knowledge, technology, techniques and models are developed					
52.	Easy access to information					
53.	Significant budget is allocated for training and learning activities					
54.	Budget is utilized effectively					
55.	Grants are always available for learning events and innovation					

Bibliography

Agrawal & Sakesna (1989), Study habits and achievement motivation in relation to academic achievement of polytechnic students of Madhya Pradesh, Barkatullah University, Bhopal.

Agrawal V.M. & Jain P.C. (1987), A fact-finding survey for determining collaboration of industry with polytechnics of Madhya Pradesh, Technical Teachers Training Institute Bhopal– 462002.

Alison Wolf (2004), Vacational Education is not About Tackling Social Exclusion. In Conor Ryan (ed) *Bac or Basics, Challenges for the 14-19 Curriculum.* Wolf, A. London, Social Market Foundation

Allan C. Ornstein & Francis P. Hunkins (1988), Curriculum: foundations, principles, and issues, Allyn Bacon Boston.

Armarkar R.P. & Saksena Kiran (2002), Design of strategies for effective implementation of curriculum in autonomous polytechnics of Maharashtra State, Barkatullah University, Bhopal.

Barry Harley (1973), *A Synthesis of teaching methods*, McGraw Hill Book Company, Sydney.

Bob Wilson (1987), *Methods of training: individualized instructions*, Parthenon Publishing Group Limited, Park Ridge.

Boyatzis R.E. (1982), *The competent manager, A model for effective performance*, John Wiley, New York, NY.

Bruce Joyce, Marsha Weil and Beverly Showers (1992), Models of teaching, Prentice Hall of India Private Limited, New Delhi.

Charles E. Skinner (1995), *Educational Psychology*, Prentice Hall Private Limited, New Delhi.

Chaudhary G.P. & Gupta B.L. (1994), A study on formulation of staff development plan for Government Polytechnic Jalgaon, Barkatullah University, Bhopal.

Chondhikar D.M. & Lahiri Shikha (1999), Design of competency based curriculum with emphasis on assessment scheme for a course of mechanical engineering diploma programme, Barkatullah University, Bhopal.

Dale P.D. & Kudesia U.C. (1998), A study on factors affecting job satisfaction of teachers in technician education institutes of Madhya Pradesh, Barkatullah University, Bhopal.

Dandoti S.Z., Mahashabde R.S., & Jain K.K. (1995), Identification of skills and developing programme structure for diploma in textile manufacture for Maharashtra State, Barkatullah University, Bhopal.

Ganjoo S.M. & Verma P. (1999), A study of existing attitudes towards self-learning among polytechnic teachers of Madhya Pradesh, Barkatullah University, Bhopal.

Gupta B.L. & Jain P.C. (1992), A study on utility of industrial training of polytechnic teachers, Barkatullah University, Bhopal.

International Labour Office Geneva (1983), *An introductory course in teaching and training methods for management development*, Sterling Publishers (P) Ltd., India New Delhi.

J. William Pfeiffer, Arlette C. Ballew (1998), *Using case studies, simulations, and games in human resources development*, Aditya Books Private Limited New Delhi.

Jamuar A.K. & Gupta B.L. (1997), A study on role conflict in polytechnic teachers and designing strategies to minimize role conflict, Barkatullah University, Bhopal.

Jha K.N. & Khambayat R.P. (1997), Development of cases on the present state of the art about industry institute interaction in selected polytechnics of Madhya Pradesh, Barkatullah University, Bhopal.

John W. Newstrom, Edward E. Scannell (1980), *Games trainers play*, McGraw Hills Book Company New York.

Jon Wiles & Joseph Bondi, (1989), *Curriculum development*, Macmillan Publishing Company New York.

Joshua Earnest & Soni S.K. (2001), Reengineering technician education programmes for labour market orientation through competency-based curriculum development in polytechnics, Barkatullah University, Bhopal.

Kagan J. (1964), *Information processing in the child, significance of analysis and reflective attitudes,* psychol, monograph.

Kapse C.P., Saxena S.K. & Khambayat R.P. (2001), Designing of industrial training programme with a view to develop relevant competencies for non sandwich engineering diploma programmes, Barkatullah University, Bhopal.

Kechkar G.M. & Saxena S.K. (1998), Utility of industrial training experienced by polytechnic teachers, Barkatullah University, Bhopal.

Khartri K.R. & Haider S.Z. (1993), A study of different facets of flexibility under multipoint entry credit system in diploma programme in mechanical engineering of selected polytechnics in Gujarat State, Barkatullah University, Bhopal.

Kolb D.A. (1972), *Organisational psychology, an experienced approach*, Prentice Hall, London.

Kulkarni B.B. & Khambayat R.P. (2000), A study of the impact of industry institute interaction on promoting industrial work culture in Maharashtra Polytechnics, Barkatullah University, Bhopal.

Leslie J. Chamberlin (1969), *Team teaching*, Charles E. Merril Publishing Company. A Bell & Howell Company, Columbus, Ohio.

Leslie Rae (1998) *Techniques of training*, Jaico Publishing House Mumbai.

Leslie Rae (2002), *The art of training and development in management*, Crest Publishing House, New Delhi.

Mani R.K. (1994), Module on case method, Cement Industry, HRD Project, Technical Teachers' Training Institute, Bhopal.

Mary, Brown Allgood (1965), *Demonstration Techniques*, Prentice Hall of India Private Ltd New Delhi.

Maslow A. (1970), Motivation and Personality, 2nd edition, Harper & Row.

Maxwell, G.W. *et al.* (1980), Handbook for California Vocational Educators. US, San Jose State Univ. California, Microfiche No. ED 210-518.

Melissa Towner, David Muller, Tony Simon and Marie Stewart (1987), *Learner psychology in training*, Parthenon Publishing Group Inc Park Ridge U.S.A.

Michael J. Marquardt (2003), *Action learning in action*, Jaico Publishing House Mumbai.

Mike Pedler (1993), Action learning in practice, 2nd edition, Grower Publishing Company Limited Hants England.

Nafade R.M. & Mathew Susan S. (1999), A study on utilisation of time in different activities by the teachers of government polytechnics and formulating the strategies for effective time utilisation, Barkatullah University, Bhopal.

Nayak B.S. & Kudesia U.C. (1995), Competencies required for laboratory technicians as viewed by polytechnic teachers, Barkatullah University, Bhogal.

Pagare Sanjay P. & Rawlley Anju (2000), A critical study of the curriculum document and its implementation in an autonomous polytechnic, performance of passouts and their employability, Barkatullah University, Bhopal.

Pandey H.S. & Gupta B.L. (1998), A study on the commitment level of polytechnic teachers and formulating strategies to enhance the commitment level, Barkatullah University, Bhopal.

Pat Hedges (1997), *Increasing profitability by effective use of learning*, Kogan Page London.

Pater Lassey (1998), *Developing a learning organisation*, Kogan Page Limited, London.

Pathade R. & Shivagunde R.B. (2002), A study of facilitating and constraining factors influencing the choice and continuance of technical teaching as a career by graduate engineers in Raigad District of Maharashtra, Barkatullah University, Bhopal.

Paul Hersey & Kenneth H.Blanchard (1992), *Management of organisational behaviour*, Prentice Hall of India Private Limited, New Delhi.

Perry G.W. (1969), *Case studies in teaching*, Sir Isaac Pitman and Sons Limited, London.

Peter F. Oliva (1992), *Developing the curriculum,* Harper Collins Publishers New York.

Peter Senge (1994), *The fifth discipline, Field book*, Nicholas Brealey Publishing, London.

Pfeiffer J. William and Arlette C. Ballew (1993), *Using case studies, simulation and games in human resource development*, Aditya Books Private Limited, New Delhi.

Piget J. (1963), *The child's conception of the world*, Paterson, N J Littlefield, Adams.

Race Phil (2005), *Making learning happen*, SAGE Publication.

Raymond L. Hilgert, Sterling H. Schoen, Joseph W. Towle, (1978), *Cases and Policies in human resources management*, Houghton Mifflin Company Boston Dallas.

Reynolds J. (1980), Case method in Management Development, ILO Geneva.

Robert F. Mager (1990), *Making instruction work*, Kogan Page, London.

Robert K. Yin (1984), *Case Study research design and methods*, SAGE Publications, New Delhi.

Roger C.R. (1880), *A way of being*. Boston, Houghton Mifflin.

Rosella Linskie (1977), *The learning process*, D. Van Nostrand Company New York.

Sahu S.D. & Lalla G.T. (1996), A study on design of industrial training of diploma students of mining engineering, Barkatullah University, Bhopal.

Saxena S.K. & Jain P.C. (2003), Developing a model for enhancing institutional flexibility in order to provide optimal academic services, Barkatullah University, Bhopal.

Soni O.P. & Kudesia U.C. (1996), Utilisation of industrial training experiences by polytechnic teachers, Barkatullah University, Bhopal.

Soni S.K. (2004), *An information resource on educational technology for technical & vocational education and training*, Sarup and Sons New Delhi.

Suraweera D.D.D., Tiwari N.P. and Ganorkar S.R. (2001), A study on competencies required by technical teachers of Sri Lanka and suggesting alternative strategies of teacher training, Barkatullah University, Bhopal.

Timothy S. Mescon & George S. Vozikis (1988), *Cases in Management*, Harper & Row, Publishers, New York.

Umale G.V. & Gupta B.L. (2002), A study on performance appraisal of government polytechnic teachers in Amravati region of Maharashtra State, Barkatullah University, Bhopal

Vedanayagam E.G. (1988), *Teaching technology for college teachers*, Sterling Publishers Private Limited, New Delhi.

W. Douglas Seymour (1968), *Skills analysis training*, Sir Issac Pitman and Sons Ltd, London.

Yasin Masooda & Jain P.C. (1993), A study of entrepreneurial attitudes among polytechnic final year students (boys and girls) and perception of girls regarding problems of women entrepreneurs—Barkatullah University, Bhopal.

Index